*f*P

ME AND HANK

A BOY AND HIS HERO, TWENTY-FIVE YEARS LATER

◆

SANDY TOLAN

THE FREE PRESS

New York   London   Toronto   Sydney   Singapore

THE FREE PRESS
A Division of Simon & Schuster Inc.
1230 Avenue of the Americas
New York, NY 10020

THE FREE PRESS and colophon are trademarks of Simon & Schuster Inc.

Book design by Ellen R. Sasahara

Photo editing by William Tolan

Manufactured in the United States of America

10   9   8   7   6   5   4   3   2   1

Library of Congress Cataloging-in-Publication Data

Tolan, Sandy.
Me and Hank: a boy and his hero, twenty-five years later / Sandy Tolan.
p.   cm.
1. Aaron, Hank, 1934–   2. Baseball players—United States—Biography.
3. Tolan, Sandy. I. Title.

GV865.A25 T65 2000
796.357'092—dc21
[B]   00-026484

ISBN 0-684-87130-0

To my mother, Sally Tolan,
and to the memory of my father,
Thomas Lawrence Tolan, Jr.

CONTENTS

BRAVES

HANK AARON   outfield

When I was a kid, I had three heroes: my dad; Bart Starr, the quarterback of the Green Bay Packers; and the man who played right field in my hometown—Henry Aaron of the Milwaukee Braves. Hammerin' Hank hailed from Mobile, Alabama. He was six feet tall and 180 pounds, unremarkable

1

compared to today's Paul Bunyans of the weight room. But Hank possessed wrists of lightning. In his powerful hands, the bat *snapped* across the plate, turning a baseball into a bullet: fired past the pitcher's ear, streaking six feet over second base, and smoking into the first row of the center field bleachers. Facing the pitcher, he looked to some like he was sleeping. But when the pitch came, he pounced. Trying to sneak a fastball past Henry Aaron, an opposing pitcher once said, was like trying to sneak the sun past a rooster.

Number 44 didn't have the stout flamboyance of Babe Ruth, the electricity of Jackie Robinson, or the flash of Willie Mays. But Hank was our jewel in the Milwaukee outfield, a man of speed, and power, and grace, and brilliance. Hank was as good as anyone; he was just quiet about it. Willie Mays's fans forever point to his astonishing catch in the 1954 World Series off the drive from Cleveland's Vic Wertz. Sprinting to the center field wall, his back to home plate, Mays caught the ball over his shoulder. As he turned to throw back toward the infield, his cap fell off.

Hank Aaron, said a teammate, would have made the same catch.

Except he would have kept his cap on.

O

My life with Hank began on a warm Saturday afternoon in May 1964. I was eight years old. My big sister Kathy decided it was time I learned about baseball.

There were eight of us—Mom and Dad; Tom, the oldest at fourteen; then Kathleen; Mary; me; John; and Willy, born in 1963. Up to then, anyway, we were faithful, obedient Irish-German Catholics—fish on Fridays, mass on Sundays, birth control never. We filled up a huge six-bedroom, three-story brick-and-stucco house my parents bought for $29,500 in 1959. Maple tree in the side yard, basketball hoop on the garage, and across the street, a county park, with steps through a dark ravine to the lakefront, and the beach at Lake Michigan. Down the street were bigger houses still, on the bluff, overlooking the lake.

In 1964, my dad, left leg shriveled from polio at age six, could still limp around okay with leg braces and a cane. He could still make it down to the basement, where now and then we'd saw and pound together our great wooden ships, to launch in the bathtub. He could still swing a bat on the front lawn, sending us skittering after ground balls through the middle and into the neighbors' yard.

It was blue-skied and quiet that afternoon Kath took me for my lesson in baseball. We walked down Terrace Avenue beneath a canopy of giant elm trees. The way I remember it, I wore double-kneed jeans with the elastic waist and the too-long belt my mom had poked extra holes in. Kathy pounded her Duke Snider glove, playing catch with a hardball she tossed toward the leaves. She was thirteen, and a lefty, like me—and like Eddie Mathews of the Braves, Number 41, her hero.

In four blocks we came to a favored spot on Earth: a tiny red and white building, with a bulbous silver fan spinning atop the tar roof. The Popcorn Stand was run from spring to fall by Mr. and Mrs. M. All winter long, we'd look at the boarded-up stand, with its hand-painted, orange-breasted bird, and its promise: *See You With The First Robin!* In April, when the robins came first, we'd get upset with Mr. and Mrs. M for not being there, too. One spring I wanted to call them—"Um, excuse me, hi, when are you opening?"—but nobody could remember what came after the "M." It stood for some long foreign name none of us could pronounce. Probably German—like Maier, my middle name, after my mom's father. I wondered if the M's knew Grandpa Irv, for they each ran important businesses: for Grandpa, it was the daily newspaper, the *Milwaukee Journal,* where he was the publisher; for Mr. and Mrs. M, The Popcorn Stand.

We liked listening to Mrs. M's accent. John Topetzes, my buddy since kindergarten (who went by the nickname T), had innumerable ways to get her to say the word "three."

"How much is that pack of pumpkin seeds?" T would ask, standing on the "kids' step" in front of the sliding glass window.

"Tree." The old lady peered down over specs, wisps of gray hair escaping from a bun.

"What if I got four red coins and one swizzle stick?"

"Tree." Frowning now, wiping her hands on her apron.

"Three Bazooka Joes?"

"Tree."

"Six red coins?"

"Tr—" And then Mrs. M would lose her temper and tell T to order or let the next kid step up.

Our trips to The Stand were daily—for candy necklaces, candy Lucky Strikes, Pez, gumballs, jawbreakers, Sweet-Tarts, Sugar Daddys, Sugar Mamas, Sugar Babies, and popcorn: small buttered, ten cents; with coconut oil only, a nickel. Sometimes, laden with our haul, we'd walk the block to T's house, before setting down for a rest. If T's father was back from the university, he'd puff his cigar and tell us, "I just talked to Vince"—Lombardi, the Packers' coach—"and he's got a secret play for Sunday. I promised him I wouldn't reveal it." Or, "Hammering Hank and I chatted the other night. He's requested my assistance in adjusting his batting stance." We'd bask in this for a while—did Dr. Topetzes teach *sports* at Marquette?—then go upstairs to the shoe boxes full of olive green army men, which were off limits at my house. "I don't want you kids playing war," my mom would say.

The consumables from The Stand quickly took a seat way in the back starting that May morning in 1964. For as Kath was about to show me, at The Popcorn Stand there was another prized item: Topps baseball cards, ten per pack, with the long slabs of pink bubble gum that made the cards smell sweet.

"Two packs, please," Kathy told Mrs. M that afternoon. (She didn't know about *"tree."*) She gave one pack to me and we went and sat on the grass. "What we want," Kath told me, "is guys from our team." I knew this much about the Braves: they were strong men in white wool uniforms who sometimes didn't shave. "If we're really lucky, we'll get Eddie Mathews or Hank Aaron." I remembered that Hank hit a lot of home runs, and that he was the star of the team, even better than Kath's hero. For me, Hank was the guy to get.

I tore open the pack, shoved the gum in my mouth, and

scanned the cards: TWINS . . . ANGELS . . . PHILLIES . . . CARDINALS . . . no BRAVES in my pack. But Kath was smiling. She had Hank.

She showed me the card. Henry Aaron stood in uniform, blue cap with the red bill, and a white "M" sewn on the front, for Milwaukee. No scowling out at the pitcher's mound with bat in hand, like some of the cards; no posed leap for a fly ball, like others. He was just standing there, on the field, smiling—warm, unassuming, real. Like I could talk to the man.

"Here," Kath said, holding out a gift. "You got Hank Aaron in your first pack of baseball cards."

From that day I had a new hero. Wherever I could, I soaked in his story: about how, as a teenager in Mobile, he delivered 100-pound blocks of ice, hauling them with tongs up many flights of stairs, forging those powerful wrists; about how he trained his batting eye with the modest tools available—he'd hit bottlecaps with a broomstick; about how he learned to bat with the Mobile Black Bears by facing the pitchers cross-handed; about the day he left home to play ball, riding the train with two dollars, two pairs of pants and two sandwiches; and most of all, about his heroics in the 1957 season. That year, Hank hit a home run to win the pennant, starred as the Braves beat the Yankees in seven games in the World Series, and captured the MVP of the National League. The Braves' pennant years were treasured oral history, passed down by the family elders.

Dad would tell the story of Nippy Jones, the obscure infielder who pinch hit for Warren Spahn in the tenth inning of Game Four of the '57 Series. Nippy insisted he was hit in the foot by a pitch. To prove it, he showed the disbelieving umpire the ball. And there, between the seams, was Nippy's shoe polish. The ump reversed himself, and Nippy trotted to first base. That proved to be the tying run, and the Braves, down two games to one, went on to win the game, and the Series. "That's why we *love* Nippy Jones," Dad would say for years.

Mom remembered the elegant New Yorker who sat next to her during Game Three at County Stadium. The woman declared, haughtily, that *of course* the Yankees would prevail. "You could just hear it in her voice—they all thought we were so bush league," Mom said. Vindication came when the Braves won it all with a 5–0 shutout in Game Seven at Yankee Stadium.

Tom recalled the hundreds of thousands of Milwaukeeans that filled the downtown streets that night, the love frenzy that brought Milwaukee, once and for all, into the major leagues—in its own eyes, and, it seemed, in the eyes of the nation.

My times with the Braves were more modest. By 1964, Mathews, the veteran third baseman, was starting to lose his power. Spahn, the once-great lefty, was old and fading. And the team was mediocre. As they declined, the fans stayed away. The home attendance had dropped off so sharply— barely 750,000 for all of 1963—that there was even talk of the Braves leaving town. *That*, I refused to believe.

Most games I listened to on my late grandpa Tom's portable transistor radio, the old black Zenith, with Earl Gillespie and Blaine Walsh calling the action. From the press box, they caught foul balls with a fishnet—or tried to. A batter would foul one back and Gillespie would yell, "Get the fishnet, Blainer!" You'd hear great clunking and scrambling, but never, as I recall, "I got it!" Which was okay; I never caught a foul ball either.

A few times, we made it out to County Stadium. Before the games and afterward I'd wait for Hank and the other Braves at a chain link fence, along the walkway between the Braves dugout and their clubhouse. I'd stick a program through the links of the fence, calling out with the other kids: *Hey Frank! Hey Eddie! Hey Joe! Hey Mr. Aaron!* By this time, there was more talk of the Braves leaving. Nobody seemed very happy and I didn't get many autographs. Hank didn't stop to sign, not when I was there.

By late 1964, the papers were full of the unthinkable— the Braves really did want to move to Atlanta. Milwaukee officials vowed to fight the move. We were worried.

So was Hank. "Aaron Plans to Investigate Problems of Atlanta Negro," said an October headline in the *Journal*. "I have lived in the south and don't want to live there again," Hank told the Milwaukee sportswriters. "I don't want to go on the road and find out one day that some Ku Klux Klan group has exploded a bomb in the area where my family is living. There have been a lot of bombings down south and nothing has been done to find the people responsible." The year before, four little black girls had been murdered in an explosion in a Birmingham, Alabama, church. And Bull Connor, the Birmingham public safety commissioner, had turned the dogs and fire hoses on black demonstrators. In Georgia, Lester Maddox, an up-and-coming segregationist politician who headed a group called Georgians Unwilling to Surrender (known by its initials, GUTS), was vowing never to abide by the 1964 Civil Rights Act. When three young black ministers showed up to try to integrate Maddox's Pickrick restaurant, he threatened them with a pistol. Two years later, Maddox was elected governor. Martin Luther King, Jr., proclaimed that he was "ashamed to be a Georgian."

In early 1965, when the move was all but inevitable, Hank was invited to Atlanta by more moderate local officials, including the city's white mayor, Ivan Allen, and Georgia's lone black state legislator, Leroy Johnson. Before Hank left, he said that if the new Braves stadium were not completely integrated, he would refuse to play there.

Hank returned saying he could live and play in Atlanta after all. "Actually, Atlanta is not the south," he told a *Journal* sportswriter. "What I mean is, it isn't like the rest of the south. The only thing bad about it is it happens to be in Georgia. They have made tremendous progress in all phases" in Atlanta, Hank said. "The Negroes there are way ahead of the Negroes here. It's no contest. Sure they've got segregation problems there, but they've got them in Milwaukee, too. Up here they call it 'de facto segregation.' Down there they just call it segregation."

Still, Hank said, he didn't want to go if he could help it. "This is my home," he told the papers.

There was talk of suing the Braves to keep them in Milwaukee. But most people seemed resigned to the departure. Attendance was pathetic, a fact Braves officials were always quick to point out. In 1965 the team owners had the audacity to schedule five exhibition games in Atlanta, and these outdrew Milwaukee's first twenty-eight home games of the season.

A few times that year, the big crowds came. On Bat Day at County Stadium, at the urging of the public address announcer, we children held our wood aloft: 15,000 matchsticks, steady and silent in the late afternoon sun. It may have seemed like a final plea, or threat. Whatever it was, it didn't work. The Braves were leaving.

In one of my last trips out to see the Braves, a young outfielder named Rico Carty hit a pair of homers and a double. After the game I waited with Kath and a bunch of other kids for his autograph behind the Braves dugout. Rico was laughing and joking in Spanish with a teammate I can't remember. I was three kids away when he ducked his head and disappeared.

The Braves' last game in Milwaukee was September 22, 1965. Twelve thousand, five hundred seventy-seven mourners came to pay last respects. They gave Eddie Mathews a three-minute standing ovation when he came to bat in the eighth. The next inning, Hank and teammate Joe Torre got their own long cheers. "This I've never seen before," Hank said after the game. "Words can't describe the way I felt."

The Braves lost to the Los Angeles Dodgers in eleven innings. Hank hit the final pitch, a line drive out to center field. A bugler played "Taps" on the Braves' dugout. The next morning the *Milwaukee Sentinel* ran a picture of Aaron and Mathews: Number 44 and Number 41, side by side, backs to the camera, on the long cement corridor to the Braves' clubhouse. Walking away.

"Great While It Lasted," said an editorial in the *Journal*. The mayor sought to reassure us that we were still a major league town: "Big league baseball teams do not make big league cities." If we judged ourselves on that basis, the mayor warned, "heaven help us!"

"Let 'em go," my brother Tom said, covering the wound of abandonment with disdain. "They stink now anyway." It was true; those who abandoned us were losers and no-names. Names like Spahn and Burdette and Bruton and Shoendienst had given way to Bolling and Woodward and Gonder and De La Hoz. But of course there was another name, which is why for me the sting wouldn't fade. The man who patrolled right field in my hometown, the great Henry Aaron, was leaving. What was I going to do with my hero 800 miles away?

O

When the 1966 season began, Milwaukee, like a wounded lover, tried to move on. My friend T started rooting for the Chicago White Sox, ninety miles down the road. My dad suggested that perhaps I could pull for the Cubs, as he had as a boy, when there was only a minor league team in Milwaukee. The Cubs were okay; they had Ernie Banks and Billy Williams and Ron Santo—but no Hank. Anyway, I couldn't pull for a Chicago team. I had to find a way to follow the Braves.

In that first season without them, I'd wait for dark, and scour the AM radio dial. Night after night, I'd pull in country preachers, and trucker talk shows, and distant oldies stations playing greaser music . . . and finally, one spring evening, a faint signal, coming in at 650 AM: *"Felipe Alou the batter . . . Hammer on deck . . ."*

The Hammer on deck! Hammerin' Henry Aaron! The Atlanta Braves, coming through the speakers in Milwaukee! Alone in the living room, I jumped up and down, again and again, pure elation surging through me. Now I could relax; I'd found Hank again.

Season after season, I'd listen through the pop and crackle of distant thunderstorms in Indiana or Tennessee. The station was WSM out of Nashville, 650, the voice of the Grand Ole Opry. When the signal faded, I'd flip over to 750, WSB in Atlanta. Chin on the living room rug, I'd scrawl on homemade scorecards, recording walks, hits, strikeouts and home runs, keeping track of my distant hero and his teammates: Phil Niekro, Ralph Garr, Dusty Baker, Cecil Upshaw, Felix Millan. Sometimes my mom or my sister Mary would come in and shake their heads in amazement. All they could hear was static. But through the buzzing I could make out the voice of Milo Hamilton, the Braves' new play-by-play man: *"Here's the pitch to the Hammer. . . . There's a drive, deep into the power alley in left. . . . That thing is . . . OUTTA HERE!"*

Great as it was to follow Hank from afar, these were my baseball-formative years, and I was deprived of a home team. So was the rest of Milwaukee. In the summer of 1967, a young car dealer tried to come to our rescue. Bud Selig of Knippel-Selig Ford arranged for an exhibition game between the Chicago White Sox and the Minnesota Twins to be played at County Stadium.

I went to the game with my mom. Dad couldn't come;

lately, he was having trouble walking. We were worried, and so were the doctors. They said that Dad would probably need a special diet and some kind of exercise. Beyond that, they weren't sure what would help.

Mom and I sat in the lower grandstand behind home plate. We yelled a lot. We stomped our feet. The grandstands were packed, the box seats were packed, the upper deck and the bleachers were packed. Selig roped off standing-room-only fans four and five deep along the outfield warning track. When Twins left fielder Bobby Allison went back on a fly ball and spiked a kid, drawing blood on the boy's shin, I was jealous: Allison escorted the boy off the field, to the cheers of 50,000. The kid got to sit in the Twins' dugout and get patched up by the trainer.

It was the biggest crowd ever to see a game at the stadium: 51,114. Five thousand more were turned away at the gate. The Twins won, but nobody cared. We cared about sending a message. "MILWAUKEE:" shouted a big home-made sign in the bleachers. "We Deserve a Major League Team."

Milwaukee was to get a big-league image that summer—but not one it wanted. This was a summer of unrest in America: riots and civil conflicts, dozens of them, broke out across the country, including the huge conflagrations in Newark and Detroit. A week after the baseball game, Milwaukee joined the list, when a riot broke out in the city's "Inner Core." The mayor, and others, preferred to call it a civil disturbance. Seventeen hundred were arrested, nearly a hundred injured, and four dead: a young man, two old women, a cop.

ME AND HANK

On a muggy August night, we heeded the mayor's curfew, eating quietly at a picnic table in the backyard, spraying *Off!* on our arms and legs. The city's most improbable civil rights leader, a Catholic priest named James Groppi, was in the *Journal*, calling the riot a "revolt."

It was our last summer in the backyard. Soon, we'd pay to put an indoor pool where the yard was now. The doctors now thought that what Dad had was multiple sclerosis. Unlike the polio that got his left side, the M.S. hit his strong right side. He was already losing some of those powerful muscles in his right leg, the one that compensated. The only way to slow the right leg's deterioration, the doctors said, was by exercise, and the only way to exercise was to swim.

We had time to think that night: to slap at mosquitos, and chew slowly on burgers, and look at Dad's crutches, lying in the grass; to imagine the electric shovels, soon to breach the moist soil and make a hole beneath our feet; to wonder about the riot, and the curfew, and what Father Groppi was calling a revolt.

Would this revolt reach us? And if it did, what would we do? Mom and Dad believed in integration. Since the fifties, they'd sent us to an integrated grade school, the Campus School of the University of Wisconsin–Milwaukee. But this riot, this "revolt"—no one had taught us anything about that.

At the heart of the battles that summer—as I learned from my fifth-grade classmate Dale Phillips—was the right for blacks to live wherever they wanted in the city. Dale's mom, Vel Phillips, the first black and first woman on the Milwaukee Common Council (and a friend of Hank's), had many times introduced a bill to allow open housing in the city. As Hank had said in the paper, there was "de facto segregation" in our town. Certainly I'd never noticed any blacks living in my neighborhood. Again and again Dale's mom put forward the open housing resolution. Again and again it was defeated, 18–1, by aldermen saying they feared that if the resolution passed, the whites would move to the suburbs, where no such laws existed. The mayor agreed.

By that summer, the battle was in the streets. One day Dale took me to a rally where Father Groppi was shouting from the podium. He was flanked by the Commandoes of the NAACP Youth Council, young black men standing straight, black berets tilted over one eye. The Commandoes, Dale told me, ran the street demonstrations with discipline. They were unarmed, but Dale said, "Nobody messes with them." Sometimes even the police would back down from a confrontation. Other times, the cops wielded their long billy clubs.

On the stage, Father Groppi was enraged, roaring into the microphone, going on about black power and the need to fight *whitey*. I looked at my skin and at the skin of the man on the podium. I felt strange; wasn't Groppi himself a white man? Wasn't his father an Italian grocer? "He's white, but he's *black*," Dale told me. "I mean, the dude's *white*, but he's *black*." But who, I wondered, was *whitey*? Was *whitey* the bigot on the south side who wouldn't let the black man live in his neighborhood? Or was I, this eleven-year-old kid from the east side, was I *whitey*, too?

O

ME AND HANK

In 1968 the Chicago White Sox, starved for fans in their hometown, agreed to play ten games a year in County Stadium. It was another coup for Bud Selig, the car dealer and up-and-coming baseball entrepreneur. I saved up money from my *Journal* route, and bought a single ticket, lower grandstand, for each of the games. I'd ride the #30 Jackson-Downer bus, transferring at Capitol Drive to the Stadium Freeway Flier and the thirty-minute ride west. Through the open window I could smell the Ambrosia chocolate factory as we went by, the rising loaves of the Wonder Bread plant, the sweet pungence of the Red Star Yeast factory, and the smoky hops of the breweries: Schlitz, Miller High Life and Pabst Blue Ribbon. The Harley-Davidson plant belched smoke, and so did the steel foundry of the Falk Corporation's factory, where they made the giant gears for mines, bridges and ships. We passed the vast rail yard of the old Milwaukee Road, and the bars and auto repair shops of Pigsville in the Menominee River Valley. The bus slowed, daylight faded, I pounded my freshly oiled glove, and the banks of stadium lights came into view.

The first year of the "Chilwaukee White Sox," the crowds at County Stadium were big. I sat amidst them, by myself, smacking my fist into the deep pocket of my Rick Monday glove, always ready to pounce on the foul ball that never came.

The next year, 1969, T and I went to the games together. We'd sit in the upper grandstand, our programs rolled into microphones:

T: *"This is Red Rush . . ."*

Sandy: *"And I'm Bahhhhhhb Elston, with your Go-Go White Sox!"*

T: *"Hey, friends, for all your insurance needs, call Friendly Bob Adams, at Andover three, two-oh, two-oh."*

From our announcer's perch in the upper deck, we could look beyond the outfield bleachers to the Johnston cookie factory and its flashing red lights: "Cookies, Crackers, Candies, Chocolate." Farther south stood the giant clockface of the Allen Bradley company.

"The largest four-faced clock in the world, Red, in case there's anyone out there who doesn't know this important big-league fact about Milwaukee."

"That's right, Bob, even bigger than Big Ben in London, England!"

The crowds were thinner that year, and after a few innings we'd try to sneak down into the first few rows behind the ChiSox dugout. Just as I was into the Braves, T was into his White Sox: Carlos May, Bill Melton, Wilbur Wood, Leon "Daddy Wags" Wagner, and Walter "No-Neck" Williams, a five-foot six-inch fireplug whose head appeared truly buried inside his shoulders. All game long I'd keep an eye on the sausage-shaped Patrick Cudahy Hot Dog Scoreboard, scanning for news from Atlanta.

By now the open housing battle was over; Milwaukee and most of the suburbs had passed strong ordinances giving blacks the rights to move where they wanted. Father Groppi had taken his fight to the state capitol, marching with welfare mothers, occupying the state assembly building and getting himself arrested. Soon he'd take on one of our favorite teams, the Marquette Warriors, chastising them for their mascot, Willie Wampum, a Marquette student who'd do a war dance at halftime during the basketball games, wearing a giant, papier-mâché head of an Indian "warrior." As a result of Groppi's pressure, that dance would stop, and Willie Wampum would be no more.

The same year, 1969, Hank and the Braves enjoyed a brief resurgence: they won the National League Western Division, only to lose in the league championship series to the Miracle Mets, three games to none. You couldn't blame that on Hank: he hit a home run in each game.

The next year, Bud Selig brought baseball back to Milwaukee, luring the Seattle Pilots to the Great Lakes. "Milwaukee has a great setup there and the people there are major league," one player told the *Sentinel*. "Milwaukee is a major league town," said another. "The people there are real good major league fans." Those of us who cried about how Atlanta stole our Braves four years earlier were only too happy now to scoop up a franchise from Seattle, which was promptly renamed the Brewers, after our city's most famous industry. Apologies now to any young Seattle fans who felt robbed the way we did. On the other hand, it should be noted, the Seattle Pilots played only one year in the American League, in a place called Sick's Stadium, and the team, upon arrival, appeared truly ill. Despite the blind hope of spring and sportswriters' gushing over a new team in town ("the infield should be the Brewers' showpiece"; "Gene Brabender, native Wisconsin son, figures to head up a sound staff which shouldn't disgrace itself"), the 1970 Brewers were basically a patched-up band of has-beens and never-would-bes.

But just as Milwaukee's love affair with the Braves was likened to Brooklyn's for its Dodgers, so our new team's embarrassments on the field endeared us to them—just as New

York took to those early Mets. We felt bad for our boys. On a cold April opening day, between trips to the men's room to stand under the heaters, I watched the California Angels pound our new team, 12–0. In that whole sorry season, one play stands out. Gene Brabender, the would-be favorite son from Black Earth, Wisconsin, was on the mound. The bases were loaded, one out.

"A swing and a chop back toward the mound. Double play ball, this should end the inning. Brabender turns to throw to second . . . and he throws the ball over Kubiak's head! It's into center field! One run is in! Here comes another one! . . . And now it's nine to nothing!" Forever I will recall the afflicted Brabender, running off the mound to back up the throw from center field, raising his arms to the heavens like Job.

As we watched the Brewers lose, I kept up on news from the South. Through the static of Nashville radio, and the fine print of the morning box scores, I knew something momentous was happening: Hank was piling up the homers, and slowly climbing up the list of all-time home run greats. By 1970 he'd already passed some of the greatest home run hitters ever: Stan Musial, Lou Gehrig, Mel Ott, Ted Williams, Jimmie Foxx and Mickey Mantle. In 1970 he hit 38, and 47 the next season, and 34 in 1972, eclipsing his longtime rival, Willie Mays. At the end of the 1972 season, Hank was alone in second place with 673 homers. He was thirty-eight years old, and it was clear he had a shot at the greatest record in sports: the all-time career home run record of 714, held by the immortal one, Babe Ruth. My hero, passing the Bambino. What a great thing that would be.

In the spring of 1973, I was seventeen, a junior in high

school. The baseball season was new; Hank had hit a few homers already. One morning I came downstairs for breakfast, heading, as always, for the sports section first. It was early. My mom was in the poolroom, easing my father out of the pool and into his wheelchair. Every morning at six o'clock, she'd crank him down into the shallow waters in a small overhead lift. He'd swim for twenty-five minutes, then she'd crank him back up again. By now Dad couldn't walk at all. But in the water, he still looked strong. Sometimes I'd look out at him through the windows in the dining room, as he pulled himself through the water, back and forth with those powerful arms. The water on his biceps would glisten.

I sat at the table, by the bananas and the sugar bowl and the box of Wheat Chex. I opened the sports page to find the following headline: "Aaron Hit by Hate Mail."

The article didn't reveal what the letters said, but Hank gave some idea: "It's very offensive. They call me 'nigger' and every bad word you can come up with. You can't ignore them." The article was clear: the hate was being delivered to Hank because he was challenging Babe Ruth's record. The record of a white man.

Dad was out of the pool, half dressed, the back of his wheelchair poking out of the bathroom. His right hand sat in his lap, frozen in place. With his left hand, he fiddled with an electric razor, finally freeing the blades and blowing old whiskers into the sink. Mom was drying his hair with a towel.

I read slowly. "This is just the way things are for black people in America," my hero was saying. "It's something you battle all your life. If I was white, all America would be proud of me."

I looked over at Mom. She was struggling with Dad's top

button, flipping up his collar, measuring the right length to tie his tie.

I looked again at the headline. I knew enough not to be shocked. It was 1973 and I lived in America. But I was shocked anyway. It seemed incredible that people could be this unfair.

Hank's chase, it was clear, had grown larger than baseball. I told my parents: I want to do something.

I went out and I bought a scrapbook: fake leather with string binding; red, with gold letters. On the first page I scrawled "HENRY'S HOMERS." Over the months the pages filled with clips from the *Sentinel*, the *Journal* and the *Sporting News*: a chronicle of the countdown to 715.

And then I wrote Hank a letter: *Don't listen to them, Mr. Aaron. We're in your corner. You're my hero. I believe in you.*

I sent the letter off, expecting perhaps a Braves team picture in return, or maybe a form letter:

> *The Atlanta Braves*
> *Thank You!*
> *For your interest.*

Weeks passed. I read more ugly news of the hate and the threats against Hank. Inning after inning, in his spot in left field in hometown Atlanta, he'd heard the slurs, burning into the back of his neck. Who was this black man, these fans wanted to know, who thought he was better than Babe Ruth? He couldn't touch the Babe with a ten-foot pole. Why didn't he just go away, quit the game now, get the hell out? While he still could.

By June, the record was within reach. I pasted more of Hank's home runs in my scrapbook: Number 680, 685, 687. Twenty-eight more to go.

In late June 1973—I remember it being around noon, warm and muggy—I went out to the porch to get the mail. In the stack I saw a letter postmarked Atlanta, Georgia. Return address: Fulton County Stadium. Must be the "thank you for your interest" note from the Braves. Or maybe not. I opened the letter, carefully. And read:

> *Dear Sandy:*
>
> *I want you to know how very much I appreciate the concern and best wishes of people like yourself. If you will excuse my sentimentality, your letter of support and encouragement meant much more to me than I can adequately express in words . . .*

I scanned to the bottom:

> *Most sincerely,*
> *Hank Aaron*

Hank Aaron. His signature, in blue ink.

My mouth was half open, frozen that way. Cicadas called from the trees. An old convertible cruised by, Stevie Wonder blaring out, and fading. I stood motionless, at the doorway, holding my letter from Hank.

1

THE ENCOUNTER

Prescott, Arizona, September 1998

I stand with a lock in my hand, gazing past an open aluminum door at the boxes of an old life and a failed marriage. I duck my head and step into the must. Files, mementos, books, cassettes and reel-to-reel tapes are in heaps, strewn across the tiny storage shed. The last time I was here, it seems, I couldn't wait to leave.

The boxes house seventeen years of my political and environmental reporting, from trips I have made to South America, the Middle East, American Indian country, and along the campaign trail. They are piled up to the ceiling, each marked in a hasty scrawl: REHNQUIST (an investigation of the Supreme Court justice for challenging the rights of blacks to vote, as a lawyer in Phoenix in 1964), SANCTUARY (trial transcripts of the American church workers who were convicted of smuggling Central American refugees into the U.S.), DOMINICAN REPUBLIC (Haitians held against their will in the sugarcane fields). High in a corner, a box says, FBI SURVEILLANCE, and next to that, URANIUM SPILL and GOLD MINES and NAVAJO-HOPI LAND DISPUTE.

Boxes and boxes and things I'd forgotten, coated with dust: tapes from my last jazz show on college radio, a reporters' "Stylebook" from the Associated Press, a few old journalism awards mounted on dark-stained wood. And photographs, loose and scattered: palm trees in the Mojave Desert, a wonder from an early solo trip west; an old friend, on the porch of a Tucson bungalow where I once lived; and me, bleary-eyed and wired, one late night, singing "Mack the Knife" into an empty Budweiser bottle.

I've come for none of this. There's something else, the one thing from this mess I want most. But I'm afraid it's lost, a casualty of my life as an itinerant radio producer: ten addresses in seven years, belongings scattered from Costa Rica to Arizona to Wisconsin to Massachusetts.

Perhaps this thing I've come for can't be found here. But if it is here, I'll find it. I'll need to go through the mountain of boxes, one by one.

And there it is, the first thing I touch in the first box I reach for: my old red Hank Aaron scrapbook. I rub my hand softly across its cover, tracing my finger along the gold cursive letters: "Scrap Book." I open it, carefully, and see "HENRY'S HOMERS," traced by my hand with my father's blue fountain pen. And there, taped into the inside cover, is my letter from Henry Aaron, dated June 20, 1973. Standing there in the unsettled dust, I read:

> *It is very heart warming to know that you are in my corner. I will always be grateful for the interest you have shown in me. As the so called "countdown" begins, please be assured I will try to live up to the expectations of my friends.*

I feel peaceful, and supremely happy, sort of the way I felt that night in 1966 when I discovered the Braves on long-distance radio. I'd found Hank again; I could relax. I have again, in my hands, the tactile details of an early connection: the roots of something. And I have the physical evidence that will make my next step possible.

I want to travel to Atlanta to meet my old hero, where he's now a senior vice president of the Braves. I want to find out, really, what he went through. I want to learn something about how all that hate hit him, what stayed with him, what he let go, what the whole experience says about what we were doing then, in America, how we are doing now. Of course, I want to bring along my old scrapbook, and the letter that was lost and found.

I trash most of the boxes, ship a few back home to the East Coast, where I now live. Then I sit down and write Hank Aaron a letter: my second, coming a generation after the first.

> *Dear Mr. Aaron,*
> *Surely you won't remember me, but 25 years ago you wrote me a letter . . .*

I tell Hank that when the Braves left Milwaukee there was a big hole in our lives; that I followed him for years through the static of Nashville radio; that I watched him climbing up the list of home run greats, passing one after another; that I remembered "the sick thing that still makes me angry"; that I've been thinking of him all season, during the happier home run chase of Mark McGwire and Sammy Sosa, and how that reminded me of what he went through in '74. I tell him how I've grown up to be a journalist and radio producer, and how, now, finally, I'd like to meet my old hero.

The letter goes on for three pages. It's polite, but a bit like the first letter must have sounded: "I think I cried when the Braves left town, but I was only nine so I really don't remember. . . . With all due respect to McGwire and Sosa, let's face it, yours is still The Record. . . . Chasing the greatest record in all of sports, you were dealing with *this* . . ."

I mail it off to Turner Field. I'm so proud of it, I send a

copy to my brother Will, whom we all call Yam. "He'll either love it," Yam says, "or he'll think you're out of your mind."

O

Weeks later, and still no word from Hank. My wife, Lamis, and I fly back to Milwaukee for Christmas. One night Lamis goes to bed early, and my mom and I sit up talking at the kitchen table. I pour her a glass of red wine, and myself a bourbon on the rocks.

"The first time I saw Henry Aaron," Mom says, "your father and I were at the stadium with some friends. This would have been in the fifties."

Probably '54, I tell her, Hank's first year with the Braves.

"Probably. And the only thing I remember about that first game was that he got caught between the bases trying to steal. I turned to someone and said, 'I don't think that kid is going to last.'" She laughs. "I guess I was wrong about *that* one!" Hank was twenty then; Mom was twenty-seven.

The Green Bay Packers were big in our family, too—a Sunday ritual of faith following hours of suffering: Mass, where Monsignor Grasser would drone on and on, and I'd shift my bony butt in the hard pew; Sunday School, where the road to heaven was drawn on the chalkboard, with little chalk gas pumps along the way called "confession" and "communion." Late on fall Sunday mornings I'd get home and tear off my stiff clothes and slip on the green jersey with the number 15 that Mom had sewn on. And then I'd have these pretend huddles where I got to play Bart Starr: *Okay, Boyd—*

you go out deep and cut across the middle. Marv, go straight up-field and do a buttonhook. Carroll, you do a fly pattern. I'll fake it to Marv and throw deep. On two. Blue, 52! Blue, 52! HUT! HUT! Then the real game would come on. Tom and Mary and John and Dad and I would sit in front of the new color RCA. In later years, Dad would be in his wheelchair. Mom would bring us cold pears and Triscuits and slabs of sharp cheddar cheese, and she'd pour Dad a glass of Miller High Life from a tall clear bottle. I'd watch it foam up. "Thanks, Sal," Larry Tolan would say, in that warm, low voice honed by Camel non-filters.

Mom remembers further back, to the first baseball game I went to, with our next-door neighbor, Cliff Randall, in his Volkswagen. "You must have been four or five," she says. "He came home and said you were most into the treats." That seems right. I remember nothing of the game—maybe they were playing the Dodgers?—but I seem to recall a hot dog and a block of caramel corn and a frozen malt in a plastic cup. It was a doubleheader, probably in 1961; I got bored early and we came home. That season there were no whispers of the Braves leaving town. Later, Mom says, as the leaving talk grew loud, that's when I really got into the Braves. "You were so in love with them," she says. "You know, math was not one of your strong suits. But boy could you handle those batting averages and earned run averages!"

I was into the numbers for sure. I remind Mom about Strat-O-Matic, the board game played with three dice, two white and one red, and computerized player cards based on the previous year's performance. In winter, when the new cards arrived, my brother John (then nicknamed Yan, short

28

for Johann) and my buddies T, Che, Zan, and Freak would gather in John's bedroom for the annual draft. We all had mythical home parks: Yan-kee Stadium, Zan-kee Stadium, Che Stadium, and T-ger Stadium. Freak's team played at Freak Field. (His real name was Jim Ladky; he got the nickname because he was built long and narrow and had a big shock of bushy brown hair.) My nickname was Ace, so even though I preferred that my team play on real grass, I had no choice but to play in the Acetrodome.

We sorted the players by positions and then made selections, like real team owners. Of course, I always had my eye on Hank, but then, so did everybody else. One year we had to veto a proposal by John to conduct ninety-six rounds, with complete farm systems and minor league rosters. And I thought *I* was crazy. It took long enough just to choose twenty-five guys. We wanted to start rolling the three little dice.

"Shaking, one-two, against the lefty pitcher: triple ones, baby, it's outta here!"

"Home run?! That's ridiculous! He only hit three homers last year! Let me see that!"

"Look! It says right here! Sorry, it's a home run!"

Once, on such a long-shot homer, I kicked John hard under the Strat-O table. My younger brother had been gloating. Or so I'd thought. Quietly, with huge tears in his eyes, he kept playing. In college, I sent him a letter and apologized.

More than once Freak and I got into rows over Hank's chase for the Babe's record. *Babe played part of his career in the dead-ball era*, Freak would say. *Much harder to hit home runs. And now, there are more teams. Diluted talent. No comparison.* I'd come back: *What about all the night games Hank's had to play? What about the short porch in right at Yankee Sta-dium? Two hundred ninety-five feet! Who knows how many cheap home runs Ruth got? And what do you mean, superior talent back then? Blacks couldn't even play in the majors! And where is your loyalty to Hank, anyway?*

Only once do I remember our shouted arguments getting my parents' attention. It may have been the time Che and our buddy Gar nearly came to blows over which was the better recreation: pinball or batting machines? Mom came storming upstairs and laid into us. *Everyone is always welcome in our house. But you have to show some respect. This is too much, boys, just far, far too much.* Dad's voice, strong and sharp, came flying upstairs in support. Afterward, barely whispering, we all agreed we'd had it coming. "I can't *believe* the stuff your mom put up with," T would remember thirty years later.

Mom has cut up some pears and laid a bowl of grapes be-tween us. Remember, Mom, I say, that the next year, to keep the peace, we took the Strat-O games up to the Yellow Room on the third floor? Yeah, she tells me, and so John could have his bedroom not filled with all those stacks of little player cards! And isn't the Yellow Room where you would have "spring cleaning" for all your baseball cards? Right, I say. Dusting them off, sorting them and putting rubber bands around them. Until one year I sold them, all 5,000 of them, for thirty-five dollars. I kept only my six or seven Hank cards—including the one of a smiling Hank that Kathy gave me in 1964, the year before the Braves left town.

"I remember feeling like we'd been had," Mom says of the team's departure. "We felt abandoned, annoyed. And angry.

But you said, 'I'm still going to be for them anyway. I'm still going to be for Hank.'"

I tell Mom I've dug out the letter and scrapbook from the storage shed in Arizona. She recalls something about a letter from Hank. "But you know," she goes on, "I don't remember that you were keeping a scrapbook." At first, I am amazed to hear this. How could she forget such an important chronicle—this great, red, fake-leather piece of history, attended to so painstakingly?

I think about it for a minute. I was taping Henry's homers into the scrapbook from April 1973 until the following April. Here's what Mom had going then: a son in grade school (Yam) and two in high school (me and John), a daughter (Mary) in college, another daughter (Kathy) launching an acting career in New York, a son (Tom) working as a longshoreman and a cabbie while mulling graduate school, and a husband going downhill. Once an up-and-coming lawyer—second in his class at Michigan Law School, former clerk for United States Supreme Court Justices Frank Murphy and Thomas C. Clark—Dad was down to short hours in the office at the courtesy of the firm. Our future uncertain, Mom had gone back to school for her Master's, and was teaching English at the University of Wisconsin–Milwaukee.

I tell Mom about a memory I have of that time. All eight of us—Mom and Dad and the six kids—are sitting around the table after dinner. Chicken bones lie on plates, and there's a layer of custard sauce in the china pitcher, the one with blue flowers. And then Dad suddenly says he's feeling really good today, he's feeling strong, and he is just going to try to stand up and walk. And we are all surprised, because Dad hasn't walked in years. *Sally, hon, can you get my crutches? I think they're still in the vestibule.* And she does, Mom goes out and gets them, and while she hovers, while we watch, Dad slowly stands up. Out of that wheelchair at the head of the table, he pulls himself up by those metal crutches, and he staggers, smiling, laughing now, he staggers around the dinner table, and out into the front hall. And as he lurches, on his feet, he cries out, "I can walk! I can walk! I can walk!"

Mom is shaking her head, slowly, frowning, trying to remember this. Her fingers cradle the stem of her wineglass.

My mother says she has no memory of the story I just told. None. As it happens, none of my brothers and sisters do either. "Sweetheart," Mom says gently. "Do you think maybe you *dreamed* that?"

It's past midnight—late for both of us these days. I put away the whiskey and the wine. Mom wraps up the fruits we've been nibbling on.

"I hope you get to see Henry, dear," Mom says as we trudge upstairs to bed. "That would really be wonderful."

A week later, back home near Boston, I get an e-mail from Hank Aaron's secretary: Mr. Aaron can see me on January 11. I'll have forty-five minutes.

O

It's strange. I've reported from seventeen countries: along back roads laid with mines during the Nicaraguan *contra* war; near the Serbian shells falling on Mostar in Bosnia-Herzegovina; amidst the smoky roadblocks and flying stones of a West Bank on the verge of explosion. But not in eighteen years as a journalist have I been more nervous before an interview than I am for my encounter with Henry Louis Aaron. Certainly I've felt more pure terror, like the moment the plane landed in Sarajevo, and the BBC correspondent looked at my ghostly face and asked, "Sure you're all right, old chap?" But never with sweatier palms, never more like a nervous kid, never groping so, for the words to make a sentence

"Um . . . ahh . . . um," I begin. "And, uhh, I, uhhn . . ."

Clearing my throat, starting again:

"Aside from the fact that you were my hero when I was little, and now I've grown to be a reporter, I feel like I'm here for two reasons."

"Well, thank you," Henry Aaron says.

I am, truly, in Hank Aaron's office. For the moment, this fact is too much to absorb. For the moment, I have forgotten how to be a journalist. I look at him: tailored tan suit, broad, handsome, gentle face, hair flecked with gray. Large hands, and the lightning wrists, resting on his lap. On a wall, a framed collage of the 1957 Braves.

"I grew up in Milwaukee," I tell him.

"Did you really?" he says, with a big smile. "Nothing like Milwaukee."

And then I start telling Hank Aaron my story. It seems he hasn't connected my recent letter with the overgrown kid sitting in front of him. I reach into my bag, and pull out the old scrapbook.

He laughs. It seems this isn't the typical interview for him, either. I place the collected memories between us, and open them up again.

The first thing is his letter to me—still in the inside cover, loose now, with yellowed tape marks on the corners. He reads it aloud, his voice rich and deep. When he finishes— "Wishing you only the best, I am most sincerely, Hank Aaron"—he sets the letter down and looks at me.

"It's been quite a while," Hank says. "Nineteen seventy-three. I tried to answer all the letters that I received—I received quite a few pieces of mail. And it was people like you that sent me encouraging letters to continue to pursue my dream. After all I was just playing baseball but I just wanted to thank you and to thank people like yourself for the support that you gave me back when, really, I needed all the support I could get."

I look down at my arms, and see gooseflesh.

"To me, it's the greatest record in sports," I tell Hank. "And yet, you were facing incredible adversity. And it made a white kid from Wisconsin just pretty upset, but I can't imagine what it would have been like for you."

"Well, it was tough," he says. "No question about it. As I mentioned before, it was people like yourself that I leaned on and that I got my moral support from. But the hardest part about the whole thing was not so much the resentment that I had from outside. It was the fact that I was separated from my kids. I couldn't do things with my kids, I couldn't go to the park with them, I had to be escorted to different places, you know."

He'd had a twenty-four-hour bodyguard. He'd had to

check into separate hotels, apart from the rest of the Braves. Teammates brought food to his room. He hardly ever saw his children. And there were death threats. Many of them.

"I don't talk about it all that much until someone brings it up. Because it's sad when you think about it. And yet you look at what McGwire and Sosa went through this year—I think they enjoyed themselves. McGwire with his son, he picked his son up out on the field. Well, my kids had to be sheltered."

During his chase, Henry Aaron got a plaque from the post office. Except for the president, no American had ever received so much mail in so short a time: 930,000 pieces in less than two years. At an ounce per piece, that comes to 58,125 pounds, or 100 pounds per day, dragged into Braves' offices in bulging mailbags. The Braves hired a secretary to open it and help Hank respond. That he wrote back to me, under the weight of this burden, is mind-boggling.

For a time back then, Hank estimated, the mail was running 60–40 against him. After a while the balance shifted, as outrage set in and Americans wrote in support. But to the end, the hate flowed:

Dear Henry Aaron, how about some sickle cell anemia, Hank?

Whites are far more superior than jungle bunnies.

You are not going to break this record established by the great Babe Ruth if I can help it. My gun is watching your every black move.

Many letters were sent neither in support nor in hatred, but in defense of Babe Ruth and the Babe's mystique. Twelve years earlier, Roger Maris had faced hostility as he assaulted the Babe's single-season home run mark. Maris, a white man and a Yankee, too, received a ton of bad press and angry mail.

As with Maris, sportswriters and letterwriters said Hank could never really beat Babe's record, because the Bambino didn't come to bat as many times. To them, it was just an honest discussion about baseball. But Henry Aaron grew up in segregated Mobile. He played in the twilight of the Negro Leagues with men who'd been denied a fair shot at playing in the majors, men too old to go on. A year later he endured the abuse inherent in breaking the color barrier in the Deep South Sally (South Atlantic) League, the last bastion of segregated ball. For Hank, it had not often been just about baseball.

"No matter what it is," he tells me, "you talk about Jackie Robinson having to go through that period, of telling people, just give me a chance, I can play as well as anybody else, Dr. King, civil rights marching, telling people, don't judge me by the color of my skin but by my character, and then in '74 I break this record. So it was a lot for people to keep swallowing."

Hank Aaron pauses. Then: "You couldn't drink at this fountain, couldn't go to this restaurant. And people just thought that separate was supposed to be the right thing to do. When they saw a black ballplayer, white players or white reporters just didn't kin to him.

"It was some tough times. It was some tough times for blacks. It was some tough times in this country."

I tell Hank that for me, his struggle was part of my own awareness. I tell him about Dale Phillips, the fifth-grade classmate who took me to see Father Groppi and the Commandoes, and about Dale's mother, Vel, Milwaukee's first black council member and later, the city's first black judge and the first black to serve as Wisconsin's secretary of state. (She was also the first woman to serve in these posts.)

"I know Vel Phillips very well," Hank interjects.

There was something about the struggle of those times, I tell him, that his record seemed a part of. "It seemed like your struggle, what you were doing was about racial justice. Did you feel that way at the time?"

He thinks about the question, and responds slowly: "I don't know that I felt that way, but it certainly was caught up in the time of what was happening in this country, no question about it. I did feel like the struggle in which I was in was one that I had as much on my shoulders as some of the other civil rights leaders, because had I failed or had Jackie Robinson failed, then it would have set baseball back a hundred years."

I remembered a story I'd heard not long before, about how Dr. King had once thanked Jackie Robinson for making his job easier. Like Jackie, a friend of Hank's would tell me later, Henry Aaron kept his eyes on the prize.

"If I had gone through this period trying to accomplish what I did, and if I had showed any malice whatsoever, I would have been just the same as anybody else. They would have said, I told you so. I felt like I was in the middle of something."

And something was in the middle of him.

"It left, it left—it carved a part of me out that I will never restore, never regain."

"And what part is that?"

"Well, just, not trusting people, I guess."

O

I start turning the pages, to some of the landmarks in his career, and my boyhood. The brittle paper is beginning to crumble; little flakes fall on the glass top of Hank's desk. He brushes them off.

"Sorry," I say.

"That's all right."

I read the headlines aloud: " 'Aaron Hits 700th,' there's a picture of you . . . 'Aaron Clubs 701st; Braves Fall' . . . 'Aaron To Get Nixon Letter' . . . Do you remember that?"

Hank reads quickly, under his breath:

Dear Hank,

It must be deeply satisfying for you to near the end of your exhilarating quest, to which you have directed your finest efforts for so many years. Your quiet determination and professional excellence have earned you the respect and admiration of millions of Americans. . . .

He looks up at me. "I don't remember," he says.

Aaron Slurred As He Assaults Ruth's Mark . . . Mrs.

Ruth Wishes Aaron Good Luck, Health . . . Aaron Shakes Ghost of Ruth.

"Do you remember that feeling, that day, that moment?"

"Oh, God, I don't know that I had any feeling," Hank replies, with a short single-syllable burst of laughter. "I was just glad that it was over with, really." But he allows himself another thought: "I wouldn't have minded, if my mind had been at ease."

The forty-five minutes are over in a couple of blinks. Toward the end of our time, in the back pages of the scrapbook, I can that see the headlines and images are more interesting to me than to Hank. He remains gracious, but our time is up.

I thank him—five or six times—and tell him that I hope to talk to others who might help me understand what he went through, what his record meant to blacks in Atlanta and the South, how the record still echoes in America. He gives me a few names. Maynard Jackson, the former mayor of Atlanta. Andy Young, Jackson's successor and the former U.N. ambassador and member of Congress. Felix Mantilla, an old teammate from Milwaukee and the Sally League. He says I could start my search with his daughter, Gaile Aaron, who lives here in Atlanta.

Someone's with us in the office now, asking for a moment of his time. I make my way out, carrying an old dream in a new package, and forming a plan for a journey.

2

BITTERSWEET EMBRACE

Atlanta, Georgia, January 1999

I float out of the Braves offices, emerging onto a plaza of heroes—legendary Braves, represented by red and blue numerals, four feet high: 3, Dale Murphy; 21, Warren Spahn; 35,

Phil Niekro; 41, Eddie Mathews; and Number 44. Beyond is the entrance to the Braves museum. I'll stop in for a look.

The door is locked. I turn around. A man—scraggly beard, dark blue jacket—is walking toward me.

"Tryin' to get in to see the legends?" he calls out. "Place ain't open very much this time of year. What're you doing?"

I look at the man in front of me. Wild strands of black and gray fly from his beard like wires. His windbreaker is spotted with stains, tennis shoes busted up, pants too short. His right eye is glazed and cloudy.

I'm wearing a dark suit and a red tie, canvas bag over my shoulder.

He's wearing a half smile, like he's curious.

"What're you up to, man?"

For a moment, I think, homeless guy, street person. On some days, I would put up my guard, or just be on my way. But today, something tells me, *Stay.*

"I'm a journalist," I tell him. "I just came from interviewing Hank Aaron."

"You just talked to Hank Aaron?!" he shouts. "You interviewed Hank Aaron? You serious, man?"

"Yeah!" I tell him. "Yeah, actually Hank was my hero when I was little."

I pull out my scrapbook. We sit beneath a bronze statue of Hank, and the swing for 715. I tell him my story; he tells me his. His name is James McClain, and he lives on the street. He's from Jacksonville, Florida, originally, and he had a wife and a kid down there. But it was a bad marriage, he says. She took his baby boy, and that took a lot out of his stride. He's been around Atlanta most of the last thirty years.

During the season, he says, he hangs out by the stadium, collecting autographs.

"When Hank Aaron hit that ball, I was there—I was in that stadium over there," James says, pointing to the empty parking lot where Fulton County Stadium stood in April 1974. "And when he came up to the plate, it seemed like it was me. It was me hittin' that ball. And when he swung, it seemed like he stood at home plate for a hour. The ball stayed in space—seemed like it was in suspended animation. He put all he had into that lick. You'd like to hear him grunt from home plate.

"And when I seen him hit the ball, I seen everybody look up. It felt like he passed the civil rights bill to me. That this is the way it's going to be, that we're here and this is it. And that we are great athletes as well. And to prove it he broke a world record.

"I felt real good."

When Hank was in the middle of his pursuit of 715, James was just back from a tour of duty in Vietnam. "We wasn't getting hate mail over there," he says, "but we was getting a lot of repercussions from Vietnamese soldiers at the time. One day, they stopped us on the Ho Chi Minh trail and asked us why were we fighting here on the trail and not at home."

Around the time James came home, President Nixon declared, "We stand on the threshold of a new era of peace." It was to be a "peace with honor." But this wasn't long after a presidential commission released the Kerner Report, declaring that America was in fact becoming "two societies, one black, one white—separate and unequal." The America

James returned to was still nursing deep wounds: the massacre of thirty-three inmates, most of them black, during the Attica prison uprising in New York; the "justifiable homicide" of Black Panther Fred Hampton, in a fusillade of bullets by Chicago police and federal agents, as he lay in bed; the shootings of two Jackson State students by the Mississippi Highway Patrol; the assassination of Dr. King.

"At the time, Martin Luther King hadn't been too long assassinated, and people had lost their spirit," James remembers. "They didn't have idols, and Hank Aaron was coming up in the ranks. And Hank Aaron, that day he hit that ball, I myself was so tense that I thought that he would be assassinated. I could actually feel shots. And when he hit it and I looked at him after he hit the ball, I could actually see him being shot going around them bases. I could actually see him being shot down. But for some reason it didn't actually happen. Today I still wonder why."

When Hank crossed home plate, alive and standing, Vin Scully, the play-by-play announcer for the visiting Los Angeles Dodgers, let the cheers and fireworks ride for nearly two minutes. Then he said, "What a marvelous moment for baseball; what a marvelous moment for Atlanta and the state of Georgia; what a marvelous moment for the country and the world. A black man is getting a standing ovation in the Deep South for breaking a record of an all-time baseball idol. And it is a great moment for all of us."

Of course, it was only a home run. Great as it was, it couldn't begin to be a salve for all those fresh racial wounds. Still, James agrees with Vin Scully. Something shifted that day.

"We'd go to games and all the white kids didn't want to sit

with blacks. You could feel the racial tension in the stadium. They thought they were far greater than we was. But it seemed like in the stadium that day the whole personality changed, and blacks and whites began to actually come together." He speaks softly, intently, the raspy edge in his voice pushing it beyond a whisper. "And the people in this community, and Georgia society, it changed. And I knew then that everybody had a chance. Seemed like he broke more than a world's record of baseball. He broke a barrier between whites and blacks that day."

I squint, at the optimism of this homeless man. "Do you really think so?"

"I know so in my heart."

"What makes you say that?"

"Because I begin to see that young white kids want to be like Hank Aaron. All of them begin to wear number 44, Hank Aaron. And that was something I'd never seen. I'd never seen white kids with Hank Aaron on them. They were saying, 'I knew he could do it.' And a lot of them today still idolize Hank Aaron. They want to be like Hank. Me myself," James laughs, "I still want to be like Hank."

The smile stays with him. He's looking at me. "And here you are, twenty years later. From a boy to a man."

James looks down at the scrapbook between us. I consider the randomness of our encounter. How is it he just appeared in front of me? What were the chances? Could there be some fate in this, some plan at work?

"Excuse me, man," James is saying. "I'm wondering if you could help me out a little bit. I mean, I'd like to get something to eat."

James is hungry. So I help him out a little bit. Enough for a meal and maybe a night off the street.

We say our goodbyes. I tell James, I'm coming back for Hank's birthday gala in February; maybe we could get together again. "Oh, man, I'll take you all around Hank Aaron's old neighborhood!" James promises. "And you should come during the season. We could go see some games!" I agree. It sounds great. I give him my card, and ask him to call me, collect, any time.

And then we move in our separate directions.

"You know what?" James calls out, as we drift apart. "I think when he hit that ball that day, I think he hit it for you as well."

O

A few years ago I traveled to Denver to teach a training seminar for Native American journalists and producers in public radio. When I got to the station, KUVO, I was told that if I needed anything I should ask the production manager, Rodney Franks.

I had known a Rodney Franks in Milwaukee. We had gone to the Campus School together, during the years of Father Groppi and the Commandoes and the open housing battles in the city. Turns out it was the same guy. My old friend Rodney and I had both ended up in public radio, and here we were again, in Denver, a generation down the road. We went out one night for pizza, to catch up on a piece of the last twenty-seven years.

I remembered Rodney as a tall skinny kid with a long

stride. He had little brothers named Stevie and Ricky. They were at Campus School, too.

"I remember, man, you were allergic to peanuts," Rodney was saying with a laugh. "You broke out in hives or something, right? And so whenever we'd have peanut butter cookies for dessert in the cafeteria, I'd know to sidle up to old Sandy and get some of that extra dessert."

Campus Elementary was started as a teachers training school by educators at the University of Wisconsin–Milwaukee, where my mom would later teach English composition and literature classes. The school was rooted in the ideals of progressive education and independent learning, and by the early 1960s had incorporated racially integrated eduation as a core value. "There were a lot of white kids in the school and I hadn't really gone to school with white kids before," Rodney said. "And there were teachers' sons and daughters from Colombia, from India, Norway, Venezuela. That was really a springboard for me to interact with people from different cultures."

There were no grades given at Campus, just evaluations, and many classes were made up of "teams" of older and younger students. Miss Blakely's ten-year-olds operated the school store, and in Mrs. Bergdorf's class, the eleven-year-olds ran an actual savings bank: a single kid-sized teller's booth, with a hole in the glass to make your deposits and withdrawals.

Rodney came to Campus in 1963. We were classmates starting in second grade. For me, going to school meant a walk through the neighborhood. "And what I remember most," said Rodney, "were the bus rides. Heading down Center Street, and noticing that the further east you got the nicer the houses got, the bigger the houses got. Better manicured the lawns were. And I also remember the ride back. The faces change. The color of the faces change. And I kind of felt, in the neighborhood you had to be one certain way, you had to wear one kind of suit, and when you went to school you had to wear a different kind. It was a kind of dualism. You had to be a little bit tighter coming back. Especially if you were a bookie type of kid."

In the early Campus years, the Braves were still in town. When they left, Rodney said, "I kind of lost interest. But everybody was keeping up on Hank's career." Rodney remembered the exhibition game in 1967, when 51,000 people filled up County Stadium to show we were still a major league town. "I was at that game," he said. "And the place was packed. We're talking about the White Sox and the Twins. Man, oh man. I just recall the excitement. That was my first professional baseball game. I hadn't really gone to any of the Braves games."

That fall, we went back to school in the wake of the riots. Mr. Vance—our new teacher, a black man with a degree in education, who, I learned later, had been trying for years to get a job, any kind of teaching job—held a piece of chalk in his hand. "And I remember him writing up on the board, CIVIL DISTURBANCE," Rodney told me. "And then all the kids would sit around and talk about what a civil disturbance was." Teams were assigned to write papers. Some focused on the war in Vietnam. Rodney and one of the Gerardo sisters decided to study the turmoil wrought by the approach of Halley's Comet in 1910. My report was on the devastation of the Great Chicago Fire. (It appeared Mrs. O'Leary had been

slandered, and that neither she nor her cow were to blame.)
It struck me, these many years later, how Rodney and I both
focused on the power of fire. It was the aftermath of the riots
that lived with us then, two eleven-year-old Milwaukee boys,
each in his own way.

I tell Rodney about the time in my family's backyard during the civil disturbance. The whole city was under curfew.
Taverns were closed, gas stations shut down; there was no
mail and the buses stopped running. The streets of Milwaukee were empty. I remembered how uncertain, how out of
my league I'd felt. Beyond that, I couldn't figure out what to
think about the unrest. Except to wonder, would the city
burn? Could it come to our side of town?

On the east side, we harbored vague fears of a siege. In
Rodney's part of town, it felt like martial law.

"Armored personnel carriers were rolling down the streets
during the curfew," Rodney recalled. "We lived on 25th and
Keefe. And one evening I stayed down with my cousins on
4th and Chambers, and I remember armored personnel carriers there, too. I thought they were tanks. My father said,
'No, they carry soldiers inside of those vehicles.' It was during that time that we came to understand what the inter-
state highways were for. You remember feeling very kind of
white—isn't that what you said?—and I remember me feeling very kind of trapped."

Rodney's grandparents came up from southern Georgia
and northern Florida in the 1920s, part of an early wave of
the great African American migration north. "Their motiva-
tion for moving up was like a lot of people: for what they perceived as a better life," Rodney told me. "A life in the North."

Rodney's grandfather worked in a Milwaukee steel foundry, at Continental Can, and as a meatcutter for Plankinton Meat Company. My grandfather had arrived in Milwaukee around the same time, down from Mellon in the northern part of the state by way of a degree in business from the University of Wisconsin. He set to working at the *Milwaukee Journal* in 1924—the only job he ever had.

The summer of 1967 was a touchstone in our conversation: A Braves-less, Hank-less summer; a summer when a big crowd again filled County Stadium; a summer of anticipation for another Packer NFL championship; a summer of riots—of marching for open housing, of a long walk over a bridge and the smell of tear gas.

"That's a smell you don't forget," Rodney said. "Acrid, almost like baby diapers. Ammonia kind of smell." The march was for open housing. Groppi and the Commandoes and Vel Phillips and other community leaders went across the 16th Street Viaduct, linking the black neighborhoods with the segregated south side. At the time some people called it "the longest bridge in the world—the one that connects Africa to Poland."

Rodney and his dad marched, too. "I remember hanging real close with my dad. It was a pretty long walk, but things didn't get really hairy until we got on the other side of this bridge. I'd never seen hostility from people like that before, from white folks like that before. There was a park that we all finally ended up in, Kosciuszko Park. And I remember us being kind of huddled there, and people throwing stuff at us. And we never knew whether those bottles they were throwing would be filled with gasoline or not."

I asked Rodney if he remembered when George Wallace came to the Milwaukee Auditorium during his presidential campaign in 1968. He did. I told him I went downtown that night, got off the bus, and plunged myself into the middle of a heated argument between a white nun and a Wallace supporter. When I tried to speak up, the Wallace man looked down at me: "Get lost, pumpkinhead," he snarled. I went across the street to see the Commandoes—strong young black men, a few years older than I was. Black berets pulled low to one side, they marched in step, clapped in step, barked out chants in unison. They looked sharp. They sent a message of power. I had a feeling that night that power and justice were on the same side. The enemy—a southern segregationist—was so easy to see.

I told Rodney what I would tell Hank several years later: that the years at Campus, and what I learned from my parents and saw on the streets in Milwaukee and on TV were all tied up in my own understanding of what Hank went through. That what Hank did, ultimately, was about civil rights. Rodney agreed. "There was definitely a sense of pride, but also a sense of worry from folks in the community," he told me. "Hank Aaron and Willie Mays—they were like the princes, man." I mentioned my scrapbook, and the letter I'd gotten from Hank, and my own pride when Hank had done it. Rodney smiled.

"When he hit it, man, I got chills. Because Babe Ruth is the icon of baseball achievement. You know, Maya Angelou has this saying that's so profound. She said that 'black people thrive and survive in direct proportion to the heroes and sheroes that they have. Always, and in all ways.'

"There's a saying: that people exist on the shoulders of people that came before them. When Hank Aaron made that 715 back in April of '74, he was running on the shoulders of all these people that came before him." The men of the Negro Leagues. "So when he made that run around the diamond, he was running on the shoulders of Satchel Paige, running on the shoulders of Cool Papa Bell, he was running on the shoulders of Rube Foster, Josh Gibson, Buck O'Neil. He was running on Jackie Robinson's shoulders."

Which is not to say the running came without a price. "There's certain avenues of advance and certain things that you can do as an African American," Rodney told me. "And there's certain things that you can do but you will also be putting yourself in harm's way by doing it. One of them is marrying a white woman. Or it's moving into a neighborhood where you're not allowed to live—and you move in there anyway. And for Hank Aaron it was hitting 715."

O

He's sittin' on 714. Here's the pitch by Downing.
Swinging, there's a drive into left-center field,
that ball is gonna beeeee . . . outta here! It's gone!
There's a new home run champion of all time,
and it's Henry Aaron!
(sound of fireworks popping)

—Milo Hamilton, Atlanta Braves play-by-play
announcer, April 8, 1974

"I saw it on TV, just like everybody else," says Hank Aaron's eldest daughter. "And what I remember was, like my father said, 'Thank God it is *over*.'"

Gaile Aaron and I are sitting on a couch in the lobby of her downtown Atlanta condo building. I've got the scrapbook out again. It's getting a bit dog-eared as I haul it all around Atlanta. We turn the pages, beginning with the first entry, home run number 674.

"Isn't that *something*?" she says, looking over yellowed box scores.

We begin moving through the countdown: 697, 698, 699. Number 700, and a picture of her dad with a big smile. "Look how *young* he looks," Gaile says.

"Yeah," I say, looking over at Gaile. Her eyes are brimmed, filled to capacity.

Then number 701, 702, 703. Next to the article for homer 707, there's a small picture of her father: alone in the dugout, hand on his chin, frowning, gazing down. "Got a lot on *his* mind," Gaile says.

Seven hundred ten, 712, 713. "There's 714 right there," Gaile says. "'Shakes Ghost of Ruth.'"

"And look," I say, "'Hank is King of Swat.'" There's her father, in a broad smile of relief after 715. We can see the back of his mother's head, her arms flung around Hank, squeezing him tight. It looks like a picture of a proud mother congratulating her son. It isn't.

"See how she's holding him? She was *huggin'* him. He's glad it's over. She has something else on her mind."

"Yes. While he rounded the bases, there was a cannon

that went off in the outfield. My grandmother thought it was a gun. She thought someone was *shooting* at Daddy. And she's holding him like that, because she was saying, if they're gonna kill him, we're gonna go down together. She was going to go down with him."

I think about this: At the moment Hank Aaron established the greatest record in sports, he didn't celebrate, his mom didn't celebrate, and his daughter Gaile didn't celebrate. She couldn't even be there. Instead, Gaile says, "I was with the FBI."

She was a student at Fisk University in Nashville. For two years, she'd been under the FBI's protective surveillance, after callers threatened to kidnap her if her father didn't quit the chase. The Braves, and the FBI, moved swiftly. "I'll never forget my father calling me one day and he said, 'Gaile, where are you?' And I'm like, 'Where am I? You called me!'"

As Gaile came back from class one day, she saw five men waiting with her dorm mother.

"They flashed their badges and closed the door. They said, 'Miss Aaron, we're concerned about a kidnapping threat. So what we're gonna do is just transform the whole campus. The men that you see cutting the grass, those are FBI men. The men that are painting in the student union, those are FBI men.' And they're telling me all this and I'm like in shock and the only thing I could say was, 'Does my father know you're here?'"

The same day, her friends were taken to get mug shots at the FBI office in Nashville. Anyone else around Gaile was a suspect. The FBI men told Gaile, "If the kidnappers do make a move, they will probably put you in a car. They will probably have guns. Just do whatever they say. And please know that we are right behind you."

That was half her college life, played out as I composed my scrapbook in Milwaukee.

While Gaile went to college with the FBI, her younger brothers and sisters were being escorted to school in Atlanta by armed guards. "My sister, she was about ten or eleven. She said what scared her the most was that if Daddy went on the field and he had his back turned and somebody tried to do something to him and he couldn't defend himself. Now that's a scary thing for a child. I know it was scary for Daddy.

"It was a lonely time for him. I know it was. I know."

These memories are not spoken as if they were twenty-five years distant. They lie, potent, just beneath the surface. I see them reflected when Gaile narrows her eyes; I hear them emerge in a long, slow "mmmm-hmmmm." Or, they will burst out as tears, quickly blinked away.

"Baseball has always been like the all-American white sport, the hot dog, the apple pie," Gaile says. "And when Daddy began to close in on the record, white people were angry at my father. They took it personal."

I recall the famous quote by the literary critic Jacques Barzun: "Whoever wants to know the heart and mind of America had better learn baseball." Barzun didn't have the Aaron family's experience in mind: malicious letters by the ton, racial slurs shouted nightly from the bleachers, threats to kidnap a man's daughter, the promise to kill. In Gaile's experience, in her family's, you could read Barzun's remark differently.

"They'd rather not say who is the home run king. They have not forgotten who he is. They just don't want to remember," Gaile says.

I tell Gaile what her father said to me: that his experience carved something out of him that can't be regained. "Mmmmhmmmm," she says. "*Carved out*. And that void will never be filled. It's just the scar of playing baseball being black, and going after Babe Ruth's record. Now, you cannot do anything but accept it and realize that it's there. It's a void. And I know. I know how it affected our whole family. It just makes you fearful. It's hard to trust people."

It's not that Gaile has drawn conclusions about white people in general, she says: she's been around them since she was a girl, starting in grade school in suburban Milwaukee. "I look at people as human beings. And I'm glad that is a quality that all of my brothers and my sisters have. We got it from Daddy. That's good."

Yet she has come to understand how little many of her white friends understand about her experience, or her father's. She remembers the night a few years ago when Denzel Washington and Turner Broadcasting released *Chasing the Dream*, a film about Hank's pursuit. "You would not believe the people that came up to me the next day at work that said to me, 'Gaile, I am so sorry'—these are white people—'I am so sorry, I had no idea all of that was going on.' That's hard for me to believe. They can just detach themselves from it, you know?"

Her experience has also taught Gaile something about the reality of separation. In one world, a baseball hero is named Babe Ruth. In another, his name is Henry Aaron. "Even when you look at certain TV shows or sitcoms, and they're talking about baseball, they say Babe Ruth, they never say Hank Aaron. I pay attention to that because I went through that. So I have a keen eye for that. Now, I tell you, if you look at some black shows, *Cosby* and all of that, they always said Hank Aaron. See? There's a difference."

Baseball experts and social historians point out that Babe Ruth's mythology goes beyond race. But it is not only blacks who find Ruth's long white shadow, cast for decades now, a bit odd. One night, a few months after interviewing Gaile, I went up to the press box in Milwaukee during a Brewers game. The announcer was Bob Uecker, an old friend and teammate of Hank's. Uecker, a white guy from Milwaukee, is one of the funniest men in baseball. He says he can make Hank laugh just by saying hello. When they were teammates on the Braves, Uecker says, he'd hit a weak little pop-up, come back to the dugout, walk past Hank and act like he'd just smacked one out of the park. "How far did it go?" he'd ask Hank. "I didn't see it."

During his break for the third and fourth innings, Uecker came out of the booth and talked to me. "I never say anything about Babe Ruth," Uecker told me. "If I say anything, it's about Henry Aaron. Babe Ruth doesn't have a record anymore."

A career .200 hitter, Uecker turned his lousy stats into shtick, and made his post-baseball career a lot more successful. For years he appeared on the *Tonight Show*. He'd tell Johnny Carson how his bats were put to best use as barbecue wood. Or he'd relate his biggest thrill in baseball: the homer he hit with the bases loaded in the bottom of the ninth, to win the intrasquad game. But tonight Uecker seems irritated, almost angry, that Hank remains obscured by Ruth. "I don't want this to sound like I'm knocking Babe Ruth," he says. "Babe Ruth was a legend. But when I talk about records and home runs—Henry Aaron is the guy. That's it!"

I understand how Uecker feels. For decades, Hank seemed virtually forgotten. Three years after he retired, *Baseball* magazine rated Hank, with the most homers, most RBIs, most doubles, most total bases, second most hits, second most runs scored, as the twelfth best player of all time. As the slugger Reggie Jackson once said, Hank has been given "the least credit for greatness."

When I was a kid, there was magic in saying the number "seven-fourteen." It seemed it was a magic that the whole world could own, something hallowed and unapproachable. But "seven-fifty-five" is not spoken with such reverence. It is not even a number that evokes much recognition.

But ask Bob Uecker, or ask Gaile Aaron. They will tell you what it stands for: the total number of home runs belonging to Henry Aaron. "I just think he did something spectacular," Gaile says. "He broke Babe Ruth's record. It's Hank Aaron's record now. Just read the books. Hank Aaron is the home run king."

3

SHADOW OF THE BABE

Elizabeth, New Jersey, August 1973

One late summer evening, around the time I was pasting homer 701 into the scrapbook, and Gaile Aaron was getting ready to go back to college with the FBI, and a congressional resolution was laying out grounds to impeach the president, Ed Wojciak was watching his beloved New York Yankees on the television in his parents' bar.

ME AND HANK

The bar was called the Club Froghollow. Ed grew up in the apartment upstairs. The place had been in the family since 1919, when Ed's grandparents opened it, in the heart of a Polish enclave in Elizabeth, to serve the thousands of factory workers in the neighborhood. For decades, the place thrived. Ed's grandmother opened at six in the morning to catch workers coming off the graveyard shift. In those days the Singer sewing machine factory employed nearly 10,000; the Phelps-Dodge copper-wire plant another 3,000. Every night, the joint was jammed. MEET ME AT THE *Club Froghollow,* an old calling card invited; 72 BUS TO FRONT DOOR . . . TELEVISION NIGHTLY.

Ed sat on a stool at the horseshoe bar, sipping a birch beer. He was back for the summer from college at Holy Cross. In his absence, he noticed, a few neighborhood places had gone out of business: Sam the barber, Billik's Butcher Shop, Pop's candy store. His cousin Jeff and his family had moved out to Pequannock, joining others from the neighborhood in the Jersey burbs. And Ed's dad, who for years had been opening the place at 8:00 A.M., now didn't flip the sign until ten. Ed had a sense that the high times in the Club Froghollow were all in the past: the wee hours when Elizabeth jitterbugged to the live bands in the dance hall out back; the evenings his grandparents would invite couples to listen to the radio in the family parlor; the night his parents unveiled the first color TV in the neighborhood; the night just after they'd remodeled the bar, all in black and white linoleum, and his dad, Ed senior, stood in the well, surrounded by customers, looking trim in his white apron. More and more, now, the place was about nostalgia. Even though he was an only child, Ed Wojciak (rhymes with "Kojak," he liked to say) had no intention of becoming a third-generation proprietor of the Club Froghollow.

He stared up at the TV as Thurman Munson fouled off a pitch. It wasn't possible that someone could love baseball more. Ed knew the stats: the Yanks were going nowhere with weak-hitting Gene Michael and Horace Clarke up the middle; Bobby Murcer was having a good year, but he'd never fill the Mick's shoes in center field. He knew the strategies: field boss Ralph Houk liked to rely more on power than on speed; he managed without flair, always by the book. Ed had even picked up some things on his own about the way the game was played, like how to hit a fastball. He'd learned that two blocks away, under the iron railroad bridge, playing stickball with his friend Greg Arek.

Above all, what Ed loved about baseball was the Yankees, and their astonishing history of greatness: twenty-nine pennants, twenty world championships, and a legion of pinstriped Hall of Famers that could fill this bar. Sitting on his stool, Ed liked to consider the names, the way they sounded together: Gehrig and Hoyt; Gomez and Ruffing; Combs and Dickey and Baker. And Joe D., and Yogi. And Mickey and Whitey, soon to join the rest. What a squad they would make—anchored, of course, by the greatest of them all, George Herman "Babe" Ruth.

Ed got this love from his mom, who was tending bar at the moment, pouring a gin and tonic for Linoleum Joe, one eye on the game. Irene had been going to The House That Ruth Built since the 1940s. As a teenager, she'd take the train with her girlfriends to Jersey City, catch a ferry across the Hudson, and ride the subway to the Bronx. After the games, the girls would wait for autographs outside the clubhouse. Nearby stood the players' wives. They looked so good, then, with their wide-brimmed hats and white gloves. It was different today.

Irene saw Connie Mack, and Hank Greenberg, and Bob Feller, and Bill Dickey. And Early Wynn, and Eddie Lopat, and Joe Gordon, and Tommy Henrich. And Reynolds and Lemon and Blackwell and Stirnweiss. And Colavito and DiMaggio and Rizzuto and Raschi; Vic Raschi, boy, could he pitch.

By 1960, Ed was a fan. That summer he turned eight years old, and Irene started taking him to Yankee Stadium. Sometimes Greg would come with them. She held the boys' hands as they changed trains in Manhattan. One Sunday afternoon they went to an old-timers' game. A bunch of fat guys whose faces had fallen now stood along the foul line, their names echoing over loudspeakers. To Ed, these knobby old pin-striped men seemed comical. But his mom told him each man's legacy, what each had done when he was limber: who hit for average, who hit for power, who threw a curveball that fell off the table. Who crashed the walls, who speared the liners, who saved a run with his glove, in the clutch.

Who delivered, when it mattered.

One time, Ed and Irene sat in the right field bleachers, and Ed caught a check-swing home run from Harmon Killebrew, the slugger from Minnesota. Grown men fought Ed for the ball. His mother peeled them off like a cop at a riot. Or a bartender at the Club Froghollow. In the end, Ed held the ball.

Now there was a station break, and an announcer came on with news from Atlanta: Henry Aaron had hit another home run. It seemed inevitable: the greatest record of them all, held by the greatest hero of them all—Yankee hero, family hero, hero of the Club Froghollow—this record was going to fall. And it would not be broken by a favorite son, like Mickey Mantle, but by this—outsider, this guy from Atlanta.

"Goddamn nigger," Ed heard a man at the bar saying to everyone in general and no one in particular.

Ed looked around the bar. He loved the Babe, loved what he stood for, loved that he was the greatest symbol of the greatest team in the greatest game in the world. But, Ed figured, Hank Aaron has earned this. Give the guy his due. It's his.

Ed had no company that day. Around the bar were angry people.

"This nigger has no claim," another man said. "He shouldn't be doing this."

"It's a shame," said a third man, shaking his head.

Ed looked at his mom.

As he remembers it, she was shaking her head, too.

O

I was pissed," Ed remembers, twenty-six years later. "I figured, give me a break, this guy can *play*. I don't think anyone saw beyond the color thing, and realized that this guy could play baseball better than almost everybody. Let's be *serious*."

We're in Elizabeth, under the rusted iron railroad bridge.

Ed, his son Bret, and I are idling in a rented Ford Windstar. This is Ed's first time back to Elizabeth since the Yanks were in the World Series in 1996. It's my first time ever to visit his folks, even though we've been talking about it since we first met in 1977, just four years after that afternoon at the Club Froghollow.

When he graduated from Holy Cross, Ed took off out west, landing in the mountain town of Flagstaff, Arizona. With some help from his parents, he bought a little sub shop. At the time I was going to college in Flagstaff, and Ed's place was a short walk from class. It was a simple operation, at the start—Ed taking orders, Ed at the grill, Ed at the register. Though he had bigger notions, for now it was just subs and burgers, menu in plastic letters on a plastic Coke sign overhead. Like a stromboli place in Jersey. With his full beard and laser gaze, Ed would pull the order out of you quickly. "Uh, well, uh—I'll have Mom's Burger!" I'd sputter. Well, did I want cheese? What *kind* of cheese? "Please *specify*," Ed would say.

Then Ed met Brandy Bronson, the deli manager at Cheese Aplenty on the east side. They had a lot of the same ideas, and before long they had turned his place into their place and renamed it La Bellavia, Italian for "the beautiful way." Cool jazz, hanging plants, deep-fried zucchini, Brandy's cinnamon apple pie, and imported beers you could drink in the sun at their sidewalk café. There was no place like it in town. I liked it so much I asked for a job. They put me to work waiting tables.

Two decades later, we peer through tinted glass, to the spot where Ed used try to fire a pink rubber ball past his friend Greg. The Pensie Pinkie, they called it. It was sold at Pop's candy store. If you hit it on the ground past the pitcher, it was a single. Off the wall across the street, a double. Pulled hard and off the wall, a triple. Over the wall, a homer. If you hit it real hard, you could split the Pinkie in half.

Ed recalls the time in the bar in 1973, when the people stood against Hank. "I told my mom, you know, you were in there too," Ed remembers. "And she said, 'Well, that's how it was back then.' But everybody wasn't like that. There were people that were more accepting and said that it was about time that blacks got their rights. But these people were a little slow. They didn't get it."

What did you say, I ask Ed, when they spoke like that against Hank? "You're kind of in an environment where everybody feels that way," he says. "You can't exactly stand up and fight against the whole barful of people that are against you. I just shook my head and said, 'Oh, well . . .'"

But baseball remains a strong bond between Ed and his mom. For years—for most of Ed's life—mother and son have been talking about a pilgrimage to the statues and the legends of the game: a church called the National Baseball Hall of Fame. Now, they actually have the trip planned. Before long, the Wojciaks will be heading north to Cooperstown. They've invited me to come along.

We look at the layers of chalk on the wall. Probably no one has played here in ages, Ed says, not since they put the turnpike in here and made the neighborhood real different. But there it is, a rectangle traced again and again by Ed and Greg and other kids: the outlines of the strike zone. "Still there," Ed says. "Oh, yeah."

○

Along the ragged industrial edge of Elizabeth, one monolith stands out: the old Singer sewing machine plant, five stories high by four blocks long. We ride along its width—Irene Wojciak at the wheel, Ed senior alongside her, me in the back. I have never seen such a long building. Endless lines of wire-mesh windows stare out from the drab brick façade. During the war, Ed senior tells me, thousands of men and women churned out the M-1 Directors, guidance systems for the big antiaircraft guns. There was money here, then, and on paydays the neighborhood joints would spill over.

The Wojciaks inhabited a white world; the neighborhoods were segregated and baseball was segregated, too. It was on the cusp of the time of Jackie Robinson, in the wave of victory after the war, still in the flush of the heroic American century of George Herman Ruth.

Irene never saw the Babe play; she was only five when he retired. But she grew up in the shadow of his legacy.

To Irene's generation, and to her father's, Babe Ruth was the man who saved baseball from the disastrous "Black Sox" betting scandal of 1919, breathing new life into the game with the wind of his monstrous home runs. With his strong arms, huge torso, and stick legs, he hit more homers than some entire teams. The incorrigible child from the Baltimore waterfront, unloved and abandoned by his parents, became the most famous, most photographed, most celebrated man in America. He was so big, so *Ruthian*, that headline writers couldn't think of enough nicknames: the Bambino, the Behemoth of Bust, the Wazir of Wham, the Wali of Wallop, the Rajah of Rap, the Maharajah of Mash, the Sultan of Swat.

Babe roared like the twenties. In *Baseball: An Illustrated History,* Geoffrey C. Ward and Ken Burns tell how: First Ruth parked his wife and adopted daughter in a rural Massachusetts farmhouse. Then he moved into an eleven-room hotel suite on Manhattan's Upper West Side, and drove around in his twelve-cylinder Packard. He partied hard, "drinking bourbon and ginger ale before breakfast, changing silk shirts six and seven times a day, and becoming a favored customer in whorehouses all across the country." When the Depression hit, the Babe kept going, earning a record $80,000 in 1930. This was more than President Herbert Hoover made. "Why not?" asked the Babe. "I had a better year than he did."

We drive past a boarded-up place they used to call Grant's. "They cashed so many checks, they had the money all over the sink and the change fallin' in the water and everything," Ed senior says. A few doors down, there was Bartley Brown's. He was the police court judge. "The judge liked me," Ed senior recalls. "I went in there when I was in the service and he wouldn't let me spend a dollar buying the drinks." The bar was L-shaped, he says, maybe thirty feet long, lined with sawdust, with a brass rail and polished spittoons—the kind of place where, a decade earlier, the Babe himself might have enjoyed a few drinks. "It had the big old-fashioned mirrors and mahogany back bar. He had a double drawer National Cash Register, all brass, shiny like a son-of-a-gun. On top of the ledge there, it was loaded with pennies, because his drinks were twenty-eight cents for the cheaper shots and thirty-three cents for the expensive ones, and he served you a mug of beer and it was strictly Ballantine." Women were not allowed at the bar; they had to drink in the back room. Blacks didn't come at all.

This was the time the ballplayers came back from the war. One of Irene's favorites, George "Snuffy" Stirnweiss, had been playing second base in place of Joe Gordon, who was off fighting. Snuffy had been 4-F because of ulcers. In 1945 he led the American League in hitting. "He was from Red Bank, New Jersey, just down the shore here," Irene says. Snuffy was one of the few wartime players who could still compete with the big boys when they came back from Europe and Asia. Even the Babe said so: "That sawed-off runt playing second base is the only ballplayer who could've gotten a uniform when the Yankees really had a ballclub." In '46, with Joe Gordon back, they moved Snuffy to third, and he made it to the All-Star Game. Snuffy watched that day as the great Ted Williams, back from the war, put on a show: four for four, including a towering homer off Rip Sewell's infamous "ephus pitch," a twenty-five-foot-high blooper that ordinarily drove hitters mad. Snuffy didn't do so badly himself; he went one for three.

Stirnweiss played with the Yanks until 1949. Irene recalls that he rode the commuter train from Jersey to work at Yankee Stadium. It was on one of those trains, a few years after his playing days, that he died. It was 1958. "I remember reading about it the next day," Irene says. "It was on the Central Railroad that went into New York. The train went right over the bridge and into the water. That was a big thing."

We drive in quiet for a while, moving through a neighborhood once familiar to Ed senior. He delivered the mail here after the war. Then it was mostly a Jewish neighborhood, with a mix of other white ethnics. Now, the faces are black and brown. Irene powerlocks the doors. And checks them. Three times.

Irene comes from the coal town of Nanticoke in eastern Pennsylvania, white working-class country where nearly everyone knew hard times. This is where she first loved baseball. "I was a little kid then, and we'd run to Litt's Field and go sit in the bleachers because there was nothing else to do." As a girl she watched a star player, a local kid called Pete Wyshner, who played a magnificent outfield even though he had just one arm. "He *roamed* that outfield," she remembers. "He was something to watch." He wore his glove on his fingertips. In one motion, he'd make the catch, stick the glove under the stump of his right arm, grab the ball with his left hand, and fire it back to the infield. "It was amazing, you know?" Pete had lost his arm as a six-year-old during the Depression. "The boxcars would go by loaded with coal," Irene says. "Probably delivering to the cities. And kids would jump on it and walk off with a mound of coal." Irene figured Pete had lost his arm in a fall off a coal car. But he kept playing, teaching himself to bat and throw left-handed.

In 1944, when Irene was fourteen, Pete was voted the most valuable player in the Southern Association, batting .333 and stealing 68 bases. In 1945, Irene remembers, Pete made it to the major leagues. The war was still on, and the talent pool was shallow, but there he was, a major leaguer, now going by the name of Pete Gray: a one-armed man from

Nanticoke, Irene's hometown, swinging the bat for the St. Louis Browns. (Pete Wyshner had become Pete Gray at a time when ethnicity was looked on with disdain in mainstream America. In 1939, *Life* magazine praised the young Joe DiMaggio, baseball's first Italian-American superstar, for his conformity: "Joe, now 24, speaks English without an accent, and is otherwise well adapted to most U.S. mores. Instead of olive oil or smelly bear grease, he keeps his hair slick with water. He never reeks of garlic and prefers chicken chow mein to spaghetti.")

We drive past an old community dance hall. In Pete Gray's day, in Snuffy's, in Ed's and Irene's, big bands played there. "Xavier Cugat," Ed tells me. "He was the rhumba guy. That was before your time." Ed even got into it himself for a while.

"He was a crooner." Irene smiles.

"I was a crooner," Ed admits. I think of his old picture: hair in a pompadour, he's standing slim, in the well of the bar, in his white apron. He kind of looked like a crooner.

In 1948, in the back hall of the Club Froghollow, Ed would sing Sinatra to Irene and her girlfriends, while they practiced dancing for the prom. Afterward, Ed would drive them home. The girlfriends rode four across in the backseat of his mother's '46 Hudson.

That year Irene turned eighteen. She saw the Babe that spring, at Yankee Stadium. "I remember him being in his camel hair coat and hat," she says. "He was kind of hunched up—he had already lost a lot of weight. He was ailing." A few weeks later the Yanks honored Babe Ruth for the last time in The House That Ruth Built. By then, cancer had riddled Babe's throat. "The termites have got me," he told Connie

Mack, the ancient manager of the Philadelphia Athletics. With his bat as a cane, he hobbled to the microphone, managing a few words. Irene heard him on the radio. "His voice was real weak, and hoarse," she says. Babe made his way back through the dugout and into the clubhouse. An old teammate, Joe Dugan, poured him a beer and asked how things were going. Babe Ruth started to cry. "I'm gone, Joe," he said. Three months later he was dead.

"During his magnificent career, pitchers frequently struck out the great Bambino, but he quickly struck back with prodigious wallops," Frederick G. Lieb nearly shouted in Babe Ruth's obituary for *The Sporting News*. "But when the Grim Reaper struck Babe out at New York Memorial Hospital on Monday, August 16, there was no home run to hit in reprisal. . . . A shocked nation heard the verdict, 'You're out,' with a sense of personal loss one feels when advised of the passing of one's kin or a dear personal friend." Honorary pallbearers included Governor Dewey, Mayor O'Dwyer, William Bendix (who had starred in *The Babe Ruth Story*), Connie Mack, Jack Dempsey, Joe DiMaggio, and a score of newspapermen who helped to make him famous. One of them, sportswriter-poet Grantland Rice, wrote *Game Called*:

> *The big guy's left us with the night to face,*
> *And there is no one who can take his place.*

We drive past the old and abandoned, the new and unfamiliar—"That's a colored bar now," Ed senior says—and pull up at an island, safe and familiar to the old Elizabethans: Big Stash's, a Polish deli and bar. We go in for pastrami.

At a table in the back, Ed tells Irene about a problem in the Club Froghollow last night. Ed was tending bar, but he was running his ass off and didn't catch what really happened. Irene heard about it from Tony, the guy who sweeps up after closing. "And it was so—not funny," she says. "It was awful."

The bar was busier than usual, Irene says, and a black guy, Cal, a regular now, was having a drink. "We never had any black customers," she says. "But the few that come in are very nice, decent people." Two white guys, Yosh and Perry, were riding each other. Yosh was feeling pretty good. "Yosh called Perry a white nigger," Irene says. "So Yosh turns around and he says to Cal, 'Oh, I don't mean you, Cal. You're a nice guy.' So Cal says, 'I don't have to be insulted like this.'"

"So he got up and left," Ed says.

Ed and Irene say they want to talk to Cal next time he comes in.

Will he come back in? I ask.

"Oh, yeah," Ed says. "He'll get over it."

○

Earlier that afternoon I was sitting having a cold draught when an old man wheezed into the Club Froghollow, gasping for air as he crept toward his stool. He mounted it slowly, and took a long puff from an inhaler. As his breath returned, he ordered a beer and looked around. Short white hairs stood up on his head like a bristle brush.

We got to talking—the inhaler guy, me, and Staś, another old-timer. I asked them about the old neighborhood.

"Things was rough," Staś told me. "We used to go to the railroad tracks over there during the Depression and push the coal off the cars, to heat our houses."

"Everybody had their own neighborhood," said the man with the inhaler. "The Poles had theirs. The Irish had theirs. The Italians, the Jews, the Lithuanians."

Irene was tending bar, half-listening.

"You couldn't walk in a Lithuanian neighborhood," Staś told me. "I'd get beat up if I went there."

And now? Now, they said, it was all gone. All mixed together. Christ, there was barely anything left. The Puerto Ricans came in. And the Central Americans. And the niggers.

I looked around the bar. Everyone seemed unfazed. Except Irene. She approached the offender. "Don't you know you're not supposed to say that word?" she hissed.

They didn't pay her much mind. "Yeah," said a younger bearded guy at the end of the bar. "Now it's all South Americans. Go out to the park on a Sunday. There isn't a green card between 'em. But if immigration comes, they'll get away. They all run fast from playing soccer." He laughed.

A few minutes later, one of the black regulars came in and ordered a whiskey. He sat by himself. The conversation turned to other subjects.

At the table at Big Stash's, over corned beef, I tell Irene there's something I've been wanting to ask her, about that time in 1973, when Hank was going for the record. Was it hard for you? I ask. People's attitudes often change over time. It was a different time. Is there anything you remember about how you felt then?

Actually, no, she says. She didn't have a problem with

Hank breaking the record. And she can't remember anyone in the bar having a problem with it either. Ed, she asks her husband, do you remember anything like that?

No, Ed senior says. He doesn't remember anything like that either.

"They're embarrassed about it," young Ed, my old friend, tells me later. "My folks would like to forget how they acted. They really don't want to remember."

○

My memory is made sharp by the images on the brittle pages of my scrapbook: a powerful swing, on a chilly night in Atlanta; a strong man, looking up in hope, at the path of the ball he hit; a mother's fierce embrace, near home plate; three large block numerals, made in red with my own hand: 715.

That night it was cold in Milwaukee, too, below freezing. I was alone, I think, watching on television. It was a school night. I was two months away from high school graduation. I seem to remember Curt Gowdy's voice, calling over the crowd—"It's gone! He did it!"—as Hank crossed home plate and was mobbed by his teammates.

4

HOMETOWN

Harry's Bar, Milwaukee, December 1998

Four old friends sit around a table, laughing hard. A half-empty pitcher of amber and a basket of onion rings sit between them. Coats are piled in a mound on an extra chair.

Outside it's unbelievably cold, nearly so cold you could spit and watch it freeze before it hit the ground.

"And remember this?" asks T, my friend since kindergarten, picking up a fork for his play-by-play: "'We'll be back for the bottom of the eighth in just a minute.' . . . 'Hey, friends, this is Friendly Bob Adams, at Andover three—'" He looks over at me. "Ace?"

I swallow an onion ring, grab T's fist and speak into the fork: "'Two-oh, two-oh!'"

"'For all your insurance needs!'"

In the world, we're known as John Topetzes, Tony Grueninger, Victor Thomas and Sandy Tolan. In a warm bar, with cold beers, three nights before Christmas, nearly twenty-five years after our high school graduation, we are known by our names of 1974: T, Gar, Vic and Ace.

T is laughing, tapping Gar on the shoulder, remembering something else. I look at his long fingers, curling around a cigar. He first came to my house when we were five years old. With shovels, by the maple tree, we tried to dig to China. We hit roots and began to argue; when he threw the shovel down and stormed away, my mom called after him: "But John! You're not allowed to cross the street!"

Years later, we'd spend a night each summer sleeping on lawn furniture downtown—camping out on the sidewalk at the *Journal* building, waiting for Packer tickets to go on sale the next morning. The Green Bay Packers played three home games at Milwaukee County Stadium each year, and the games usually sold out in a matter of hours. Across the street, in winter, we'd buy basketball tickets from a cross-eyed scalper, who'd deal us "toilet seats" at high prices. In the heavyweight lull, when Muhammad Ali was stripped of his title for refusing to serve in Vietnam, we'd listen to computerized boxing matches on the radio: Joe Louis vs. John L. Sullivan, Floyd Patterson vs. Jack Dempsey, Ali vs. Rocky Marciano, complete with a rabid crowd and a frothing ringside announcer. (*"The bell has sounded at the end of Round 15, but they're still fighting! Ali and Rocky are still fighting!! The referee is trying to stop the fight!!!"*) The night Ali came back, in his first title fight against Joe Frazier at Madison Square Garden, T and I were headed downtown to a Milwaukee Bucks game. We'd brought a transistor radio, and tuned in for round-by-round reports as we walked from the bus stop toward the Milwaukee Arena. The scalper wore his corduroy coat, collar turned up against a bitter wind. Frazier won by a decision. T celebrated; I was crushed.

T would keep me company on my paper route. At five on a Sunday morning, we'd take turns pulling a laden red wagon through the unshoveled sidewalks, going up the service elevators, walking down the carpeted hallways, laying the Sunday *Journals* at the apartment doors. Afterward, we'd go to my house and announce pretend football games into my new Superscope cassette recorder. *"This is Charley Jones in Philadelphia!"* T would say, his voice in a stage whisper so as not to wake my parents. "And I'm Curt Gowdy!" I'd announce. T was pushing six feet, with the voice of a man. I was four foot eleven and high-pitched. We'd go on for hours, a high-low combination, making it up as we went along.

We order another pitcher. T remembers something from 1968. Or maybe '69. "Like it was yesterday, Ace: We'd be hanging out at your house and it'd get to be eight or nine o'clock at night, and, determined as ever, you'd zero in on that WBCS or whatever it was, and who was that announcer, Harry Calloway or something?"

"Milo Hamilton," I say.

"*Mye*-low *Ham*-ilton!" T shouts, high-fiving me. "Milo Hamilton! But you would sit there, Ace, and literally listen— and I can remember, 'Oh, wait, Hank's up.' In fact, I remember one night Hank hit a home run on an 0–2 pitch in the bottom of the ninth. He nailed this 0–2 pitch to beat the Cubs. Isn't that weird how you remember stupid stuff like that?"

"I remember when I was a kid, sitting on the front porch of our house on Murray Avenue," Gar says of the days before the Braves left town. "We had this little hand-held transistor radio and we'd listen to Earl Gillespie and Blaine Walsh. My sister and I used to suit up in full uniforms. My sister wore 41, Eddie Mathews, and I had the Hammer Aaron, 44. They were wool, the legit wool uniforms," Gar says, laughing.

"I wish we still had those things!"

We get together once every couple of years. Our professions and our politics have put us on separate roads, but we have strong bridges: shared history, shared loss, the agonies and triumphs of our teams. Usually, when I come home at Christmas, we'll talk football: who did well for the Packers that year, who let us down, what were the team's prospects in the playoffs. Two years earlier I returned to Milwaukee for the Super Bowl. Friends back east didn't understand why I'd fly a thousand miles to watch a game on TV. If I was that excited about the Packers, why didn't I go to the actual game in

New Orleans? They didn't get the part about coming back to the place of the old legends, where boys once watched the games with their fathers.

But tonight, at my request, we've gathered to discuss a man of summer: the great Henry Aaron, and what he's meant to our town.

"Hank Aaron," T declares, "is the most underrated athlete of the twentieth century."

"I mean, if there was *ever* a guy who was underrated, it's Hank Aaron," says Gar. "I mean, honest to God, if you look at any meaningful statistic in baseball, big statistics that really matter, he's up there in the top five in probably ten different categories."

None of us can think of a man whose excellence has been so overlooked. How much, I ask, is this because Hank Aaron is black?

"I don't know that race had really that much to do with it," says Gar, who's white. "If it's race, I don't think Willie Mays would be as well known as he is. I think part of it is Hank played in Milwaukee."

"Some of it *was* that he spent a lot of his career in Milwaukee," says Vic, who is black. "But as far as people not allowing him his due, when he was going for the record, I think race had to do with that. I remember those times. It was like, 'Hank Aaron can't do this.' I think that some of this was just with the times. Just like black quarterbacks in football. Now it's a non-issue. We don't even think about it. But I think for Hank during those years, it was an issue. A black guy beating Babe Ruth. To me it was a big thing. I thought, hey, if the guy could do the do, if he could belt more home runs, give him his props. But there were a lot of people that didn't want to give the guy his proper due."

"It's just that it's hard to relate to that," says Gar, "because I don't think that was the sentiment up here. I think people here have a sentimental feeling for guys like Hank Aaron. The thing about Hank is that he was kind of an understated, quiet guy. I don't know if that's Hank or that's a function of playing in a town like Milwaukee, because we've had other players like that. Robin Yount was one. But there's kind of a quiet quality to the way he goes about his business."

I tell the story, attributed to the old Braves pitcher Lew Burdette, about how Hank could have made the same famous catch as Willie Mays in the 1954 World Series—except that Hank would not have lost his cap.

"Right." Gar laughs. "That's it." To Gar, Hank was an emblem of Milwaukee: hardworking, unassuming. You produced things, but you didn't waste time talking about it. "Substantial, agreeable, well-ordered," as a writer once said of Milwaukee. But not boastful. I remember what Gaile Aaron told me: that her father never brought his work home with him. Would a man who dug ditches for a living, he'd ask, come home and talk about how many he'd dug that day?

"This is the kind of town that appreciates that," Gar says. "Because it's certainly not a flashy town. It's kind of a quiet old midwestern industrial rust belt town. And maybe you just don't generate the kind of flash that you generate in other towns."

"He wasn't the flash of the league," Vic agrees. "He wasn't

flashy at all. He went about his job. In many ways, he's the kind of hero that we all would like to see. He's not a showoff, he's not a braggart, he didn't hold out for huge salary demands. He didn't make $100,000 until the very end of his career. I mean compared to now, who's this pitcher who got $105 million? Kevin Brown, or something like that? I really think Hank's like the end of the Golden Age."

We sound like the men that our fathers were, yearning for uncomplicated times in an uncomplicated place. When ballplayers made human salaries. When they spent their careers on one or two teams. When they reflected the values of their community. When hard work was good enough.

"Hank Aaron kind of fell between the cracks," T says. "When he really plateaued at 715 in the seventies, that was a transition time for sports. I think twenty-five, thirty years ago people did respect the quiet guy. That's the kind of guy that the people looked up to and was put on a pedestal, whereas in the eighties and nineties it almost became, you had to be a loud-talking kind of a flashy guy. The more you talked, the more attention you got. Sort of the Joe Louis vs. Muhammad Ali type of thing, whereas Joe Louis was just this solid great fighter, but he was a quiet gentleman type. Ali was also a great fighter but has become so much more publicized because he was loud, and brash, and flashy." It occurred to me later that these very qualities—loud, brash, flashy—were precisely what people had admired in the Babe, decades before Hank Aaron or Muhammad Ali came on the scene.

O

But Hank Aaron's understated way did not necessarily put him in the same camp as a Joe Louis, whose measured humility in the 1940s went over well with a white press and a white public always on the lookout for a great white hope. Quite the contrary: by the end of his career, and after it, Hank was speaking out forcefully about the hate mail he received, and about institutional racism in baseball. But as a twenty-year-old rookie left fielder for the Braves in 1954, Hank entered into a white world, even in the more "enlightened" North, that had certain expectations of how a black player ought to behave.

"It sure tastes like home cooking," Hank told a *Milwaukee Journal* sportswriter for a profile about the "Very Tasty Table" of the "Negro Members of Braves Squad." The article, about "Mother Gibson's," where Hank and his black teammates boarded during 1954 spring training in Bradenton, Florida, didn't bother to mention why these Braves couldn't stay with the rest of the team. Instead, it focused on the quality of Mother Gibson's fried chicken, bacon, eggs, and hot biscuits. "Mrs. Gibson's must be the original home of southern fried chicken," said the Braves' property custodian. "Her's [*sic*] is the best I've ever eaten."

In early articles, Hank was the "Negro second baseman," dubbed "Little Henry Aaron" by one headline writer. "We could realize a big profit on that boy if we wanted to sell him to any one of at least 10 major league clubs," said the Braves general manager, John Quinn, watching Hank work in the Florida sun. Other baseball people focused on his ability and promise: "He's going to be one of the greatest hitters in the game," said his manager in the South Atlantic (Sally) League, the prophet Ben Geraghty, before Hank had ever swung his bat in the majors. "His wrists are the quickest I've ever seen."

Hank struck some Milwaukee sportswriters as "delightfully" ignorant, a southern black hayseed from the Alabama backwaters. For these white men, Hank was entertainment, a one-man minstrel show. Aaron "runs the bases like Stepan Fetchit with a hopped-up motor," one article said. Another day's headline picked up on the reference: "He Just Keeps Shuffling Along." One amused sportswriter called him "Baseball's Great Philosopher," claiming, falsely, that Hank once threw away a telegram when he didn't recognize the name of the sender: Ford Frick, the commissioner of baseball.

But the city's attitude toward race relations in the early 1950s was not merely patronizing. The Milwaukee that Hank moved to had just been through a divisive mayoral election in which race was the central factor. "The Braves were coming here just as there was a large African American movement out of the South," remembers Frank Zeidler, who served three terms as the socialist mayor of what was, back then, a union town. "A lot of people came to Chicago, and Milwaukee got a major spillover. This was not well received."

We are sitting in Zeidler's vinyl-sided duplex in the largely black neighborhood of central Milwaukee. Zeidler has lived here for fifty-three years, longer than the European mountain ash has stood by the chain link fence in his small front yard. The ex-mayor is about to turn eighty-seven. He wears a rumpled dark suit, suspenders and a bolo tie. A handful of pens stick out like straws from his shirt pocket. On the bookshelf behind him are Harvard Classic editions of Dante, Plutarch, Homer, Emerson and Edmund Burke.

The smear campaign in the 1952 elections, and again in 1956, included claims that Zeidler was paying for billboards in the rural South to invite blacks to move to Milwaukee. In fact it was jobs in the Milwaukee foundries and tanneries that drew blacks north. An additional attraction, Zeidler says, was "because of the socialist movement here, there was a place to come. You had a chance for good treatment."

By this time the city had developed a dual image regarding race relations. In some quarters it had earned a reputation for racial tolerance. Wisconsin had been a leading abolitionist state before and during the Civil War, sending 80,000 troops into the Union army. Booker T. Washington and Frederick Douglass had given speeches at the University of Wisconsin. And blacks voted in early state elections. But African Americans coming north to Milwaukee in the late 1940s and early 1950s encountered white communities quite satisfied with their substantial, agreeable, well-ordered lives. "It was like two galaxies coming together," Zeidler remembers. One galaxy was inhabited by ethnic whites—mostly Poles and Germans, like my grandfather Irv Maier, the publisher of the *Journal*—people who, according to a 1947 book, *Our Fair City,* had forged a town "so comfortable, so pleasantly Old World, so free of false pretentions and the travails of ambition that only the vain, the restless and the conscience-stricken want to change things." It was about this time that blacks in numbers started moving to town. The white resistance to change—or what Milwaukee historian John Gurda calls a "brittleness-slash-stability"—helped fuel the racial friction that Frank Zeidler felt in the mayoral races. This resistance, Gurda says, combined with the relative newness of the black community in the city, made Milwaukee ripe for more overt racism than other northern cities.

Hank Aaron's arrival into a racially charged Milwaukee, Zeidler believes, offered some opportunity for whites to reassess the capabilities of blacks—something that had already begun happening on the baseball field. The Braves came to town in 1953, six years after Jackie Robinson broke in with the Brooklyn Dodgers. By then, Zeidler says, "there was a well-spoken belief that the greatest team in baseball was the Kansas City Monarchs [of the Negro Leagues] and the greatest pitcher was Satchel Paige. So there was already a little bit of social acceptance."

Adding to this was the virtual worship of Braves players, black or white, by a community and a state deeply grateful to have entered the major leagues. "The reaction of Wisconsin residents," writes Gurda in *The Making of Milwaukee*, "bordered on hysteria." On a Sunday in March 1953, after learning that the Braves would soon be moving from Boston, "nearly 60,000 people drove out to County Stadium just to peer over the third-base fence and watch the grass grow . . . as many as 15,000 fans showed up before every game to cheer infield practice. Comparable crowds formed at Union Station or Mitchell Field to welcome the team home from routine road trips. The players were showered with beer, cheese, sausage, clothing, pens, jewelry, outboard motors." The black Braves players were no exception, says Gurda. Billy Bruton, the first black Milwaukee Brave, was once the guest of honor at a shopping center opening. "The team's success allowed people to overlook issues of race," Gurda had told me earlier. "Billy Bruton, Wes Covington, Aaron—if you got a chance to see any one of those guys, including the black ballplayers, it was like seeing God in the flesh." Here Gurda was speaking from memory. He is a close friend of my brother Tom and is old enough to remember the glory years of the 1950s. "The pride," he said, thinking back. "The adulation."

In 1957, Hank's success—winning the National League most valuable player award and leading Milwaukee to a World Series victory over the Yanks—provided further evidence of black excellence to skeptical whites. "He made contact between whites and African Americans far more acceptable, just by his success," Zeidler says. "Psychologically, you could say that because of his success, it was possible for whites to understand inherently that blacks were capable of great achievements—and that made social contact more acceptable."

At best, Hank's contribution to racial harmony in Milwaukee was small and anecdotal. For one thing, all the adulation did not prevent the black Braves from being the butt of popular racist jokes: *What's black, has six legs, and catches flies? The Braves' outfield.* (Covington, Bruton, and Aaron.) The joke was attributed to teammate Warren Spahn, who later apologized to Hank. More important, no ballplayer could reverse the larger trends that prevailed in the city for decades: endemic job discrimination, especially in the traditionally white trade industries (carpentry, plumbing, electrical work); substandard housing in the black neighborhoods; white flight to the suburbs; and continued "de facto segregation," as Hank himself put it before leaving town for Atlanta.

O

To get a better picture of the black community in the twelve years Hank played in Milwaukee, I call an old associate of my mom's from the University of Wisconsin–Milwaukee (UWM): Reuben Harpole, the founder of a UWM outreach program called the Center for Urban Community Development. Some refer to Harpole as a community activist, but that doesn't describe his range. To African Americans in town, where he has deep ties to almost every part of the community, he's known simply as "the black mayor of Milwaukee."

"Sally, our children are taking over for us," Harpole says, laughing, leaving a message for me on my mom's answering machine. I call him back and we meet for breakfast the next morning at the Hyatt downtown, a half block from the *Journal Sentinel* building, home of the new, merged paper.

Harpole tells me that by the mid-1950s, when Hank first arrived, many African American men in Milwaukee were supporting their families with work in the steel foundries and tanneries. The grandfather of my schoolmate Rodney Franks poured steel and cut meat; Vic Thomas's dad was a welder and a handyman at the industrial giant, A. O. Smith. But the good jobs in the trades, Harpole says, where the real money was, were closed off. "Everybody in the community always knew that racism was there lying under the surface, because they couldn't get a job—unless they had something like sweeping the floor or shining shoes," Harpole remembers. At one point during the 1950s, he tells me, "there were two black people working down at city hall." One was Frank Ziedler's secretary; the other was the elevator operator. Well into the 1960s, Harpole says, one of the biggest banks in the state, First Wisconsin, wasn't hiring black tellers. And the department store, Gimbels-Schuster's, "only hired light-skinned African Americans. The black skinned ones—'we don't want you.'"

By 1964, the demonstrations had begun. "King had started marching," Harpole recalls. "The American revolution was on TV." Over the next few years, he tells me, the Milwaukee protests would encompass the hiring practices of the bank, the local A&P, and the white-run trade industries; the quality of public education; and access to open housing. Harpole marched with the Commandoes and Father Groppi, and with a lot of black leaders who "didn't get the ink." The press, he recalls, preferred to focus on "a white priest leading a black revolution. They made a hero out of him." (Some stories also made him into a villain.) "But the others who'd been fighting for years got no play: Lloyd Barbee, Cecil Brown, John Givens, Walter G. Beach, O. C. White, James Dorsey, Clarence L. Johnson, Wesley Scott, Bill Kelly, Mrs. Bernice Lindsey." Only a couple of these names are familiar to me.

"The feeling was excitement," Harpole says of those days. "It looked like we were gonna crack through this mess."

At the heart of the movement in Milwaukee were the battles for open housing, and the marches across the 16th Street Viaduct to Kosciuszko Park on the south side. The issue was the desegregation of neighborhoods. Here, Hank had laid a little groundwork.

Not long after Hank moved to Milwaukee, the Aarons became one of the first black families to move north of the "de facto" segregation line of Capitol Drive. (The first black family to do so, Harpole tells me, had been welcomed with a burning cross on their front lawn.) According to one early report, Hank, who had known segregation his whole life, was nervous at first, then relieved by the reception he and his young wife Barbara received. "I couldn't have picked a nicer place to live," he told reporters at the time. "These are real nice, warm, friendly folks." Apparently, a lot of them were.

By the time he left town, Hank had begun talking frankly about the racial attitudes and tensions that so disturbed him. His father had once told him that no one would want to hear what he had to say until he proved himself, but now, as he would tell his friend Joe Kennedy, he was beginning to get that respect, and he could build a platform from which to speak. He was reading the reflections of Dr. King and the moral anger of James Baldwin. He had also joined a progressive Catholic parish in the inner city—St. Boniface, where a young priest named James Groppi would soon take the pulpit. Despite Milwaukee's self-image of racial tolerance, despite its genuine affection for the young ballplayer from Mobile, Hank had begun to feel a chill across the color line.

O

One morning I ride out to see Thomas Cheeks, a retired realtor and schoolteacher. He lives in an assisted living center on the city's northeast side. We sit in a quiet conference room off the main lobby.

Tom Cheeks looks to be in his late eighties or early

nineties, though when I ask he only smiles. Before I sit down, he's pulling something out of a plastic bag. It's a signed, framed picture of Hank, wearing a Braves uniform with the number 5 on it—the number Hank wore at the beginning, before switching to 44. Next, he unsheaths some forty-year-old documents—incorporation papers for the investment company he started with Hank and Billy Bruton. "You know, Billy passed away," Cheeks tells me. "He was out driving one Sunday afternoon, pulled over to the side of the road, and that was it."

Cheeks peers intently through his glasses, smiling in a bemused, checking-you-out kind of way. His skin is a light tan color, and I spend a good part of the interview trying to determine whether he is white or black. As we talk, his experience tells me: he is black.

"I knew your grandfather," Cheeks tells me. As civil rights demonstrations went on almost daily in the streets, Cheeks and his group, the Committee of Concern, started talking up equal opportunity to the white power brokers in town. My grandpa Irv Maier was one of them.

"You've never been in a Jim Crow car, have you?" Cheeks recalls asking my grandfather.

"No."

"Well, suppose I'm the conductor, and I say to you, 'Sit here!' *Why?* 'Because I said so!'" How would Irwin Maier have liked that?

I am certain Irwin Maier would not have liked that one bit.

"He was one of the most powerful men in the state of Wisconsin," Cheeks tells me.

I had never thought of Grandpa Irv in quite that way. But I do remember him dedicating the new train station once. I recall him talking about how he was going to help revitalize downtown. And he had raised money for our new Performing Arts Center (PAC). Years later, when I worked as an usher at the PAC, I'd walk past his portrait on the way to the auditorium.

I also knew that Grandpa liked our Sunday family gatherings to be tranquil and well ordered: some light recreation for the children, perhaps, alongside pleasant adult conversation, with Grandpa at the center, in his coat and tie, rocking under the apple tree in the backyard. Writing this, more than twenty-five years later, I cannot conjure up a picture of my grandfather without a tie. Even in his last years, in the rest home, ninety-four years old, I remember him dressed to go to the *Journal,* where he had worked for fifty-six years.

And we knew without asking that Grandpa Irv was not to be challenged. We'd learned. In 1967, my sister Kathy was a junior at Riverside High. She had rebelled against Catholic high school and enrolled in the public school for her sophomore year. She was co-chair, with a black student, of the school's Human Relations Committee, which was formed to help ease racial tensions around the time of the riots and the open housing marches. They put on a dance, and Kath wore a black and white dress. Later, when black students demanded to see their people's story reflected in the history curriculum, a reporter for the *Journal* called and asked Kathy for a comment. She said she supported the black students and suggested that the reporter talk to them directly.

That Sunday, when Kath told Grandpa about the reporter's call, he exploded. *What do you know?* he asked my sister, as the rest of us—his wife, his daughter, his son-in-law, and his grandchildren—looked on in extreme discomfort at this breach in the tranquility. He, *Grandpa,* was meeting with other community leaders. *These* are the people the reporters should be talking to. Not *high school students.* Kathy was furious. She remembers yelling back at him in tears: *I sit next to these guys in school. I know things you don't know. If your group doesn't listen to groups like mine, they are going to get nowhere.* I remember her crying and getting up from the table, and Grandma Lorraine following her, doting, flustered, like a nervous bird, trying to settle things down. But Kath stormed out of the house. She said she was late for her editorial meeting at the *Riverside Rocket.* Years later, Kath tells me that she had felt silent support from Mom and Dad; though they hadn't challenged Grandpa, they had let her speak her piece.

Later, Grandpa Irv wrote Kath a note of apology, and invited her to lunch; Mom encouraged her to go. "I never responded," Kath wrote me a while back. "I was afraid he'd try to win his argument in a restaurant somewhere and I'd hold back, afraid I'd cry in public." They never talked much after that. As far as I remember, the incident was never brought up again. As with my father's M.S., which dawned on us in earnest that same summer of 1967, we didn't discuss it. We bucked up and moved on.

Tom Cheeks has his gaze fixed on Irv Maier's grandson. I ask him what else they discussed thirty-some years ago. "I told him that some of our people would like the world to stop so they can get on."

"You mean, stop the world so they can get *off*," Grandpa had said, correcting him on the old phrase.

"No, I mean, get *on*," Cheeks replied.

"Oh," said Irv Maier. "I see what you mean."

Out of those meetings came a group called "We-Milwaukeeans." Cheeks and my grandfather were the co-chairs.

"He was very open-minded," Cheeks says of the family patriarch.

I'd never thought of Grandpa quite in that way, either.

O

Long before Tom Cheeks sat down with Irv Maier, he was the realtor for Hank's first move into white Milwaukee, just north of Capitol Drive: "4025 North 14th Street," he remembers. "Let me tell you about that house, it was something. It had the most beautiful, built-in, walk-in shower." A couple of years later, he helped arrange for Hank to address a Boy Scout troop in the northwest suburb of Mequon. Hank liked the rural surroundings. "And Hank said, 'Tom, look around and see what you can find out here.'" Cheeks met a builder who was putting up houses in Mequon. They found one to suit Hank's needs. They made a deal. And then the builder told him, No, I don't want to sell this house directly to Henry Aaron. I'll sell it to your real estate company, and *you* sell it to Henry Aaron.

"I was the straw person," Cheeks remembers some forty years later. "The builder was afraid of criticism of selling to minorities." Sure enough, on the day of the deal, Cheeks says he hadn't been home for fifteen minutes before he got a call from one of Hank's new neighbors. "She really 'blessed' me," he says.

For Gaile Aaron, for years the only black child in her school, Mequon seemed fine at first. "I didn't realize I was any different," she had told me when I saw her in Atlanta. Gaile remembered sleep-overs with white friends. She remembered welcoming white neighbors. The mayor, Jim Egan, a close friend of my parents, had made a point of welcoming Hank into the community. And the Aarons had no trouble making the place their own. They laid out the backyard patio in the shape of a baseball field, with the barbecue pit in dead center. Hank's brother Tommie joined the family in Mequon for his brief stint with the Braves in Milwaukee. And yet some people in the suburb made it clear the Aarons were not welcome. Gaile recalled the day in school when someone slit her boots with a razor. She was eight years old. "I'm getting off the bus, I'm going down the driveway, I'm not thinking anything about it," she recalled. "My father's standing and watching in the picture window. He says, 'What happened to your boots?' I mean, someone had purposely done that. But, see, I wasn't in tune with the racism." Gaile wasn't the first member of the family to experience such treatment in the Mequon schools; her aunt Alfredia, Hank's younger sister, had endured so much taunting that she had to pack up and go back home to Alabama. Before she left, Hank and Barbara had gone to the Mequon school to talk about the abuse. In Hank's autobiography, *I Had a Hammer*, Alfredia Aaron Scott recalled: "The principal looked at Henry right in the face and said, 'There wouldn't be a problem if you hadn't brought her to this school.'"

Tom Cheeks prefers to remember what Henry Aaron did: the way he carried himself; the way he gave back to the community; the way people would look at him and find nothing to criticize, even in failure. He remembers being at County Stadium once when Hank struck out with the bases loaded. He lightly tossed his bat up, caught it, and went back to the dugout with his head high. The next time at bat, he smashed one out of the park. "That's one of the best lessons I ever learned from Henry," he tells me.

Cheeks would rather not revisit the painful details of the Aaron family's early encounters with racism in Milwaukee—especially since so much of the city embraced Hank from the start. "Some things are better left unsaid," he tells me. He thinks this is advice I'd do well to consider. "A silent man is never strangled by his own tongue," Cheeks admonishes me, before moving in short, slow steps down the long hallway to his room.

○

"I remember when my dad came home screaming about how a realtor in Wauwatosa wouldn't show a house to Hank Aaron," Terry Perry is telling me. It was 1956, she says, the year before Hank and his family broke the color line in Milwaukee. Apparently the house Tom Cheeks found for Hank wasn't the family's first try. "It was the first awareness I had of people being treated differently because of being black," Terry says.

The baseball season has begun. Terry and I are sitting in box seats near the field, watching the Brewers battle the Kansas City Royals in the first game of a doubleheader. She and my brother Tom have been close friends since college days.

Terry Perry is Milwaukee much like Hank Aaron was Milwaukee: doing instead of just talking about it. When she thought about her kids growing up knowing only white people, Terry and her husband moved the family into Sherman Park, one of the city's few integrated neighborhoods. To help connect their four-year-old girl to her heritage, Terry entered the child in Irish dancing classes. A few years later, Mary Catharine was performing for Johnny Carson on the *Tonight Show*. Terry has been involved in politics for most of her life, getting her start knocking on doors for John F. Kennedy at age nine. "It was the 'ask not' thing," she remembers, quoting Kennedy's inaugural call to "Ask not what your country can do for you; ask what you can do for your country." Terry later worked for Legal Action of Wisconsin, advocating for the poor, and after that ran a city task force on domestic violence. Now she runs the Milwaukee office of U.S. Representative Thomas Barrett.

"I remember my dad just being *spitting mad*," Terry says, recalling the incident with the realtor. "My father was *screaming*. And the only thing he could think of to do was to sell our house, and sell it *only* to a Negro family. We'd just bought the house. My mother was pregnant with kid number six." In the end, they stayed in the house. A few months later, kid number six, my old friend Joe Perry, was born, narrowly escaping a birth in the upper deck of County Stadium.

"It was July 13," Terry says. "My parents came to a twi-night doubleheader between the Brooklyn Dodgers and the Milwaukee Braves. My mom was nine months pregnant, but she loved baseball. They walked up and up the ramps to the upper deck. And during the game she went into contractions." At first, she refused to leave: "They were having such a great night at the old ball yard." Soon Terry's mom started leaking amniotic fluid. When the Perrys finally got up to go to the hospital, the fans around them gave them a standing ovation. The Braves won both games that night, 8–6 and 6–5, The next day, Hank launched a twenty-five-game hitting streak. (Joe, by the way, also came out very well.)

The next year, the Braves were in the World Series against the Yanks. "I was in Catholic grade school and our principal, Sister Damien, put it on the loudspeakers," Terry remembers. "We had to get on our knees and say our Hail Marys before the game."

Summers in the late 1960s and early seventies, and into the fall, Tom, Terry, her brother John, their friend John McKeon and a bunch of other buddies would hang out together. A lot of them played softball for the West Side Crusties of the Unamerican League, a team I'd been told was named after dirty underwear. (Later, in checking this fact, I conferred with another family journalist: No, Tom said, he'd consulted with a Crusty historian, and was unable to confirm said derivation; its origin, according to a man named Crusty Ed, was simply in "a way of life.") A couple of times I got to play for the Crusties. McKeon, a slick-fielding shortstop from Philly with a cool paintbrush mustache, even let me take his position for a couple of innings. This I took utterly seriously, though I may have been the only one. Everyone played with a beer at their position; at one game, the rule was, If you hit someone's beer with a batted ball, it would be an automatic out. Priorities.

Tom and his friends lived on the west side, but they often hung out at our house. I was fired up that they called me "Ace," and relieved that they didn't find it weird that I followed Hank through the static on the radio. When I got older, and when Mom and Dad were at the theater or the symphony, Tom would sometimes let me roll a smoke from his yellow can of Top tobacco. Other times I'd steal a pack of Camel straights from my father's carton in the bottom left-hand drawer of the desk in the library. With our new silver butane lighter, T and I would sneak down into the ravine across the street in Lake Park. A passerby could have heard us in convulsions of coughing, and perhaps spotted puffs of our smoke floating up from the thicket below.

Terry buys us a couple of cold ones. She recalls sitting in our family's kitchen with my mom and dad and Tom. "Larry and Sal, they always really liked their kids' friends," she says. "They were completely welcoming." They'd talk about Vietnam and the civil rights movement and the presidential race between George McGovern and Richard Nixon. Mom was all for the Democrat; slowly, Dad came to agree. "Your dad loved to discuss issues," Terry recalls. "He would ask questions. He seemed to be pondering people's answers." I remember that, too. The kitchen table, at cocktail hour: Dad in his horn-rims, with his dark hair and shining eyes, leaning forward, listening intently, laughing, questioning, responding. Mom would stand, sipping a drink, hand on the back of someone's chair, or weigh in, stirring a wooden spoon in front of the stove.

It's a warm night and the Brewers are ahead. Jose Valentin, the Brewers' erratic shortstop, spears one in the hole and nails his man by half a step. Suddenly the Brew Crew's defense and pitching are looking sharp. They have been winning for a change, and with a victory in game one of the doubleheader, they'll even their record. We aren't accustomed to seeing a whole lot of good baseball here. In their thirty years the Brewers have won but a single pennant, and that was in 1982. In these days of hundred-million-dollar contracts, the Brewers, with their small-market payroll, can't get past mediocre. The situation is grim enough that Terry has found it necessary to pass along, and repeat, a Golden Rule to her children: "Never boo the home team." She's serious about this. She hopes—a lot of Milwaukee hopes—that the new stadium being built just behind the right field bleachers will bring in enough money to allow the team finally to compete. Miller Park will have seventy luxury "suites," and the fans believe that the income from these will help save the franchise. The slogan for the 1999 season, scheduled to be County Stadium's last, is "Bringing Down the House."

○

In black Milwaukee, it was no mystery what Hank was going through as he chased the Babe. "We know what happened to him," Reuben Harpole had said as we asked for a check at the Hyatt. "Everybody in our community knows exactly how he suffered. And everybody is proud of him." But Harpole also said he didn't focus a lot on Hank's suffering at the time. First, he suggested, what happened to Hank was not all that surprising in America. "It wasn't much, compared to all the other stuff that was happening." Back then, Harpole concentrated his thinking more on the issues facing the movement in Milwaukee, and on the deeper racial traumas in America: the bombing deaths of the four black girls in the Birmingham church; the lynchings of three civil rights workers in Mississippi; the savage murder of a fifteen-year-old boy in Mississippi for saying "'bye, baby" to a white store clerk. For all Hank suffered, Harpole told me, "he wasn't getting lynched."

James Cameron would agree with Reuben Harpole there. On a suffocating August night in 1930, Cameron was sitting in an Indiana jail, suspected of being an accessory to murder. Suddenly, he was pulled out of a crowded cell block by vigilantes led by hooded Ku Klux Klansmen who beat him, dragged him down to the courthouse square, pushed him through a mob screaming, "Nigger! Nigger! Nigger!" and put a noose around his neck. Sixty-nine years later, Cameron sits before me, eighty-five and feeling it, in an office jammed with overflowing bookshelves in Milwaukee's inner city. The place is America's Black Holocaust Museum. The museum documents the devastation of the Middle Passage, when millions of slaves were packed as chattel into ships off the West African coast for their journey to the New World.

"There's a picture on a posterboard next to you," Cameron tells me. "Take it up and look at it." It's a photograph taken the night of August 7, 1930, in Marion, Indiana. Two young black men hang limp from the branch of an elm tree. Their eyes are closed, mouths half open, clothes shredded and spattered with blood. Below, the mob is gathered. A white man with a Hitler mustache and a crazed expression points to the two dead men. James Cameron, sixteen years old, was supposed to be the third. The noose was tight around his neck. He waited to die. And then, he says, came a "miraculous intervention." For reasons Cameron cannot fully explain, the vigilantes removed the rope from his neck. He stumbled back to the jail, where the sheriff whisked him off to a cell in a nearby town for safekeeping. A year later, a jury convicted him for "accessory before the fact to manslaughter"; he served four years in an Indiana penitentiary. He moved to Milwaukee in 1953. In *A Time of Terror,* his memoir of the lynching, Cameron wrote: "I understood, fully, what it meant to be a Black person in the United States of America."

I've come to talk to Cameron about Hank Aaron and what he went through, the meaning of that to black Milwaukee. I've gotten more than I expected. "Those events become traumatic events on the minds of people that go through them," Cameron tells me. "Hank Aaron will never forget what he went through. He can never forget it. Jackie Robinson could never forget what he went through."

On the other side of his office door, in the main museum gallery, lie remnants of the British slave ship *Henrietta Marie,* which sank off the coast of Florida in the 1700s. "The stowage of human cargo," one exhibit recounts. "Traders could purchase as many slaves as they wished and packed them as tightly as they desired." The collective trauma of black history in America, Cameron tells me, forges a collective understanding among blacks. Reuben Harpole had told me: "We empathize. We understand." James Cameron says: "We are no fools. There are two different psychologies, two societies in this country: one black and one white."

For nearly twenty years after he got out of prison, Cameron remained in Indiana, doing civil rights work for the NAACP and the Black Elks of Indiana. It was dangerous work at times, and after increasing threats, he moved his family to Milwaukee and took an assembly-line job at the Pabst brewery.

Cameron remembers the barnstorming days of the Negro Leagues, when Satchel Paige and Josh Gibson and Cool Papa Bell would show up in a farmer's field. "They used to go around like the old medicine shows. Snake oil! Remember that?"

I confess that I don't.

"They'd set up bleachers and charge fifty cents. They would go in and mark the diamond, and about two or three thousand people would show up. And they would have a ball, man." I recall that Hank's first professional team was in the Negro Leagues—the Indianapolis Clowns, in 1952, when he was eighteen years old. Satchel Paige had played with the Clowns, and so had Jesse Owens, hero of the 1936 Olympics in Berlin, destroyer of Hitler's myth of Aryan supremacy. (How ironic that he came home and played segregated baseball.) The catcher for the Clowns would play a couple of innings in a rocking chair behind home plate; Hank recalled how, when he came along, they still played the "shadow ball" routine, pantomiming infield practice without a ball. The team was on the road constantly, barnstorming in the tradition of the Harlem Globetrotters. "You would see some of the most fantastic plays in your life," Cameron remembers.

"They only had one or two baseballs with them, and if they knocked one into a corn field, they would have to hold up the game and go look for the ball." The old man is laughing, gazing off at something I can't see. I'm imagining a teenaged Hank, running into a corn field, chasing after a long base hit.

A year later, the Braves came to town. "I used to love to go to the ball game and see Hank Aaron," he remembers. "Especially when he hit a home run. He always hit those *line-drive* home runs. You know what I mean? Not those *blooper* home runs. He hit that ball on a line, and it would start rising, just like that," Cameron says, his arm making the *swoosh* of a jet taking off. "That was the most beautiful thing you would ever want to see."

There was a connection, then, between the team and the community. In those early days, Cameron remembers, the radio would always be on, tuned to the games. When Hank or Billy Bruton or Wes Covington would come to bat, people would stop what they were doing and listen. Cameron was so into the Braves, he'd get sick when they lost. "Man, I was just as sick as I could be."

But he hasn't seen baseball at County Stadium in more than thirty years. "I haven't been to a game," James Cameron says, "since Hank Aaron left here."

O

September 23, 1957, 11:34 P.M., is the moment frozen in time between Henry Aaron and the city of Milwaukee. It was the moment just after he'd hit an eleventh-inning home run to clinch the pennant for the Braves and send Milwaukee to its first World Series. On a day that President Eisenhower was threatening to send federal troops to Little Rock to enforce school desegregation, white and black teammates, together, raised up a young black man in triumph. I read the story for years, again and again, beneath a headline in the *Journal*. An image of the front page had been reduced and wrapped around a ceramic beer mug. It had been a gift from Grandpa Irv, and every now and then my father would drink from it. Later, so would I.

BRAVES WIN FLAG; IT'S BEDLAM! the headline shouted. And there, below, next to the article saying, "President Eisenhower Tuesday ordered federalization of the Arkansas national guard," was the news of Hank's homer. The sports page that day had featured a photograph of number 44 being held aloft. In the picture, Hank's cap is off, finally, and his face radiates joy. That image was carried in newspapers around the country, including a Youngstown, Ohio, paper, under the headline: NEGRO MOBBED IN MILWAUKEE.

That September memory must be a very uncomplicated one for Hank. Many years ago, he called it "my shiningest hour." It occurs to me that this is why he has a collage of the 1957 Braves in his office in Atlanta, and not assorted memorabilia from the Chase for 715: 1957, Hank has said over the years, was his fondest season. It was my brother Tom's, too.

"I was eight years old in the '57 Series," Tom tells me one night as we have a brew at my old Milwaukee hangout, the Y–Not II. Tom is nearing his fiftieth birthday, a milestone laden with family meaning. He was born in 1949, into a sweltering summer in the nation's capital as Dad was launching a law career as a clerk at the Supreme Court. For the new family, there was limitless potential. The next year, Mom and Dad came back to Milwaukee with Tommy, to settle down, raise kids, practice law, consider the possibilities. Kathleen came the following year, then Mary, me, John, and William.

Of the six Tolan kids, only Tom recalls the World Series in 1957. Grandpa Irv had a pair of tickets in the mezzanine. He took Tom to Game Five. "I'm eight years old, seeing Lew Burdette pitch a shutout in the World Series. In the mezzanine." He says it as if he still can't believe it. The Braves won, 1–0, and took a three-games-to-two lead in the Series. It was on a Monday, but I can imagine Dad taking off work, at home with Mom, watching on television. Three days later, when the Braves won in New York to become World Champions, the town went crazy. By nine o'clock, 225,000 people were celebrating downtown—twice the size of the celebrations on V-J Day, and fully one-third of the population of Milwaukee. On Wisconsin Avenue, it rained beer and snowed confetti. Total strangers hugged and screamed and sang and cried and danced the conga and the bunny hop. The city's main artery was choked. The Milwaukee fans, *The New York Times* remarked, were more Brooklyn than Brooklyn. As for the crowds that night, the *Journal* observed, "A bulldozer would have had a hard time getting through." At the center of one celebration was a handmade sign, made famous the next day in the *Journal*: BUSHVILLE WINS. Our town, only days earlier called "bush league" by some effete Yankee official, had at last become major league. A *Journal* columnist claimed the last word, quoting Exodus: "'And behold, the bush burned with fire, and the bush was not consumed.'"

"It was just incredible," Tom says. "Just a love feast."

ME AND HANK

My brother describes the years of the Braves in Milwaukee like the arc of a beautiful relationship that changes over time. "There was this love relationship that started up in 1953 and built up until they won the Series," he tells me. "It's a storybook thing. It's about how something rises, reaches a crescendo, and recedes." The next year, the Braves won the pennant again, and were up, three games to one, against the Yanks. They dropped the next three and lost the Series. The next year, 1959, they finished the season tied for first place but lost a best-of-three pennant playoff to the Dodgers. A year later, they finished seven games back. Attendance started to fall off, the Braves played worse, the crowds dropped further, and Braves officials announced they were leaving.

Tom looks at me. His eyes convey something in a past before my memory: a playoff game in 1959, in September, on the radio. He was on the porch with Dad. "I really remember: a salami and cheese sandwich. And having a taste of his beer. And the smell of it when he poured it in the glass."

Yeah, Tom remembers, he was more angry with the Braves for leaving than I was. Yeah, he did feel more abandoned. Because he knew how good it felt, in 1957: Hank's homer to clinch the pennant on September 23; the World Championship seventeen days later, at 2:35 in the afternoon, Milwaukee time. "These guys," he says, "could not be beat." After that, "the downhill slope." After that, "you're not as impressed." The team grew mediocre; the marriage grew stale. And yet, week after week, month after month, Milwaukee's old lover kept saying it really wasn't looking elsewhere. Finally, the evidence was overwhelming. Finally, they left.

5

NEWLY SOUTH

Atlanta, Georgia, April 1966

Andrew Young, a top aide to Dr. Martin Luther King, Jr., was standing in a crowd outside the American Hotel in downtown Atlanta, behind two white men dressed in overalls.

Good old Georgia boys, Young thought, from outside the city. It was early April 1966, the start of the baseball season, the first ever for the Atlanta Braves. From Young's vantage point, he could glance over his shoulder into the lobby of one of the recently integrated downtown hotels. He could look across the street to the Dinkler Plaza, which only a few years earlier had refused to give a room to Dr. Ralph Bunche, a United Nations official, recipient of the Nobel Peace Prize, and a black man, during the annual NAACP Convention. And he could look down the street, to the approaching convertible, where Henry Aaron sat on the backseat, waving.

As Hank came closer, the applause built. But the two men in front of Andrew Young were silent. That worried him a bit. Then one man turned to the other. "You know," he said, "we're going to have to be a big-league town. He's going to have to be able live wherever he wants to in this town."

"And I began to realize almost immediately the social impact of Hank Aaron on Atlanta," Andy Young says thirty-three years later. He looks beyond me to the soupy haze that swallows the city's horizon. We're forty-eight floors above Peachtree Street in downtown Atlanta, in the office of the former mayor, U.S. congressman and United Nations ambassador. The incident on the street in 1966, Ambassador Young tells me, "said that people understood that there was a greater significance to this baseball team than just a baseball team. It was a social statement: that Atlanta wanted to be a big-league town."

Like Milwaukee, Atlanta saw baseball as crucial big-league validation. Ivan Allen, the moderate, integrationist white mayor, who had been the only white southern politician to testify in support of the Civil Rights Act in 1964, considered the Braves a key component in making Atlanta the capital of the New South. The mayor, supported by business leaders, had bragged that "We built a stadium on ground we didn't own, with money we didn't have, for a team we hadn't signed."

"Ivan Allen knew exactly what he was doing," Young tells me. "He wanted Atlanta to be seen not as a southern hick town, but as a major city in the world. And he brought the baseball team here to try to initiate that." The white business community that supported Allen knew that a more progressive image was essential for the city to grow the way they envisioned—just as the white business leaders of Milwaukee, people like my grandfather, had known thirteen years earlier in bringing the Braves from Boston. In Atlanta, no one better exemplified the city's power elite than Coca-Cola president Robert Woodruff, known simply as "the Boss." Gary Pomerantz, author of *Where Peachtree Meets Sweet Auburn,* a biography of Atlanta and its racial conscience, called Woodruff Atlanta's "Wizard of Oz," the man Ivan Allen would always consult before making any big decisions. "Woodruff was interested in the image of Atlanta," Pomerantz had told me. "He wanted it to be a civilized place. He was trying to have the Atlanta that was stamped on the back of all these little red and white cans to be civilized."

Looking through the windows of Andy Young's corner office, we can see the results of an earlier generation's pragmatic vision. To the west is the Georgia Dome and Convention Center, Olympic Park, and a smoothed patch of red earth, awaiting new construction. To the north stands the imposing copper spire of NationsBank and the IBM Tower. Beyond lies a thick swath of green known as Piedmont Park.

While many of Atlanta's business leaders saw a reduction in racial tensions as a key to the city's growth, the Atlanta that Hank came to in 1966 was a mix of progress and friction. Mayor Allen had ordered the "white" and "colored" signs removed from city hall. The city's auditorium, downtown theaters and municipal swimming pools were formally desegregated. Seating in the new Atlanta–Fulton County Stadium was to be fully integrated, as Hank himself had insisted. And the Atlanta Chamber of Commerce had urged downtown businesses to desegregate, in the interest of a "healthy climate" for business. Many of these changes had come as the result of pressure on Atlanta's segregated restaurants and lunch counters from a student-led sit-in movement. Still, on the Braves' opening day, segregationist sentiment remained strong. Only a few years earlier, Lester Maddox, the popular segregationist, had won Atlanta's white vote in the mayor's race against Allen.

Across the South in 1966, the racial wounds were still fresh. Hank arrived just two years after Freedom Summer, when three civil rights workers in Mississippi were murdered, and hundreds more beaten, jailed, and harassed for trying to register blacks to vote. He came the year after Bloody Sunday in Selma, Alabama, when blue-helmeted state troopers clubbed and tear-gassed peaceful civil rights marchers on the Edmund Pettus Bridge. In Atlanta, Maddox had long kept pickax handles in crates by the door of his Pickrick restaurant, for customers to confront any black person trying to get service. Now, his restaurant shuttered in defiance of the 1964 Civil Rights Act, Maddox was running for governor on a segregationist plank. He campaigned across Georgia throughout 1966, was elected and took office early the next year.

"'Sixty-six," Andrew Young tells me, "was still pretty rough around the South."

In that first year for the Braves, Young recalls, he'd occasionally head out to the stadium; so would Martin Luther King. A few years earlier, Dr. King, who had led the famous bus boycotts in Montgomery, returned home to be assistant pastor to his father at Atlanta's Ebenezer Baptist Church, and to continue his work with the Southern Christian Leadership Conference. Young and King both loved baseball. "Martin Luther King used to say that it appalled him that eleven o'clock Sunday morning was the most segregated hour of the week, in church, but he was thrilled that by two o'clock in the afternoon, everybody was integrated at the ballpark." As for Young, his father had played ball in New Orleans and for semipro teams up in the Catskills, earning money that would help put him through college. In those days, Young tells me, for blacks in America, "sport was part of a survival strategy."

Before the Braves came, baseball in the city had been played by the minor league Atlanta Crackers, for decades a whites-only team, and their Negro League counterparts, called, incredibly, the Black Crackers. Now, civil rights leaders in Atlanta noticed how Hank and his white teammate Eddie Mathews, who together had hit more home runs than any two teammates in baseball history, were becoming icons of a New South. "You just always saw pictures of them together," says Young. "I don't know how conscious it was. Hank and Eddie Mathews became in many respects a symbol of the kind of brotherhood we were looking for. In those years, it was consistent with the kind of image Atlanta was trying to project. We began to enjoy the image of being a big-league town, as opposed to a racist town."

"Atlanta was not a Valhalla," former mayor Maynard Jackson says, "but it was definitely an oasis in the barren southern racist desert. The phrase was that it was a 'City Too Busy to Hate.' It basically said that if you want to ruin business, then let this hatred divide us. If you want to be a city that separates itself from the pack, ahead of Birmingham, ahead of Charlotte, ahead of all the other southern competitors by leaps and bounds, then let us negotiate these matters. So Atlanta developed a reputation of being a city that was progressive, primarily because it chose to work at how to beat the race issue."

At first, the Braves' top officials, made up largely of white men from the Chicago area, were by and large unaware of the team's role in advancing the image of racial harmony in a New South. The exception was the Braves' young assistant scouting director, Dick Cecil. He realized that this was not just a television market the team was coming into; it was a city with a 40 percent black population, and a larger black middle class than nearly any other city in the country. "They had two newspapers, a bank, an insurance company, and some great business opportunities," Cecil says. "And the black community and the white business community had a relationship that was very unusual. They worked very well together."

Cecil and I are sitting in his work studio, in a tranquil neighborhood amidst the leafy swath I'd seen from Andy Young's office. He serves bagels and cream cheese, and pours me coffee from a silver pitcher. He tells me that he had been preparing the ground in Atlanta while the Braves were still in Milwaukee. It dawns on me: Cecil was down here getting ready for the move, while up north team officials were still saying the Braves weren't going anywhere. "'We're gonna be here today, tomorrow, as long as we're welcome,'" Cecil says with a laugh, quoting the famous lie. The Braves brass had even shown Cecil secret blueprints of the new Fulton County Stadium. Did he know how to read blueprints? "I said, 'Sure, I can read these!'" he tells me. "I'd never seen a blueprint in my life!" In Atlanta, he became a different type of scout: a kind of gumshoe advance man, checking into the Dinkler Plaza Hotel under an assumed name. "I was Dick Clyde," he tells me.

"As a loyal Milwaukeean, I must protest!" I say, laughing, incredulous, and only partly joking.

"I know, I know," says Cecil, still sheepish after thirty-five years. "I love Milwaukee. I thought it was the greatest base-ball city. But the Braves were gonna move. I thought it was kind of stupid to sit there on your principle and stay in Mil-waukee. I wanted to be involved."

He got involved quickly. One of his first Atlanta memories is going to the banquet honoring Dr. King for his 1964 Nobel Peace Prize—an event attended by civil rights leaders and top white business executives. Despite many tense moments between people who had never socialized, the event spoke volumes about the strides the city had made.

Once the Braves arrived, Cecil convinced Bill Lucas, Barbara Aaron's brother, to move to Atlanta and be his liaison to the black community. "Luke probably did more than any one individual in bridging the gaps," Cecil remembers. "And it helped Henry, and it helped Barbara, because with Luke and Rubye [his wife] coming, it settled things down a lot."

Barbara at first had resisted moving from Milwaukee. She had grown up in segregated Jacksonville, Florida, where she met Hank during his days in the Sally League, and the very thought of moving back south, Cecil recalls, "just paralyzed Barbara." But the couple had come down the previous year, and realized that they could move into a good neighborhood in the city. "It helped a great deal," Cecil says.

Despite the efforts of Lucas and Cecil, the reception for black ballplayers at the new stadium was mixed. This was not just Atlanta's home for baseball, it was the South's. On opening night, the scoreboard announced: "April 12, 1861: First Shots Fired on Fort Sumter . . . April 12, 1966: The South Rises Again." In *I Had a Hammer*, Hank remembered the crowds being generally polite, with the exception of "a few crackers."

But as the season wore on, it wasn't uncommon to hear racist catcalls. "When the Braves first came, we used to say all kinds of things to the black players on the opposing team," one old fan told me. "'Hey, you black son of a bitch!' Not to be racist," the man said, smiling, "just to get them rattled."

Plenty of slurs were left over for the black men of the home team. In *I Had a Hammer*, Hank recalled worrying about his kids going to the stadium and hearing their daddy being called the same names he thought he'd left behind years earlier. Once, after Barbara Aaron had spent too long listening to a man in the next row call her husband a "nigger" and a "jigaboo," she went to a concession stand, bought a hamburger, and loaded it up with mustard. The next time the man said "nigger," she stuffed the burger in his face.

In late July of that first Atlanta season, a police guard stopped Barbara Aaron as she drove into the Braves' parking lot. She told him who she was, but he refused to let her through. She started to drive past him. The officer acknowledged that he put his hand on his revolver—Mrs. Aaron said he actually pulled the gun on her. She was arrested. When the story came out, Ivan Allen intervened. The charges were dropped.

O

In the early 1970s, two young prospects made it to the bigs. Outfielders Dusty Baker and Ralph Garr were to be the next generation of great Braves, expected to carry on for Hank. Hank took Ralph and Dusty under his wing when the two young black ballplayers came to play in Atlanta; they, in turn, would stand by Hank when he went through the hardships of the Chase. I remember rooting for both young players through the static in Milwaukee: Ralph Garr, the Roadrunner, named for his speed; Dusty Baker, the Home Run Maker, who one day, it was forecast, might even fill Hank's shoes. (Talk about pressure.)

Nearly three decades later, three hours before game time on a cloudless Saturday morning in July, I walk toward Atlanta's Turner Field, en route to an appointment with Dusty Baker in the visiting team clubhouse. Dusty is now the manager of the San Francisco Giants. I saw him the previous evening while visiting with Gaile Aaron. He told me to come back to the clubhouse before the game, and we'd talk about those early years in Atlanta.

Just inside the media gate, two dozen red-shirted concessionaires stand in a knot, listening intently to a supervisor, as if to get psyched up to sell popcorn and pennants and three-dollar bottles of water. Through the ramp, I emerge between the grandstand and boxes—a sea of blue seats, utterly empty, except for an usher scattered here and there. It's still an hour and a half before batting practice. No one is in a hurry. I gaze out at the grounds crew, watering and laying chalk in the dirt. Beneath the spray, the infield, from first to third, grows gradually darker, as if in the shadow of a drifting and invisible cloud.

I've never been a sportswriter, so this license to simply flash credentials, walk through the gate, onto the field, into the dugout and down the long walkway toward the clubhouse all feels a bit unreal, as if someone is about to stop me and ask, *Just what in the hell do you think you're doing?* Instead, Giants players, pulling on their faded black practice jerseys, barely notice when I walk in. They sit at their lockers, in their Budweiser folding chairs, or lie flopped on brown leather couches in front of a big-screen TV, watching an NFL highlights film.

In the visiting manager's office, Dusty is rolling up his socks, talking to a squat, mostly bald guy who looks oddly familiar. The guy wears shorts, and his ring of white hair flops longish and lazy over his collar. Somehow, he looks a little un-put-together, compared to what I nearly recognize. After I hear his rich voice, I realize this is Jon Miller, the national play-by-play guy and the voice of the Giants. One of my favorites. Without his tie, and his game face, he looks like a regular guy. He must be getting tidbits for the part of the broadcast when he'll say, "Well, I talked to Dusty just this morning, and you know, he told me something very interesting . . ."

I go back to watch the NFL on ESPN. Every Giant's eyes, it seems, are fixed on the big screen. Huge bodies collide amidst much grunting and crunching. A thick-necked offensive lineman describes life in "the pit." He says, "This is smash-mouth football. It's like getting into a car wreck, eighty-five times a game." The ballplayers, in their polyester uniforms and cleats, watch in silence.

Jon Miller walks past, and I slip into Dusty's office before six waiting sportswriters can react. He sits at a small desk in a small room, working on a breakfast of sausage, potatoes, bacon and biscuits. "Have a seat, dude," he says. Without his baseball cap I can see that Dusty Baker is a handsome man: strong, square features, a thin, dark mustache, the beginnings of gray up top.

Just before he signed with the Braves, Dusty tells me, West Coast universities had been courting him with football and basketball scholarships. It was 1967; he was an eighteen-year-old kid from Sacramento. He came to Atlanta with his mother. "My mom asked Hank, would he take care of me away from home? Out of trouble, keep me straight? I was a little on the wild side. Hank said yeah. He promised her he'd take care of me as if I was his own son." She asked Hank, "If he was your boy, what would you do—have him go to college, or sign with the Braves?" Dusty pressed him, too. "I didn't know what to do," he recalls. "So I asked Hank." Hank told them that it all depended on how Dusty felt. If he thought he could get to the big leagues within the next couple of years, if he was confident in himself, he should sign with the Braves. "So I ended up signing," the Giants manager says, spearing a cube of potato with his fork.

Dusty would spend the next few years between the minor leagues and Atlanta. Around the time the Braves broke spring training in 1968—Dusty's first with the club—Martin Luther King was shot down in Memphis. That day, Coca-Cola's Bob Woodruff was meeting with President Lyndon Johnson. He called Ivan Allen from Washington, reminding him that when King's body came home, the whole world would be watching Atlanta. You need to be sure, the Boss told the mayor, that everything goes right. And looks right. Whatever the city couldn't pay for, Coca-Cola would. The morning of King's funeral, Gary Pomerantz writes in *Where Peachtree Meets Sweet Auburn*, Mayor Allen looked out of his office window to the astonishing sight of Governor Maddox attempting to raise the state flag up from its half-mast tribute. With photographers documenting the segregationist's every move, the governor changed his mind. That afternoon, 50,000 people marched peacefully down Sweet Auburn, behind the mule-drawn wagon that carried King's casket.

"There were some heavy times, there," Dusty says, pushing away his plate and reaching for a pen and the lineup card. "Some very heavy times in our country." In the third month of that season, Robert Kennedy went down; later that summer, cops whaled on blacks and whites equally—reporters, civil rights marchers, antiwar demonstrators, bystanders—as the divided Democratic Party met in Chicago.

"It was a time full of peace and love but also a time full of a lot of anger and hatred," Dusty remembers. "We were having riots in the cities. Everything was either right or left, black or white. There was very little middle ground or gray area on anything." As the seventies began, the war in Vietnam bled on; students were shot down at Kent State and Jackson State. Dusty, meanwhile, was learning how to play in southern towns like West Palm Beach, Shreveport, Greenwood and Richmond. Every year, he'd make it up to the big club for a few games. "There were times I talked to Hank about what I was going through," Dusty says, recalling the confusions of a young black man new to the South. "And Hank and Ralph helped me deal with it because they're both from the South. And Hank would tell us some of the things that he'd been through. But he never dwelt on it."

By late 1971, at age twenty-two, Dusty was with Atlanta for good. Ralph Garr, his roommate from Richmond, was already starting in left field. "We were with Hank every day," Dusty says. "He took me into his home—myself, Ralph, Paul Casanova. He took care of us." As the seasons passed, Hank introduced Ralph and Dusty around. "Because of him, we met Jesse Jackson, Maynard Jackson, Andrew Young, Jimmy Carter, you name it, I met them through and around Hank Aaron."

Dusty and Ralph called Hank "Supe," for Superstar, or just "Hammer." "You tend to adopt the personalities of the superstar on your team. Hank taught us to have that burning desire to succeed, but to be humble and cool on the outside.

The thing that interested me most about Hank was that I never heard him brag on himself one time. I never heard him, not once."

Sitting next to Hank in the dugout, Ralph and Dusty learned major league baseball. Hank would tell them which pitch to wait on; which ump had the low strike zone; which outfielder dropped his head just long enough for you to take second base on a single. Without saying a word, Hank taught them how to play hurt. "I'd see him in such tremendous pain," Dusty recalls. "He'd limp in like Fred Sanford"—the old man played by Redd Foxx on *Sanford and Son*—"and run outside like he was twenty years old. Ralph and I were like, 'What happened to this guy?' And then he'd limp back in like Fred Sanford. That was the most amazing thing, day in and day out."

That season, 1971, the record talk started in earnest. Hank had begun the season just 8 homers shy of 600, behind only Babe Ruth and Willie Mays on the all-time list. Four years earlier, up in Milwaukee, a *Journal* columnist named Oliver Kuechle had made a bold observation: "Don't look now," Kuechle wrote, "but who do you suppose could, without stretching playing age too far, break Babe Ruth's record of 714 home runs? Why, your old friend Hank Aaron." Now, Kuechle looked like a prophet—or maybe just someone who could do long division. Hank was on pace to catch Ruth around the time he turned forty.

The national press cranked up. Dusty watched as reporters gathered around Hank's locker. *Could the great Babe's record fall? Was it inevitable? And, could it be considered legitimate? After all, Hank, you've played in so many more games. And they say the ball is livelier now. Hank, some of the old-*

timers say if Babe played now, he'd hit 900 homers. Do you think, Hank, you're as good as the Babe? Would this be fair, actually, to even call it a record? Typical was an Associated Press article written during the 1971 spring training, enlisting a Las Vegas oddsmaker in defense of the Sultan of Swat. "I can't help wondering how many Ruth could hit under today's conditions," Jimmy "The Greek" Snyder said, while laying even money Hank would catch him. Aaron "plays in a park that's easy to hit in," The Greek mused. Who knows, he wondered, how many fewer Hank would have hit, had he played in the days when pitchers "could spit on the ball, and apply slippery elm"? The Greek complained about the short fences Hank hit for, ignoring the shorter 295-foot right field fence in Yankee Stadium, or the 257-foot right field porch in the Polo Grounds, where the Babe played for three years, or the fact that balls that *bounced* over the fence during Babe's time were counted as homers. At the heart of the issue, for many sportswriters, was whether this man, Henry Aaron, had a true claim.

That season Aaron clubbed 47 home runs. It would be his highest single-season total in his twenty-three years in the bigs. He ended the year with 639, 75 behind Ruth. The next year, the letters, and the threats, started coming in force.

Dear Mr. Nigger,

I hope you don't break the Babe's record. How do I tell my kids that a nigger did it?

You are a real scum!! You should still be in the Negro Leagues. That's a white man's record. All you niggers are alike. Give you an inch and you take a mile.

You can hit dem home runs over dem short fences, but you caint take that black off yo face. Rite on, rite on.

Retire or die!!! The Atlanta Braves will be moving around the country and I'll move with them. You'll be in Montreal June 5 through 7. Will you die there? You will be in Shea Stadium July 6–8 and Philly July 9–11. . . . You will die in one of those games. I'll shoot you in one of them. Will I sneak a rifle into the upper deck or a .45 in the bleachers? I don't know yet. But you know you will die unless you retire.

Since you have begun the season, you already hit four home runs. I must assume you are not considering my warnings in a very serious way. However, you must not brush these forebearings off lightly. Every day that you delay your retirement, the wrath of "the ghost of Babe" increases. Every hit and each home run brings the day closer when this ghost of Babe will strike.

"He'd show us some," Dusty says, looking at me across the narrow visiting manager's desk. His gaze is strong. "Others, he wouldn't show us. Hank was like your father, and my father. They don't always tell you what's going wrong at work. You shelter some things from your kid, but you know them enough to show them what the real world's about.

"I know one thing: When you get a strong man, especially a strong black man, the more you mess with him, the stronger you make him. Even though those letters hurt, they just made him more determined."

Dusty has a story about Hank's determination and focus.

He finishes filling out the lineup card and looks up at me. "I was with Ralph. I was always with Ralph. I think we were in Atlanta. We were sitting next to Hank in the dugout. And he told Ralph and I that we'd better not sit next to him because there was a death threat. Some guy in a red coat with a high-powered rifle was going to shoot Hank. And so Hank told us, if we didn't want to sit next to him, he understood. Ralph and I were like, 'No, Hank, we're down with you, man, if you go, we got to go.' But the whole game, Ralph and I were looking around for some guy with a red coat, and Hank wasn't even paying attention!" Dusty laughs hard, eyes narrowing at the memory. "If a firecracker would have gone off, me and Ralph would have swore we were shot!" At one point, Hank recalled in *I Had a Hammer,* a firecracker did go off—behind him, in the left field bleachers. He was staring in at the infield, hands on his knees; he thought it was over. Hank flinched, slightly, but didn't move from his stance.

What strikes me most about Henry Aaron is not his determination, nor even his courage. It's this: Despite being shadowed by a twenty-four-hour bodyguard, and being whisked suddenly from one location to the next, and having food secretly brought to his room, and living with the fact that the FBI was attending college with his daughter, and hearing slurs burn the back of his neck in left field at his home stadium, and dealing with a hundred sportswriters asking him, week after week, if he was worthy, and wondering whether he would be shot rounding the bases in New York, or Philadelphia, or Montreal—he was able to focus on his work, and excel at it. In 1973 he hit 40 home runs in only 392 at-bats—his highest home run ratio in twenty-three major league seasons, a Ruthian pace in a year he was constantly being told he was no Ruth.

Hank's power of concentration was legendary. Tom House, a former teammate, now a psychologist who occasionally counsels ballplayers, says Hank had a "unique ability to compartmentalize." Ralph Garr told me, "He could separate his private life from his baseball life. His power to focus was just amazing." And George Plimpton wrote, in *One for the Record*, that Hank occasionally "takes off his baseball cap and holds it close against his face. He moves it around until he is able to peer through one of the ventholes in the crown of the cap at the opposing pitcher on the mound. The practice, like focusing through a telescope, serves to isolate the pitcher, setting him apart in a round frame so that Aaron can scrutinize him and decide how he will deal with him once he reaches the plate." But this sheer concentration—isolating a pitcher through the venthole of a baseball cap, or swinging at a bottle cap with a broomstick, or connecting with a 95-mile-an-hour fastball when a man in a red coat may be zeroing in with a high-powered rifle—does not seem sufficient to explain how Henry Aaron managed during that terrible 1973 season. Hank, it seems, was also motivated by something beyond baseball.

Andy Young had told me: "That was a time when Martin Luther King was saying to everybody, if you haven't found something you're willing to die for, you probably aren't fit to live. And I think Hank had decided that his life was vulnerable, and that if it meant dying in the course of doing his best, I don't think he actually worried about it. I think that in order to grow up black in the South, you had to learn that people were doing all kinds of things, to try to intimidate you, to make you lose your cool, to keep you from doing your best—and you can't afford to get mad. You never got angry. Anger was seen as weakness in the context of civil rights. My daddy always said, you don't get mad in a fight. If you get mad in a fight, you lose the fight."

Dusty pulls on his cap. It's time to go manage a baseball team. "I didn't see any fear in his face," he tells me, standing up. "I didn't see any fear at all. All I saw was this sheer focus, concentration, and discipline. And I saw a lot of loneliness."

O

I emerge from the dimly lit corridor and into the dugout, and a harsh blast of sunlight. On the field, they've rolled out the batting cage. Braves players take their swings. I can hear the stirrings of the early crowd. I look up into the stands: blue seats, pale, sunscreened legs, red foam tomahawks resting in laps. There are a few blacks in the stadium, but I notice that almost all of them are either on the field, or selling things. I make my way slowly up the aisles. I feel lightheaded.

I sit down next to a white couple in the field-level seats behind the first base dugout. They look like they're in their early forties. About my age. The man is chopping the air with his little tomahawk. He sets it down to talk to me. The woman lowers her binoculars. They tell me they've been in Atlanta, and huge Braves fans, since the early seventies. I ask what they remember about what Hank went through—the hate mail, the death threats, the taunts from the stands.

"If I ever heard anything like that," the woman tells me,

"it certainly didn't make any big impression on me. I'm sure there were things goin' on, but they were not things that I heard as a fan. I truly just don't have much to offer about memories of any of that."

The man doesn't, either. "Well, one thing, there wasn't that much publicity back then. You didn't have ESPN, you didn't have SportsCenter, so I think it was a lot easier, even in the seventies, to keep things quiet." True: back then, there wasn't the saturation coverage of twenty-four-hour cable sports networks. And neither the Braves nor the FBI were eager to publicize the death threats. But there were stories at the time, of the hate mail and the racial slurs, and the extra security Hank was provided, in the newspapers and magazines, on radio and television. We certainly knew about it, 800 miles north. And here, in Atlanta, the racial taunts were well documented in the local papers. Perhaps these fans missed these stories, and missed the conversations about them at the time. Or perhaps they read them and forgot. Or perhaps they *wanted* to forget, and then *tried* to forget, and then *actually* forgot.

When I had visited with Gaile Aaron back in January, she talked about two worlds, two realities, two ways of remembering. We spoke that day about a chasm in memory. Gaile told me the story about the broadcast of the *Chasing the Dream* documentary—the one that detailed the ugliness of the Chase—and how, the next day, many of her white friends at work had expressed shock. "And you know," Gaile had said, "I find that hard to believe." These people, she said, lived in Atlanta. They were old enough to remember. But they didn't.

"They can just detach themselves from it," Gaile had observed. "Just ignore it, you know?"

No doubt, a lot of white people knew something of Hank's tribulations in the harsh, lonely years before he shattered the Babe's mark. And a lot of whites understood his triumph as a triumph over racism. Bob Costas, the NBC sportscaster, had made that point forcefully when I interviewed him a few months earlier. In 1974, Costas was just out of college. He recalled how he and his buddies had been inspired by Muhammad Ali for his principled stance against the war in Vietnam, a stance that cost Ali his heavyweight title. They had supported the U.S. sprinters John Carlos and Tommy Smith when they stood, fists clenched, on the Olympic podium in 1968, as a statement of black power and protest. Likewise, Costas wrote in a later essay, when the hate mail came to Hank, he and his friends grasped its larger meaning. "I don't think he fully understands how a majority of white Americans liked him and really respected him," Costas said. "Just about every white baseball fan I knew thought he was terrific."

But it was not Bob Costas's remarks about solidarity, but rather Gaile Aaron's, about a chasm in memory, that I recalled one afternoon, heading in a cab toward New York's LaGuardia airport. I'd just been up to the Time-Life Building, visiting with a native Atlantan named John Huey. Huey is the managing editor of *Fortune* magazine. We sat in his corner office looking out over midtown Manhattan. Below, a yellow stream of taxis headed north, up Sixth Avenue toward Central Park. Huey leaned back in his chair, tossing a small leather ball in the air, thinking back.

John Huey was a big fan of the Braves, and of Hank's, long before they moved to Atlanta. "I followed them in '57 and I became a Braves fan. And I followed them in '58 and became a heartbroken Braves fan." In 1966, when they came to Atlanta, Huey was a senior in high school. "I was fucking ecstatic," he remembered. "I got to see not only Henry Aaron and Eddie Mathews, but I got to see Sandy Koufax." Huey grew up in the prosperous Buckhead section of Atlanta. At the time, it was almost exclusively white, but he doesn't recall big battles over desegregation in the city. "They had the sit-ins which lasted a week or two and everything integrated and everybody just kind of went on with it," he tells me. "It wasn't that easy, I'm sure, if you were on the other side, but from my side—a white, middle-class kid—I never felt like a redneck." He rooted for Bob Gibson and Roberto Clemente and Ernie Banks, and of course, Hank. As Huey recalls, everyone in Atlanta knew that Hank was "the real deal."

I show Huey my 1973 letter from Hank, and start telling him the history. "Wow!" he interrupts. "This is great, isn't it?" We smile, like old fans. At the time of the letter, Huey was working the cop beat at the *Atlanta Constitution*. In May and June 1973, his paper ran articles on the racial hatred directed at Henry Aaron.

But John Huey doesn't remember reading any of those. "Most of us probably read the thing, and if you were Southern, you read it and went, 'Oh, God, we don't feel that way. We want Hank Aaron to win this thing.' But we didn't realize how much of this was going on."

"And how much it hurt," I say.

"Yeah," he responds, and adds quickly: "And a lot of it didn't come from the South."

He's right about that.

"But, you know," says the editor of *Fortune,* "I thought about this before, and your talking to me now reminds me of it. I wished him so well and I was so wrapped up in his quest that I just couldn't believe that they would really be that way. I was in denial. I didn't believe that there would be mean-spirited people out there who really wouldn't want him to do it because he was black. I just—I just—I was naive."

6

SEPARATE MEMORIES

Flowery Branch, Georgia, July 1999

The day after Dusty Baker and the Giants leave town, I drive out of Atlanta, up the seven lanes of northbound I-85, through a landscape of red clay and kudzu, across the Lester and Virginia Maddox Bridge and the Chattahoochee River. I'm on my way to see another Braves legend, Phil Niekro.

I pull up at a phone booth to get directions for the last mile to his house. I'm running late, and a voice on the line tells me that Phil has changed the plan: we're to meet for lunch, at a place called Mountain Man Bar-B-Que. He's already on his way. I'll recognize the place because it has a hand-painted sign with a likeness of the Hall of Fame knuckle-baller. I hang up, slip off my tie from an earlier interview and reach into my knapsack for a more comfortable shirt. Shirtless, I look across the road, and see the picture of Number 35, and the Mountain Man sign. Beneath that, there's a man in a baseball cap, standing by his car, looking back at me changing my shirt in a phone booth. I have this feeling it's Phil Niekro, and that somehow he knows who I am, too.

"Good meeting you," Niekro says two minutes later, extending the arm that carried him to 318 major league victories. He seems not to have noticed my quick-change routine across the road. We order barbecue and sit at cement benches under a roof of corrugated tin. Waves of heat radiate down. Over his shoulder I see baskets of Georgia tomatoes and peaches. Hand-painted signs offer hawg meat and boiled peanuts, and nightcrawlers and "minner buckets" for bait. Phil looks at me through Ray-Bans, beneath a cap that says: "Major League Baseball Alumni." Sixty years old, square-jawed and clean-shaven, he looks the part.

I'd first heard his name in Milwaukee, when I was eight years old and he was twenty-five. It was the year I'd taken Hank as my hero. I remember getting Phil's rookie card that year, 1964. "Oh, really?" he says.

"Yeah. Later on I did one of those crazy things that fourteen-year-olds do—I sold my whole collection for thirty-five bucks. Five thousand cards. I still have bruises from kicking myself—I could have put kids through college on those."

The Hall of Famer commiserates. "You probably don't even remember what you had in there."

"Some of it I do. I had stuff going back. I had a Jimmie Foxx I got from my dad. I had all of Hank's cards, and there was one with Hank and Willie Mays together. Hank's cards, I saved. And I remember I had your 1964 rookie card, with you and Phil Roof on it. He was a good defensive catcher, he had quite an arm."

"Yeah, we kind of came up together," Niekro says. Phil and Phil. Like Dusty and Ralph, in another decade.

Phil Niekro grew up in Lansing, Ohio, hill country full of coal, near the Ohio River. His dad was a miner. "Solid as a rock," Niekro recalls. "He picked that coal, eight miles back in there." Phil's dad played semipro ball with the Polish National Alliance team; coal miners filled the roster. "I've got pictures of him striking out twenty, twenty-one guys in a ball game," he tells me. The old man hurt his arm, couldn't throw hard any more, and learned the knuckler from another miner. That's what he passed on to Phil, playing catch in the backyard. Phil watched the ball bob and dance and float as it came at him. "I never knew any of that other stuff," Phil tells me. "Just knuckleball." At the time, he didn't even know much about the big leagues, just the names of a few of the Cleveland Indians—Al Rosen, Bobby Avila, Early Wynn. "We didn't even have a radio or a TV. I would just go up to the

133

gas station and listen. And my dad would take us up every year or two to watch the Indians when they were playing against Ted Williams."

In 1958, when Phil was nineteen, he went to a local try-out arranged by a scout for the Milwaukee Braves. Afterward, the man sat in the Niekros' kitchen, with Phil, his mom, dad, brother, sisters, and coal-mining semipro coach. The scout, a man named Bill Maughn, offered Phil $275 a month to play baseball in the Braves farm system. "My dad said, 'There's gotta be more than two seventy-five a month.'" The Braves had just been in their second straight World Series. They'd drawn two million fans and were signing big-time contracts. "And my dad figured, 'Well, hell, my boy's going to get some of that, too.'" Phil's dad took a private conference with the scout in the next room. "And they came back in, and my dad winked at me. The guy left and my dad was holding a check for a five-hundred-dollar signing bonus. He didn't make that much money from the coal mine over two weeks, ever. That was the biggest day of my career."

Phil Niekro bites into his rib sandwich.

The next spring training, he met Hank and the other Braves in Florida. "That was when they had Spahn and Mathews and Joe Adcock and Johnny Logan and Del Crandall and all those guys. And I was just kind of—I thought they were the greatest baseball players I'd ever met. At that time, I really didn't look on Hank Aaron any different than I did on Mathews or Adcock. He was one of the players in the mix. I knew he was very special. But being a rookie coming up, your first big-league camp, you're in awe. You're just in awe. I mean, that was the Milwaukee Braves, '57, '58. It was just one big unit right there."

He came up for a "cup of coffee" in Milwaukee in '64, then stuck with the team in '65, coming out of the bullpen. I remember my dad coming home from work one day, probably in 1965. He had caught part of the game that day on the radio and swore that he had heard Earl Gillespie and Blaine Walsh talking over and over about the *Negro* pitcher, a rookie, that had just come in. Dad was amused: why do they keep telling us the pitcher is *Negro?* he wondered. What difference did it make? He didn't realize that the announcers were saying "Niekro."

When the team moved south in '66, Phil wasn't upset. "I was just happy to be there—to go anywhere." I ask him what he thought it was like for the black ballplayers. "This was only a year after Selma. What were your concerns on that?"

"You know," Phil tells me, "I really didn't pay attention to a whole lot of stuff like that. I figured baseball was something where stuff like that doesn't happen. I knew there was a lot of segregation at Selma and Jackson, but I didn't think it had any play in sports. I didn't think twice about Henry coming south, or wonder, Are they gonna accept a black ballplayer? It was the big leagues, that's all I knew. We came from Milwaukee and went to the South. I never took it any further than that. I just figured that any place Henry Aaron was gonna go, they'd just fall in love with him."

I've already told him, on the phone, about my letter to Hank in 1973, and my scrapbook, and Hank's letter to me, all prompted by the news of the hate mail. I ask Phil about that. By that time, he was the stud pitcher on the Braves, winning sixty-four games from 1971 to 1974. What was the atmosphere like then?

"I didn't know what was going on," he says. "And I don't think any players knew that. Maybe the front office, the FBI or the bodyguards. I didn't know until years later. He wouldn't have let anybody see it. He didn't want his players seeing it, getting involved. So he struggled with it. And every day he put his uniform on, his spikes, went out for batting practice and played the game. He did just one hell of a job keeping it away from his ballplayers."

I tell Phil about my conversation with Dusty Baker—how aware he and Ralph Garr and Paul Casanova had been of the death threats and the hate mail.

"If he said anything to them," Niekro replies, "they never said anything to anyone else. It was just something he told a couple of his good friends around the ball club. I didn't have the slightest idea—not one iota of what was going on."

In a way, this makes sense. Ralph Garr had told me, in a telephone interview from Houston, that Hank would check his problems at the clubhouse door, "and then come on in and play the game. He never brought them into the stadium with him. It made it easy for a person not to know what he was going through by the way he carried himself." For most of his teammates, Garr said, Hank didn't let on. "Hank Aaron was very private. And he respected his teammates. He could be in a war, or rassling bears or gorillas on the outside, and when he comes in and walks on the field, it's all baseball. And then he'd go back outside, into the war. And you'd never know it." But there were signs any teammate could pick up on: Hank was traveling with a bodyguard. Hank never stayed with the team; he was always in another hotel. And there were plenty of stories in the press about the hate mail. "A lot was made of it," the Braves public relations director, Jim Schultz, had told me a couple of nights earlier. "It wasn't a secret he was getting this hate mail." We knew about it all the way up in Milwaukee.

"I didn't know about it," Phil tells me, "until Hank got out of the game." He says that as a ballplayer in the midst of a long season, "I suppose you're kind of in a bubble—not paying that much attention."

However little Phil and other white teammates noticed about what Hank was going through, the man's talent didn't escape them.

"A lot of people looked at Henry as the greatest home run hitter of all time," Phil tells me. "Which he was. But for those people who didn't see him practicing, or as a teammate watching him play over the years, they never knew how consistent a ballplayer he was on an everyday basis. I mean, the man could hit home runs. He could hit singles, doubles, triples. He was an oustanding right fielder, he had a great arm on him, he could run the bases, he was as smart as they come. But he didn't throw it out there. You've probably heard that before. He was a quiet guy, and he played the game quiet. But then every year, 40, 45 home runs, there's his hundred RBIs, there's his stolen bases, there's his assists in the outfield. It just went on, year after year. And after a while you almost took it for granted."

I can see, now, that the man was so good, he turned his teammates into fans. "He would come to the plate, and it would just stop. Everybody in the dugout would stop what they were doing and watch him hit the ball."

I ask Phil Niekro the same question I'd asked my Milwaukee buddies back in Harry's Bar: How much is Hank's being taken for granted part of his understated style, and how much does it have to do with race?

"Maybe coming south," he replies, "maybe he thought, I better cool it down and not be a showboat and just do my thing and not give other people reasons to piss them off. Of course he never did in Milwaukee, either. If anybody had the opportunity to get the whole world to know, it was Henry. 'Cause the whole world was looking at him, and he could have put on shows that we would still be watching today. But everything remained the same. Walked up to that plate, rested his bat against his belt, put his helmet on with both his hands, took the stance, raised that bat up there, watched the pitcher, and hit the goddamn thing. The home run swing was the same. The trot around the bases was the same. The same touch at first, second and third, the same at home plate, and go sit down in the dugout. That's all there was to it.

"I never saw him get to the point where he got lots of people to applaud for him, or really recognize him for what he did."

The knuckleballer stretches. The smell of smoking meat drifts out from the kitchen. We talk a while about a ballplayer's retirement: speeches to corporate gatherings, twice-a-week golf tournaments, autograph shows. He tells me, if a Hall of Famer wanted to make some quick money, like, say, $50,000, $60,000 even $70,000, he'd need only spend one full day signing on a busy summer weekend in Cooperstown. Phil doesn't do much of that; too many guys come up and ask him to teach their kids how to throw the floating pitch. He picks his moments, preferring to stay at home, on the lake. "I like to barbecue, have a cold beer after that, watch the sun come up in the morning."

I get ready to gather up and leave. Phil looks at me. "There's a story I remember most," he says, almost shyly. "If you have a minute, I'll tell you." I am honored: a Hall of Famer is asking for a little more of my time. There is something he really wants me to know. I settle back down on the cement bench.

His story isn't about Hank, or the Braves, or Atlanta, or Milwaukee. It's about Phil, and his brother, and their dad. It was 1985, early September. Phil was with the Yankees. He was going for his 300th career win, a feat only seventeen other pitchers in baseball history had accomplished. "I've got five starts left," he remembers—five chances to make it before the season ended. Back in Ohio, his dad wasn't doing so well. He had left the coal mine to work in a steel mill. One day at the mill he slipped on ice, fell down hard and broke his arm. It didn't set and they didn't operate. He lost the use of it. Arteries began to clot in his neck; dizzy spells got so bad he had to quit work. Phlebitis took hold of his leg; they had to amputate below the knee. In the midst of this, doctors diagnosed black lung from the mines. On that early September evening in 1985, the old man was in the hospital, going downhill fast, while his son was in a hotel room in New Jersey, on the brink of win number 300. With him was his brother Joe, also a knuckleballer for the Yanks. "The phone rings," Phil remembers. "It's my mother. She starts crying." The priest was in the hospital room, giving last rites.

Phil and Joe flew home. "We drive to the hospital, of course my mom's there," Phil recalls. They looked down at the frail figure lying in bed. "Didn't even know it was my dad. He had been down to 120 pounds, from 240. Tubes everywhere." Phil and Joe stayed two nights at the hospital. "So now, the next day is the day I'm scheduled to start in New York." Not only was he going for his 300th win; the Yanks still had a shot at the pennant. George Steinbrenner, the Yankees' owner, had told Phil, "Do whatever you need to do." He couldn't decide. "Joey says, 'We can't leave. What should we do?' My dad hadn't said a word in three days. I said, 'Joe, I don't know what to do.' " Their mother said, sometimes people can't speak but they can hear.

"And I just looked at him, and I said, 'Dad, I've got a decision to make, and I don't know what the hell to do. I don't want to leave you, because I may not see you again. But I was supposed to start in New York tonight against Toronto. We're a half game out.' So Joe went over and put his head down on his lips that were barely moving. And he says, 'I can't understand him.' So Joe says, 'Dad, I'm gonna ask you a question. If the answer is yes, blink once. If the answer is no, blink twice. Do you want to write something down?' My dad does one long blink. So we get a piece of paper and a pencil and we put the pen in his hand." Agonizingly, the pencil moved across the paper. "And we just sat there, dazed. And finally he's done, and the pencil falls out of his hand."

At first, they couldn't make it out. "So we study it. And it's got a W and an I and an N. And underneath it, it has an H and an A and a P and P and a Y."

WIN HAPPY. "He meant to say, 'If you win, I'll be happy.'"

They flew back to New York. Phil walked in just in time for a rubdown and some warm-up tosses. He showed the note to the pitching coach, Bill Monbouquette. "God, you've got to win this," Monbouquette said.

He lost that night. The next day, the brothers flew home again. Their dad was hanging on. They stayed three nights, and flew back to New York. "Got my ass beat again," Phil says. His mom told him, "You're tired. Don't come back this time. Dad will be here." A few days later, in Milwaukee, he lost again. And then again. He was down to one more start. Still, his old man hung on.

"So now we go to Toronto. We've got to win all three games in Toronto for a playoff to see who's going to win our division." They won the first game but lost the second, eliminating them from the pennant race. The next day, the last game of the season, was Phil's fifth shot at number 300. "And Joe said, 'Damn, you've got to win this game.' And I said, 'I know I gotta. Hell, he ain't gonna last like this until next year.'"

The brothers stayed up until 5:00 A.M., talking. The last game was a day game. "Caught the bus, went to the ballpark, and I said to Joe, 'If I'm winning, if it looks like I've got my three hundredth game won, I want you to come out and throw at least one pitch for me. That way, you'll be in the record book, too.' We shook on it."

By the fifth inning, the Yanks were ahead, 5–0, and Phil hadn't thrown a single knuckleball. Four innings later, bottom of the ninth, the score was 9–0. Phil saw his brother walking toward the mound. "He said, 'I'm not going to do it.' I said, 'Bullshit.' He said, 'If you get this guy out, you'll be the oldest guy in the history of baseball to pitch a shutout.'" Phil was forty-six years old. "I said okay." The slugger Jeff Burroughs stepped in. Phil got two strikes on him; he still hadn't thrown a knuckleball. "I call time out, and I say, 'You know what this pitch is going to be. I can't think of a better pitch. Situation my dad's in, he taught me the knuckleball, that's why I got here.'

"I threw the knuckleball. He swung and missed."

Win number 300.

Before Phil could get off the mound, he saw his brother. "Joe grabs me and whispers in my ear: 'I got to tell you something about Dad.' I knew what he was going to say."

Earlier that day, George Steinbrenner had arranged to pipe the broadcast via telephone to the hospital room in Ohio. As Phil's dad lay there semi-comatose—he hadn't spoken in twenty-five days—his mom, telephone to her ear, passed along the play-by-play. It wasn't clear if he was hearing it.

"When I got the guy out in the bottom of the seventh inning, my dad opened his eyes and looked at my mom and said, 'Sonny's pitching one hell of a game, ain't he?'"

The next day, in the hospital, the old man was out of intensive care, sitting in bed with a smile on his face. "Didn't have a tube in him. So I took my Yankee hat off and put it on his head. And I gave him the ball."

Their father lived for two more years—long enough to see Joe pitch in the World Series for the Minnesota Twins. "Two months later, he died. Saw everything he wanted to see with his boys."

Phil stands up to leave. The owner of the barbecue joint, the Mountain Man himself, comes out to show him a page he's just printed off the Braves' Web site: a list of all the team records the knuckleballer amassed in his twenty years in Milwaukee and Atlanta. Phil smiles, hands it back, tells the man his barbecue is the best. He says goodbye. I decide to linger, and talk to the man who's built this barbecue tribute to a Hall of Famer.

○

The Mountain Man comes back with a pair of sweet ice teas. His clothes are right for the barbecue smoke and the sopping heat: T-shirt, blue jean cutoffs, a pair of Converse sneakers. He's got a gold chain with an anniversary pendant, and a Mountain Man ring: eighteen-karat gold, with diamonds in-laid. He wears a full beard and speaks in a deep southern drawl. He smiles without effort.

His real name is Don Bryant. He put his place on the land of a man named Bailey, who made boots for soldiers during the two world wars. Before he barbecued for a living, Don worked the hill country north of here, planting corn and beans, "anything that grows in the mountains." His kitchen is a converted Bluebird school bus. The lean-to, which makes shade for the benches, is built with two-by-eights and tin and an oak-slat fence. Atop the roof is the hand-painted sign: MOUNTAIN MAN BAR-B-QUE. FLOWERY BRANCH, GEORGIA. HOME OF PHIL NIEKRO. And a painting of Number 35, in his motion toward home plate on the 1973 day he tossed a no-hitter.

"Phil Niekro," he says, "is the best player who ever played for the Atlanta Braves."

The best? I say. Great, of course; one of the greatest, sure. But *the* best? I'm surprised. This is an honor, indisputably, that belongs to Henry Aaron. Moments ago, Phil said as much himself.

"No," the Mountain Man tells me. "Phil Niekro is the best they've ever had." He holds out his sheet from the Web site. "Phil's got more records than anybody."

I don't doubt this. The Atlanta records are right there, ink from the color printer barely dry on the stat sheet. And many of them are impressive. Most games won, most twenty-win seasons, most strikeouts, most shutouts. But, I point out, these records also include most losses, most hits, most walks, most runs given up. And many of the records are for longevity: most games, most innings, most years. These are nothing like the records for most all-time home runs, most all-time RBIs, third most all-time hits—records Hank holds not only for the Braves but for all of baseball. Surely, I tell him, there can be no dispute as to who was the best player ever to put on an Atlanta uniform.

The Mountain Man is steadfast: Phil was the best.

Okay, I reason, if you judge the best by who's got the most records, or who's compiled the most in a certain category, then it's clear that all that fuss, years ago, about Hank not earning the record, because he came to bat more times than Babe Ruth—all that would be silly to even consider now, right?

Wrong, says the Mountain Man. "In my mind, he didn't break the record. He played in more games than Babe did."

But wait, I say. Shouldn't that be to his credit? I mean, what's wrong with having the strength and the character to last for twenty-three years? Isn't Cal Ripken celebrated for being the Iron Man? Aren't you celebrating Phil Niekro in the same way? Shouldn't we think about Hank like that—he kept himself healthy, he earned the record?

"Not Babe's record," says Mountain Man. "Say Babe Ruth played in two thousand games and Hank Aaron played in two thousand games, and Aaron had more home runs—he broke the record. But if he played a hundred more games, he didn't break the record. If you play long enough, you can break everybody's record."

It's an argument I thought had been put to rest long ago. Instead, our conversation gets circular, quickly:

Phil's the best Brave, because he has the most records.

But these records include playing the most games, pitching the most innings. If we judge it on that basis, then of course Hank, with the most home runs, should have the undisputed record.

No, he shouldn't. He played in more games than Babe.

Around and around we go. At times it feels like one of those endless statistical arguments between baseball fans. At times it feels like something else.

Mountain Man had just told me that he'd lived in Atlanta when the Braves arrived. He'd remembered the racial tension at the stadium. Blacks and whites, he remembered, were both afraid to go to the games: whites, of getting mugged in the parking lots; blacks, of the fights in the stands, and the slurs that cut the air: "Go home, darkie. Go back home to the cotton fields. That's where you belong." It was a time in Atlanta, he'd remembered, when the schools were getting integrated; a time in America when Muhammad Ali was refusing to serve his country in Vietnam. The Mountain Man had recalled "a pretty hard matter of conflict."

I ask him, "Is part of your feeling coming from the racial attitude of the time? You mentioned resenting Muhammad Ali's stance on Vietnam at the time, and the integration in Atlanta. And here, Babe Ruth was this white hero. Did you ever think about it like that?"

"No, I never felt that. I just felt that he should earn it. And that's how I think a lot of people feel. It doesn't matter if he were Puerto Rican, black, or American. If it took him longer, he didn't do it. As far as breaking Babe Ruth's record, that's not been done." Perhaps, Mountain Man suggests, Hank Aaron should be thankful for the attention he did get. "I'd say he was very fortunate to get as far as he did, do as well as he did. He was very lucky. You walk around in front of fifty thousand fans, you never know what you're going to run into."

We say our goodbyes. He shows me a picture of his beautiful two-year-old daughter. I tell him his barbecue is great, step into the bright sun, climb into my broiling rent-a-car, and drive out of there, tasting smoke on my fingers, and mulling three words: *black, or American.*

○

The Cobb County Convention Center is a short drive from Flowery Branch. In the late afternoon, I walk in on the waning hours of a Civil War Relics show. Collectors from across the South mill around on the convention floor and the balcony overhang.

A Confederate belt buckle, found on an old battlefield near Blue Bell, Tennessee, sells for $195. Unused Civil War envelopes go for twenty bucks each. There's a Confederate coat for $495, a musician's sword for $425. And bone pocket binoculars, and a Civil War drum, and cross-sabre hat insignias, and an Original Civil War Side Spout Coffee Pot. And artists' ideas of war: Rebels advancing, bayonets fixed; Union soldiers, falling in disarray; moonlight shining on the Savannah River, beside an unblemished clock tower. And a soldier with a paintbrush, touching up the Confederate battle flag, titled *Emblems of Valor*.

"They're glorifying a lot of this," Dennis Clack tells me. He stands before two dozen rifles imported by the Confederacy: single shot, muzzle-loaded, from France, Belgium, England, Austria. "You can take a picture from one side of the mule, and it looks pretty good. But from the end of the mule, where you're flowing, you get a completely different picture." He likes this definiton of war: "One month of boredom, five seconds of sheer hell." He fought in Vietnam—First battalion, 13th Marines, I Corps, north of Da Nang.

I explain what I'm doing.

"Oh, you're talking about the hate mail," Dennis says. "You know, I'd like to see how much of it came from around here. Because I'm not sure that much of it did." True, most of the nasty letters came with northern postmarks.

Dennis tells me he spent a lot of time at the stadium when the Braves first came. "I liked Rico Carty. The Braves would be playing catch in the outfield before the game, and he'd toss the ball into the stands. And then he'd flash this big smile. And it was all teeth. I mean, his face was just pitch black, and he'd smile and all you could see was teeth. And then he'd tip his cap."

That first year, Dennis remembers, was just after Selma. "People getting beat up on that bridge—we just thought it was funny. We didn't realize it was such a world-shaking event." The next year, at the stadium, "We'd sit up and cat-call. We'd use all kinds of names. We said everything. And if you made eye contact, you knew you had 'em.

"I probably grew up racist," he tells me. "But after military service, you kind of let go of that." In Vietnam, Dennis says, it was hard to hate a man who was fighting right beside you.

He wears a graying mustache, a week's growth of beard, and a rounded belly. On his T-shirt is a list of the "Top Ten Reasons Why You Might Be a Redneck." (Three of them: family tree does not fork; porch collapses and kills more than three dogs; you think the stock market has a fence around it.) He's smiling at me, stealing a look at his shirt. "I'm really not as dumb as I look," he says, amused at the Northerner in his presence.

Dennis drew the line at hate mail. "To sit down and actually write letters threatening him like that—well, I'd have to use the word 'sickening.'" By this time, anyway, he says, he was rooting for Hank.

He takes his own relic out of its green nylon sheath:

Colonel Beardan Sharpshooter. New Model, 1859. He collects artillery shells, rifles, bullets, buttons. I ask him why he keeps these things.

"You can dig this stuff out of the ground," he tells me. "It's not like fossils. I can get more of a grip on this. You know it happened. You can actually put your hands on it."

On the balcony, I find more art: *The Diehards,* Rebels throwing stones against the Union bullets; *Victory or Death,* decimated troops, fighting to the finish; *Surrender at Appomattox,* Lee and Grant, and the end of the Rebel army.

I turn around and see a woman, about my age, sitting in an Atlanta Braves jacket, behind a display of broken coins and cracked leather holsters. Her blond hair is brushed back from her face. She wears a large diamond on her wedding finger. Her name is Susan Farrar.

"It was *the* news," she says of Hank's chase. "People were pulling for him. The racial stuff, that wasn't a real big part of what I remember. That was a small group."

I look down at a small box filled with old bullets. They are bent, as if fired through a crooked barrel. On closer look, I see that they are pockmarked. "That's what they'd give the soldiers to bite down on in the hospital," Susan tells me, "when they were going to amputate." *Bite the bullet.*

The pain must have been unimaginable. This place is filled with such testaments of anguish and loss: broken swords, bloody renderings, torn scraps of gray clothing. Things you can touch. Things that make real the sufferings of their white Rebel forbears, nearly a century and a half ago.

I tell Susan what Dusty told me, a story from twenty-six years ago—about the man in the red coat with the high-powered rifle, who said he was going to take a shot at Hank. Every time Hank hit one out, I tell her, he never knew for sure if he was going to make it home. "That just gives me *chill bumps*," she says.

A friend of Susan's has wandered over from another display of relics. His name is Steve Conrad. He remembers the night of 715; he was there. Steve's memories of the hatred directed at Henry Aaron, like Susan's, are vague. Thinking about it a generation later, he says, "Hank Aaron must have had icewater in his veins."

I pick up a bitten bullet, running my thumb, slowly, in and out of the tiny gaps. I think about a soldier, clamping down hard: an unforgotten image of suffering, nurtured and preserved to the end of the next century.

"And all he wanted to do was hit that baseball," Susan says. "We didn't know all that. He made it look so easy."

7

A HERO IN THE NEIGHBORHOOD

Atlanta, April 8, 1974

Atlanta celebrated on the chilly evening when Henry Aaron swung at a fastball down the middle and put it in the left field bullpen. But the meaning of 715 differed, in intensity and historical perspective, from one neighborhood to the next.

"Oh, it was just wonderful," an elegant, elderly white

woman told me, carefully choosing her peaches from a Jamaican selling fruit at a makeshift stand on Peachtree Street. She seemed slightly amused that I would be asking about it. "We thought it was very, very nice for him."

"We cheered," said Steve Conrad, remembering the night in Atlanta–Fulton County Stadium from a display at the Civil War Relics show. "We hugged. We patted each other on the back."

"I pissed on myself," says Albert Allen. "I thought someone might shoot him. I really was afraid." On a steamy Saturday, Allen spends the afternoon with friends at the J and P Barber Shop on Ashby Street. He was in an Atlanta pool hall that April night a generation ago. When Hank stepped up to bat, everyone put down their sticks and watched the television. "I was sitting down there drinking a Budweiser," he remembered. When Hank connected, "It was a feeling of relief. I felt good." The men around him nod, slowly fanning themselves.

No one is getting his hair cut. The barber isn't there and nobody seems to mind. The men are telling each other the news. They sit in idle barber chairs and in the seats along the window. A rusted Coke sign hangs over an unplugged Pepsi machine. A broken-down air conditioner is set on fan: the weak breeze is not nearly enough to unclench the humid fist that has grabbed hold of the afternoon. In the corner, the Braves game flickers through the television screen.

Months back, James McClain, the homeless veteran I'd met outside of Hank's office, had promised to take my brother Yam and me down Ashby when we came back to town. He wanted us to understand how Hank's record echoed in black working-class Atlanta. I've been looking around for James, with no luck; Yam and I are here on our own.

"I was in the stadium that night," says Arthur Cotton, stroking a white goatee. "I had all my family with me. Man, it was *exciting*." Next to him sits his brother A.C., wearing a yellow shirt and a yellow hat with a short lid, managing to look comfortable. My face, neck, the back of my shirt are sopping. A.C. is a deacon at the West Hunter Street Baptist Church, where the Reverend Ralph David Abernathy, the late civil rights leader and close friend of Dr. King, held forth. "All the guys around here remember it," A.C. says of Hank and the neighborhood. "They can't forget it. He had so many fans." In those days, Hank could often be seen walking down Ashby or up Martin Luther King Jr. Drive (then it was called Hunter Street), past the barber shops and rib joints and shoe repair places. "He would come over here all the time," says A.C. "I cut his hair," says a man across the room.

These are the men of Hank's generation, men who grew up in a segregated South, and watched as Hank endured things they knew well. "People have no idea what he put up with," A.C. Cotton says. "Even our young people. Today they say, 'I don't see how y'all took that.' Well, we had to take it. There wasn't a choice."

"The white man made the laws back then," says Arthur Cotton. "And he didn't make the laws to think about nobody but himself."

Albert Allen recalls meeting Hank one day while shining shoes in Montgomery, Alabama. This was two years before Rosa Parks refused to give up her seat to a white passenger on a Montgomery city bus—an act which began the famous bus boycott, led by Dr. King, whose house would soon be firebombed. Hank had come through segregated Montgomery while playing for Jacksonville of the Sally League. He walked into the shoeshine stand and asked directions to a restaurant. Allen recognized the man who was helping break the baseball color barrier in the Deep South. He pointed to the fish place across the street. A few minutes later, on break, Allen went there himself and found the place jammed. "And I was looking for a place to sit. And Henry Aaron said, 'Over here, Governor!' And I went over there and sat down with him and his teammate, Felix Mantilla."

Two decades later, living in Atlanta, Allen followed the tension of Henry Aaron's chase. He witnessed the milestones: Home run number 400, in April 1966, the day after U.S. fighter jets bombed the North Vietnamese port of Haiphong, and Vice President Hubert H. Humphrey defended the Johnson administration's poverty programs from attacks by Senator Robert F. Kennedy; number 500, in the midsummer of 1968, a month after Kennedy's assassination, as Humphrey picked up more delegates toward the Democratic presidential nomination; number 600, in April 1971, as President Richard M. Nixon named the U.S. Navy's first black admiral, and reports suggested that the Soviet Union was preparing to deploy an advanced antimissile system; number 700, late in the season of 1973, as the Shah of Iran came to Washington to request more sophisticated weaponry, and President Nixon refused to turn over key documents in the Watergate investigation.

By the end of 1973, Hank had passed all the great sluggers on the all-time home run list, until only Ruth remained. He was one home run short of 714. Albert Allen worried that something might happen to Hank over that winter. He wasn't alone. "Dear Hank," read one piece of mail during the off-season, "I hope lightning will strike you before next season."

The following spring, Allen watched on television as the Hammer tied the Babe in Cincinnati on Opening Day. It was April 4, the sixth anniversary of Dr. King's assassination. Allen remembered how Hank and his new bride, Billye (Hank and Barbara had divorced a couple of years earlier), criticized Reds' officials afterward for refusing to honor King's memory with a moment of silence before the game. "We were all very disappointed about it," said Hank, who had conferred with his friend, the Reverend Jesse Jackson, before the game. "It would have been appropriate." Billye Aaron added: "It should not have been necessary to request a moment of silence. It should have been done without asking."

Four days later, Allen sat drinking his Bud in the pool hall. For months he had known about the hate mail and the threats to kill Hank. Many of the details had made the papers; the rest had passed down the grapevine of black Atlanta—a form of communication that was so effective, according to former mayor Maynard Jackson, "it was almost like putting something on TV."

On the night of April 8, Mayor Jackson sat in the VIP section at Atlanta–Fulton County Stadium. He had just been elected as the city's first black mayor—a Deep South event of its own historical magnitude.

The newspapers that morning had reported on a president clinging to office. The House Judiciary Committee was moving closer to impeachment, while new documents revealed that the White House had been monitoring the tax records of the president's political foes. In Ohio, eight National Guardsmen denied their guilt in the shootings of four students at Kent State four years earlier. And a U.N. peacekeeping force remained in the Middle East following the 1973 Arab-Israeli War. The movie section that day ran ads for *The Sting* and *The Exorcist.* "Hooked on a Feeling" and "Midnight Train to Georgia" were playing on the radio; *Columbo, Sanford and Son* and *All in the Family,* on TV. *Jonathan Livingston Seagull, The Joy of Sex, Breakfast of Champions* and *I'm O.K., You're O.K.* were huge bestsellers.

That evening, a little after nine, Hank stepped into the batter's box. It was the bottom of the fourth inning. In the VIP section, Pearl Bailey looked on. She had flown in to sing the national anthem. Nearby sat Georgia governor Jimmy Carter. Mayor Jackson was with his guest, the entertainer Sammy Davis, Jr.

In the first row, next to the first base dugout, Herbert and Estella Aaron looked out at their son. Not far away sat A. C. Cotton and his family. And Steve Conrad. And James McClain. In the press box were Vin Scully, the Dodger announcer, and Milo Hamilton, the voice of the Braves. Curt Gowdy was calling the game for NBC. In the dugout, gazing out at Hank, sat Phil Niekro. And Ralph Garr. Dusty Baker knelt, watching, in the on-deck circle.

Gaile Aaron watched a television in Nashville. Ed Wojciak watched at Holy Cross. I watched in Milwaukee. So did my buddies: T, and Che, and Freak. Tom Cheeks watched.

And James Cameron. And Terry Perry. And my brother Tom. So, I imagine, did Grandpa Irv. Albert Allen's buddies set down their pool cues in Atlanta. Richard Nixon looked on from the White House.

The first pitch was a ball in the dirt. The crowd booed. They wanted Al Downing, the Dodgers' pitcher, to give Hank a pitch he could reach. And then Downing did. And Hank hit it. It was seven minutes after nine o'clock.

"When Hank hit that ball," Maynard Jackson told me, "Sammy must have jumped ten feet, I'm not kidding, just *flailing* his arms. He was *so* happy. It was *such* an electric moment."

As the floodlit ball curved up into the night, Bill Buckner, the Dodgers' left fielder, climbed the fence and leapt for it. Just behind him, in the Braves' bullpen, relief pitcher Tom House raised his glove. In the bleachers above, a fan began to lower his fishnet.

"And I realize it's coming right at me," House remembered twenty-five years later. "If I would have stood still, it would have hit me right in the forehead." The ball, encoded with "12-12-2-2" in invisible ink, floated downward. House made the catch. A split second later, the fishnet dropped in front of his face. Too late. House looked at the fence, and saw how high Buckner had climbed. "And then I went blank. I don't remember anything. People say I ran faster than I ever did in any windsprint, all the way to home plate."

Hank was rounding the bases. When he came around second, two young white men broke through security and ran toward him. They reached Hank, one on each side, and slapped him on his chest and shoulders. These could have been the assassins that promised to end Hank's dream. But they were students from the University of Georgia, in long hair and bell bottoms, offering first congratulations. I've seen the tape a hundred times. Even more than the stupendous breach in security, I am struck by how nonchalant Hank appeared. Following two years of death threats, and literally tons of hate mail, here came two white men, racing toward him before he could reach home with the record. Hank's only reaction was a single, subtle, forearm shiver, shaking one of the students loose. Quickly, they peeled off, and Hank rounded third.

As he headed home, the cannon went off. And the fireworks. Estella Aaron pushed her way frantically through the crowd, with Hank's bodyguard, Calvin Wardlaw, right behind her.

In the pool hall, Albert Allen watched Hank arrive, safe at home. He was so relieved, he relieved himself. "I felt that good about it. It was like if someone told you your mother had a heart attack. And you run home, and she's sitting up, and the doctor says she's going to be all right. It was *that* kind of feeling."

Months earlier, James McClain told me that he'd had the same feelings: fear that Henry Aaron would be assassinated rounding the bases, followed by intense relief, almost amazement, that Hank survived to make it home.

Moments after he stepped on home plate, Hank was surrounded by a tight knot of teammates and photographers. Governor Carter was nearby, ready to present Hank with a special Georgia license plate: HLA 715. "I don't remember running through the crowd," Tom House told me. "My next conscious moment was getting to him, and reaching across and saying, 'Here it is, Hammer.' And him looking across and saying, 'Thanks, Kid.' And that's when I saw the tears in his eyes. And I can remember being just stunned that Henry was crying. Other than a little anger once in a while—throwing a helmet, which was typical baseball stuff—I'd never seen this guy have any emotions. But here he is hugging his mother, displaying the same thing that every other athlete goes through, every other kid in America."

So it appeared.

Afterward, Henry Aaron would say of his mother's embrace, "I never knew she could hug so tight."

Eleven minutes into the applause and congratulations, the Braves flashed a message on the scoreboard: HE MADE THE GREAT CHASE POSSIBLE. LET'S HEAR IT FOR THE BABE.

An inning later, with his team at bat, Hank went back to the clubhouse, where Richard Nixon was on the telephone. "Thank you very much, Mr. President," the new home run king said. "It was a long struggle, but I finally made it." President Nixon invited Hank and Billye to the White House. They never got the chance; the president would resign four months later.

That night of April 8, the men in the J and P Barber Shop tell me, black Atlanta went crazy. "The town was on fire," says A.C. Cotton: fireworks, music, dancing and partying in the streets. He leans back in his idle barber's chair. "We needed a hero in the neighborhood."

"Hell, yeah," says Albert Allen. "It had a big effect on us."

O

"Every black knew the significance of this," Andrew Young tells me. "Because all your life, you're taught you're inferior. And everything about the structure of the society, for most people mine and Hank's age, was that you're just not good enough. You're not good enough to go to college, you're not good enough to do anything. And so every time somebody breaks one of those barriers, everybody feels good about it."

It hardly surprises Young that whites, in large part, were unaware of the racial context of Hank's record. "White people never knew, and never wanted to know, what black people were going through," he says.

Young recounts a story he heard from Hosea Williams, the civil rights leader who had been on the bridge at Selma in 1965. The story was about Joe Louis, and the 1930s, and a tiny town called Attapulgus in rural Georgia. "There was only one radio in town," Young said, "and that was in the country store. And all the white people would get in the store to listen, and the black people would be outside the windows listening." It was always Louis, the heavyweight champ, against another would-be great white hope. "And the whites would talk about when Joe Louis was going to get beat up. They were only betting on which round he was going to lose in. And Joe Louis would win, and they'd be mad. And nobody black would make a sound. They couldn't cheer, Hosea said. They would walk quietly to the edge of town. At the edge of town, down a hill, there was an old sawdust pile. And he said everybody was marching in silence till they got to the pile.

"And then they just went crazy."

In a later generation, millions of white Americans would

have no idea why blacks celebrated a home run with the intensity that they did—nor, even, that they were celebrating—just as they hadn't noticed Hank's hardships leading up to those celebrations.

"Allowing for many exceptions," says Maynard Jackson, "black people are simply mud on the radar screen of white people. I've heard some black folks say that whites get up in the morning and think about how they can hurt us. And that's simply not true. They don't think about us, period. We're just not there."

Back in Milwaukee, I would hear a story that made Jackson's point for him. I had sought out Felix Mantilla, an old friend of Hank's and his teammate in Jacksonville and Milwaukee, to discuss their days in the Sally League. I wanted to know what it was like to break the baseball color barrier in the Deep South of 1953. Andy Young had told me, "I think Hank had it worse than Jackie Robinson. He was up north. Hank was going to Jacksonville, Atlanta, Tampa, Birmingham. His struggle was in the heart of the Old South."

Felix Mantilla was eighteen years old when he arrived in Jacksonville that spring. "I wasn't used to none of this," he tells me, sitting in the empty bleachers one morning behind a backstop at the Felix Mantilla Little League on Milwaukee's south side. "In Puerto Rico, we didn't have this—'you go this way and the other one goes that way.' But I remember the principal in my school told me, 'You know, when you get to Florida, Felix, you might have to ride in the back of a bus.'" Forty-six years later, Mantilla laughs. "The thing was so *stupid* that it was funny. If you saw a fountain and it says, FOR

MEXICANS ONLY, and you're an American, you would say, 'This is stupid. It's just water. This is really *bad!*'" His hard laughter, at the sheer absurdity, is contagious.

One day, the team bus stopped at a restaurant, and the white players went inside. Felix was thirsty. He got off the bus and walked toward a water fountain. He tried the COLORED fountain. "But it was hot water coming out of it. So I tried the one that said WHITE. And it was cold. So I drank out of that one." The restaurant's manager saw him and called the sheriff. Felix nearly got himself arrested. After that, he relied on Hank and their other black teammate, Horace Garner, for guidance. "Hank was used to it and Horace was used to it," Felix remembers, "because they lived here. So they were trying to tell me a lot of things that I could do or not do." They kept telling him, *Don't get angry.* It was a hard lesson—after nightly taunts, repeated brushback pitches took on extra menace. Finally, after yet another knockdown pitch, Felix lost it and stormed the pitcher's mound. Horace Garner intercepted him before the incident triggered a race riot. "Horace used to say, if you keep on getting mad, you're going to get us killed," Felix tells me.

Pretty quickly, it had stopped being funny. "Because some of these people meant to hurt someone," Felix says.

About four days into the season in Jacksonville, Felix got a letter in the mail. Still only weeks removed from Puerto Rico, Felix had a hard time understanding English, so he showed the letter to Hank. *If you show your black ass again at the ballpark,* the writer promised, *we're going to kill you.* Someone called in the FBI. That night, a couple of agents watched from the white section of the Jacksonville Braves field. Nothing happened. Except that every night, in Macon, Montgomery, Savannah, and at the home park in Jacksonville, the young black Braves heard all kinds of horrible voices, saying things Felix had never heard. "They called you 'alligator bait.' I couldn't figure out what alligator bait was. I used to ask Hank, 'What the hell is an alligator bait?' Hank said, 'Well, this is where they grab a black person, they tie them up by the leg and dump them in the river. And then when the alligator would see . . .'" Felix can't finish the sentence; he's laughing too hard.

"That's incredible that you can laugh about it," I say.

"You have to laugh," he tells me, "because you don't want to cry." We talk for an hour that morning, on the bleachers by the ball field that bears his name. He tells me he's lived in Milwaukee since the year he arrived in town to play for the big-league Braves—1956, the year I was born.

After a while, three Latino kids arrive to hit fly balls and chase them down across the green expanse. I ask Felix if any fans, at the baseball card shows he sometimes frequents, ever ask him what he went through down south.

He pauses. "No," he says, his voice short and clipped.

How about any sportswriters? I ask.

"No."

Anybody at all?

"No. None." He pauses again. "Maybe because some of the people are ashamed about it. They don't want to ask any questions. Just let it stay like that. Or maybe they don't care."

How about back then? "Do you remember one teammate who said, I'm sorry what you're going through, this is wrong?"

"Not on our team."

"Not one player on your team?"

"No. It was like nothing was happening. You're on your own."

Blacks, over the years, have asked Felix about his role as a pioneer in American history—fans, from their roped-off section in Jacksonville in 1953; kids, at the Boys Club in Milwaukee, forty years later. In that audience, he says, "some of the guys that were white, they couldn't believe it. I had one white guy, he was very indignant, because he thought I wasn't telling the truth."

I ask Felix if he watched Hank hit his 715th home run on that cool April evening in Atlanta. Yeah, he says. At first, as he kept up on what Hank was going through, it felt like, "Here we go again with him, all over again, like in 1953." And then, when Hank swung at Al Downing's 1–0 fastball, "For me, it was a great feeling. Because we played together for a bunch of years. And I know his family was glad, because they didn't have to go through that nonsense anymore."

○

One person was missing at the stadium on April 8, 1974. His name was Bowie Kuhn. The commissioner of baseball had ordered Eddie Mathews, now the Braves' manager, to play Hank in at least two of the three games in Cincinnati before the Braves came back home. This was not popular in Atlanta, where fans, and the team's front office, wanted to see the Hammer hit both the record-tying and record-breaking homers at home. The Braves' plans to sit Hank were considered an outrage in many quarters, especially among the New

York press. Red Smith of *The New York Times* denounced the team's "brazen defiance of baseball's integrity." As it turned out, Hank hit number 714 on Opening Day, sat out the second game, and went 0-for-3 in game three in Cincinnati. When Hank and the team came back to Atlanta, the stage set for 715, the commissioner decided not to show up. Instead, he sent a black assistant, Hall-of-Famer Monte Irvin, who nearly got booed out of the stadium when he was introduced after Hank's homer. Kuhn cited a previous engagement in Cleveland. He had declined to witness the shattering of the greatest records in sports, reports said, in order to address the Wahoo Club.

Hank's anger at the commissioner lasted for years. It was the beginning of what many people, blacks in particular, began to see as baseball's official snub of the new home run king. When held by a white man, 714 was the record that couldn't be broken, the greatest in all of sport. Now, some baseball aficionados began talking about Joe DiMaggio's fifty-six-game hitting streak as the ultimate baseball achievement. (Which, when you think about it, is a ridiculous comparison.)

Hank waited for the attention, the endorsements, the praise that might finally begin to ease the hurt he'd suffered. He did land one big contract from Magnavox, and he spoke to Congress on Flag Day, 1974. But within a few years, he was a virtually forgotten man in America. Hank, one sportswriter observed, "could travel 80 miles an hour between the coasts and not be recognized by one highway patrolman. The greatest home run hitter in history is mostly likely to show up on the American Express 'Do You Know Me?' commercial."

"From all the buildup and excitement that he might break the record—this would, by normal rules, create a great deal of acceptance," Reverend Jesse Jackson tells me when I phone him one Sunday afternoon from Atlanta. "I mean, it's Wheaties box time. It's Disney World time. It's movie time. You know, Take me out to the Hank Aaron game, or *something*. But he meant almost the very opposite. As if he were the enemy. The cool reception, the death threats, you know, all those no commercial offers. I think for a moment it was like an eclipse of the Sun. Midday became midnight. Disorienting. It had to take some extra grit to deal with that rejection."

The question then, Jackson says, became, "When number one is not enough, what do you do?"

"I think baseball made a major mistake when they tried to downplay the significance of his breaking Babe Ruth's record," Andrew Young says. I ask him where that was coming from. "I think it was racial. In the early seventies, Nixon had just gotten elected, that was the white backlash period, that was the Republican 'Southern strategy,' it turned back the civil rights movement before it got going good. It was not a good racial climate. Instead of human beings like Branch Rickey taking the opportunity to advance both the cause of sport and race relations," he says, referring to the Brooklyn Dodgers' owner who brought Jackie Robinson into the major leagues, "Kuhn decided to downplay it."

This, says Maynard Jackson, after Henry Aaron had abided by all the rules. "Here is a guy that lived the way America said it wanted black people to live: obeying the law, living a constructive life, obeying all the values America said it wanted for people, especially black people. And then he has to go through this."

By contrast, Babe Ruth roared through life. "I don't want to take anything away from Babe Ruth, but he was closer to Latrell Sprewell than he was to Hank Aaron," Young says with a laugh, referring to the volatile and controversial NBA star. "I mean, Babe Ruth was a drunk, Babe Ruth was a cocky so-and-so, he was a womanizer, he was larger than life, and it was 'Fuck you, this is who I am,' and he'd point to the other player, and he'd grandstand. Babe Ruth was more like Muhammad Ali."

And if Hank Aaron had been like that?

"They would have shot him. Man, I don't think he could have stayed alive if he were that way. At that time. Look at all the flak. I mean, Muhammad Ali almost went to jail. He stood up against the war and the whole system. He was hated until just recently because he was ahead of his time. He was making too many social statements. He was a new kind of Negro, and liked to be that, and it took a long time for people to catch up to him."

After Hank tied the record, he joked that, for 715, he might just run the bases backward. For sure, Hank liked a good laugh. Once, when Dusty Baker wasn't feeling well, Hank gave him a trick pill designed to turn urine red. Dusty freaked out, thinking something was gravely wrong; when he rushed into the clubhouse to tell Hank about it, he found Hank and Ralph Garr rolling on the floor with laughter. But Hank's public temperament gave no space for showboating.

In an early memoir, he wrote, "I've never been much for clowning around." Andrew Young says that Hank and Arthur Ashe, the late tennis great, were among the last in "a breed of gentleman athletes." Ashe, Young recalled, had found racism a greater burden than the AIDS that would kill him. In *I Had a Hammer,* Hank also said he wasn't sure he would have had the temperament to take the kind of physical abuse meted out to the non-violent marchers in the civil rights movement. He was not a hot dog; he was not Martin Luther King. He was a ballplayer, who found himself "in the middle of something," as he told me when I met him. "I was just playing baseball," he said. But there he was, threatening something sacred—and facing the truth of that.

"Henry took on this role without really even wanting it or seeking it," Tom House says. "It was put on him. And he just picked it up and took it."

With this in mind, I go to see John Lewis. Lewis was a hero of the civil rights movement. He was a leader of the student sit-ins at lunch counters in Nashville in 1960. A year later, he was one of the original Freedom Riders who rode the Greyhound and Trailways buses into the Deep South, seeking to integrate the bus stations. In Montgomery, where Hank had played eight years earlier, Lewis and fellow riders endured a savage beating by a mob of hundreds of enraged whites. Others in his group came out paralyzed, or with permanent brain damage. Lewis spoke at the famous March on Washington in 1963. He faced the rage of Mississippi during Freedom Summer in 1964. With Hosea Williams, he led the procession across the Edmund Pettus Bridge on Bloody Sunday in 1965, and got his skull cracked by Alabama state

troopers. Now he is a member of Congress, representing Atlanta.

Lewis is a friend of Hank's. I mention how I'm struck that
Hank risked his life to play baseball. Lewis says, "I never discussed it with him. Probably never will." Right. They don't
need to discuss it; they both already know.

"Hank was shattering something," Lewis says. Like the
Freedom Riders before him. "And I think Hank was saying,
if Jackie Robinson could do it, if Rosa Parks could do it, if
Martin Luther King could do it, if all these people can take
it, I can take it. Sometimes I believe that maybe some force
or some power gives you that extra ounce of grace. And
maybe that's what Hank was endowed with."

John Lewis understands Henry Aaron's actions in the
context of what he calls the "Spirit of History" that guided
him to act during the civil rights era. "Others might call it
Fate. Or Destiny," Lewis writes in *Walking with the Wind,* his
1998 memoir. "This force is on the side of what is good, of
what is right and just. It is the essence of the moral force of
the universe, and at certain points in life, in the flow of human existence and circumstances, this force, this spirit, finds
you or selects you, it chases you down, and you have no
choice; you must allow yourself to be used, to be guided by
this force and to carry out what must be done."

Of course, Hank would say he was just playing baseball,
not contemplating the moral force of the universe. Still, John
Lewis says, "I think he was very much aware in his own mind
of the role he was playing, and the hand he had been dealt.
Like a textbook. He had to do it. Not just for himself, but
also for the athletes that will come behind him. And also, as

my mother would say, he had to stand up for the race. He did it with the philosophy and the thinking of the civil rights movement. He didn't make a great deal of public noise. He just kept his eyes on the prize."

○

"Life throws sticks at you," the young man says, sitting on an overturned pickle bucket beneath an Atlanta shade tree. "And you can get hit or you can catch 'em. It all goes the same way." His name is Jason Bailey. He's passing a quiet afternoon on a residential block off Ashby Street, talking with his neighbors, when Yam and I pull up in our rental car. We're wearing dress shirts and slacks; at first, it seems, Jason and the others look at these two white guys as if we're missionaries or real estate sharks.

No problem, Jason says, he'll talk to us about Hank Aaron. "The man opened it up. Even though his footsteps were behind other black footsteps, he was the first black man that broke the white man's record. But this man broke his record and kept going. Just left him back there, like, damn, scratching his head. And to this day, they still say that Babe Ruth is the greatest baseball player ever lived. How you gonna be the greatest to ever play the game, your record is just sitting back there by itself, I mean, shit, by itself, what the fuck?"

"That Babe Ruth record was made to be broken!" says an older man leaning up against an old Ford sedan. He's a slight man in his fifties, with a small round face and smiling, biting eyes. He regards me and Yam skeptically. We have arrived in the aftermath of a shooting rampage in the city by a white day trader named Mark O. Barton, who murdered his family and then nine others at office buildings in the city's fashionable Buckhead district. The papers have been running sympathetic stories about the pressures of a stockbroker's world. The man before me has another analysis: "You crackers are crazy," he says sharply, with a smile. "You probably own a bunch of guns and know how to shoot them." I tell him I don't own a gun and haven't aimed one since summer camp. (I don't think to tell him my mom wouldn't even let us play with toy soldiers.) "I bet you're lying," he says. "I bet you have plenty of guns. You motherfuckers are crazy."

We get back to baseball. Jason says, "I wasn't born back then." He's twenty-one now, three years older than I was when Hank broke the record. "But I had to read through all the history books, Black History Month, know what I'm saying? One month out of every year, we gonna sit down and talk about black history and write a report. Who stepped through the doors for the black people. I see the perseverance he had. He had a lot of courage. People were pulling a lot of shit on him. People coming up to his face, 'Nigger, don't you be doing stuff like that tonight.' I looked at the highlights on Channel 59 on cable, Sports Classic Channel, and I seen when he hit home runs and people threw beer bottles at him.

"This world is cruel. Especially back then. There still is prejudice, but you don't see it as much. I couldn't conceive of living back then. Walkin' around, you couldn't go to certain sports, couldn't go in certain restaurants."

Two sisters, about eleven and twelve, share a wobbly plastic chair in the shade of the tree. They look up at Jason with their lean faces and soft eyes; they are strikingly beautiful children.

"The man had to come through so much shit," Jason says. "Ain't no other white man gone through that, and taken so much shit, and still given back. He was hated by some people. He was a great man to me. He could probably step out there and tell me a thing or two about life."

The older man pushes off from the old Ford and starts to walk away. "I'm glad what he did," he says to us. "I'm proud of what he did. But I can't back him." He takes a hit off his Olde English 800 and strolls inside the house.

Jason explains: "Our community isn't gonna sit down and talk about something that was way in the past. You got too many problems out here already that we have to deal with. So we ain't gonna sit around and talk about this, that, and the other. Hank, Martin Luther King, these great black people who stood up for us, we ain't gonna sit around and talk about these things because they are in the past. Now we're trying to deal with what's coming up in the future."

Still, Jason, being a Braves fan, understands what Hank and Jackie Robinson and the others did. "It was only a pastime for some," he says. "It wasn't a pastime for everybody. It was the white people's game. Now people can say that the game is a pastime that can be played by all. I'm glad Mark McGwire broke the record. First the black man broke a white man's record, now maybe a white man's gonna take the black man's record. See what I'm saying? Sammy Sosa did it too, what was he, four behind Mark? It really don't matter now because everybody got a foot in the pipe, everybody got a piece of the pie in baseball. People can really say it's the American pastime."

Do you go to the games often, I ask?

"Every time I go, it's cold," says Jason. "And I'll be sittin' up in the motherfucker like, *ooh, shit!* I always catch me some fall tickets. Let me tell you, everybody is having fun out there. They've integrated it, so this black man, or this white man, is making two hundred, three hundred trillion billion dollars, for hitting the ball and throwing the ball. Ain't nobody getting on nobody's back, calling nobody nigger. Ain't nobody saying fuck you to anybody. Ain't none of that anymore. Yeah! Know what I'm saying? John Smoltz is my man, and he's a white boy. He's my favorite pitcher. The boy can throw that ball. I like him. See? It's all intertwined. Ain't no one nationality being put out because of their skin color or tone, or their beliefs. It's all a game now, just like it was supposed to be. Just like it was supposed to be in the beginning. It's all a game now."

8

HALL OF FAME

Elizabeth, New Jersey, July 1999

My old friend Ed Wojciak pulls the family rent-a-van up to the side of the Club Froghollow, and the apartment adjacent. It's nearly time to move toward Cooperstown. Everyone should be packed and ready.

We get out and look down the street, past the rowhouses, to a huge white gas tank: the emblem of industrial Jersey. "When they first put that thing in," Ed says, "before they put the fuel in, my dad says he and his friends tried to play softball in there. That's how big the thing is."

The bar is closed, shut down for two weeks by Ed's folks for the big trip—the first time Ed can remember that happening.

We open the door and Ed's wife, Brandy, bursts out with a duffel in each hand. "You guys ready?" she nearly shouts. "This is going to be a *trip*! This is going to be *great*!"

"All right!" Irene announces. "Cooperstown, here we come." This is our *hajj*, our journey to Mecca: the first for all of us; a lifelong dream for Irene and her son. We pile in: Ed at the wheel, his dad beside him; Brandy and Irene in the middle seat; and in the way back, me, squeezed between the third generation: Bret, sixteen, and Ben, just turned nineteen. I remember when Ben was born. Ed and Brandy were the first of my friends to have kids. I came to the hospital with ice cream and party hats.

We cruise past the Toca la Serra. It used to be Leonard's Place. And the Merritt Street Tavern; now it's the Casanova. And the old Union County Buick Dealer: "Now it's El Banco Whatever-Whatever," Irene says.

Soon Elizabeth is behind us. We're on the Garden State Parkway, pointed north, toward the National Baseball Hall of Fame. Exit 142, Maplewood; Exit 145, The Oranges; Exit 150, Montclair. "You know what's really funny?" Brandy asks us. "When you're around Jersey people, they don't say, 'Where are you from?' They say, 'What exit are you from?'

'Oh, I'm from Exit 150.' I just think that's so wild!" Her laugh is a high hard one, and infectious. She's into the cooler now, passing out soft drinks and juices. Brandy's been pumped for this trip for months—at least since April, when I'd last visited Flagstaff and they'd invited me to come along. For Brandy, it's a chance to take a break from the restaurant grind. Take the kids. See the country. Check out the bed-and-breakfasts. Find out what people are serving and how they're serving it. The baseball stuff is fine, too, but that's more of a taste she's acquired of necessity, being married to a baseball maniac.

"Remember when you took me to those old-timers' games?" Ed asks his mom. "Mel Allen would be the announcer. He would start saying, 'He won twenty games in 1949. This right-hander . . .' And you would go, that's *so-and-so* and *so-and-so!*"

"Allie Reynolds," Irene says. "Frankie Shea." The Naugatuck Nugget.

"And remember—Eddie Lopat?"

"Sure. And Vic Raschi. Oh, what a pitcher." I know that name: Hank hit his first major league home run off Raschi, April 23, 1954. Sixth inning in St. Louis. Nobody on base.

"And Spud Chandler," Irene is saying. "And Johnny Lindell. He was a tall outfielder."

Brandy looks at me and shrugs, and laughs.

We've crossed the New York border, into the low foothills of the Catskills. Brandy looks out at the sloping farmland and thinks of her childhood in rural Illinois: "Corn forever and ever, dirt road, pig farm, pig farm, corn. I'm sure that's all gone."

We ramble closer to the statues and legends: looking forward to looking back.

"You didn't see people wearing shorts to the ballpark," says Ed, evoking his mother's time.

"Oh, no," his mother says. "I mean, the gloves, and hats. So beautifully attired. Not like today."

"I remember seeing a picture of Yogi Berra outside the park after the game, in his suit. And his wife—"

"She was a beautiful woman," Irene says.

"She was a babe," says Ed.

Then, the players traveled by train. Then, they rode *together*. Now, Irene asks, "Did you know that Cal Ripken stays in his own hotel?" Ed says a lot of guys go solo nowadays; a pitcher scheduled to start in a couple days might fly to the next city by himself. There's no sense of common purpose any more, we lament: no loyalty by a player to a team; no understanding by the owners that a fan doesn't want to be hustled, the whole game long.

"Everything they put up on the scoreboard is brought to you by someone," Ed says. "The disabled list, brought to you by Blue Cross/Blue Shield. The farm report, brought to you by Shamrock Farms." He's quoting the message board at the Bank One Ballpark in Phoenix. Ed and Brandy and the kids have adopted a second favorite team—the Diamondbacks. Ed catches maybe twelve games a year, heading down from the Ponderosa pine country at 7,000 feet, along the smooth blacktop of the old Black Canyon Highway, through the Verde Valley, across Dead Horse Wash and Bloody Basin Road, past the forest of saguaro cactuses of the northern

Sonoran Desert, and into manicured and heavily watered Phoenix, and the $354 million stadium downtown.

"The starting lineup, brought to you by Infiniti," Ed goes on. "The defensive lineup, brought to you by Little Caesar's Pizza. Every inning is sponsored by someone. They pump the advertisements every chance they get. There's just money—ka-*ching*, ka-*ching*, ka-*ching*!—every time they change the names on that scoreboard. But if they go into extra innings, there are hardly any announcements on the scoreboard, because no one has paid for it."

"It's like, everywhere you look there's a neon sign with someone's name on it," Bret says.

"I hate that," says Brandy. "It really bothers me. Like in San Diego, it's not Jack Murphy Stadium anymore, it's Qualcomm Park. What kind of name is that?"

And Safeco Field, I say. And Cinergy Field. And Tropicana Field. And Pro Player Stadium.

"The corporations are just everywhere," Brandy says. "And the thing that's starting in some ballparks is they're changing the wall behind the catcher—a different advertisement every inning. I can't *stand* that."

I remember seeing that for the first time this year in Milwaukee. My mom and I were watching a Brewers game, and she said, "Hey, wasn't that just—" The beer ad had changed to a pitch for mutual funds.

We cruise up Route 28, past oak and sumac and elm, along the Esopus Creek. A deer darts across the road.

"They're trying to put ads on the uniforms now," Ed says. This I hadn't heard. Though I suppose the Nike swoosh is an ad all by itself. "They want to do that, so they can keep paying these guys this ridiculous money."

"If they do that," says Brandy, "I'm going to be so mad. That's disgusting."

"It's nothing but big business today," says Irene. "Money-money-money." She remembers the old Burma Shave ads at the ballparks. Bret remembers seeing a black and white picture of the Lucky Strike logo in the bleachers, with the home run bull's-eye. But it was a little more under control back then. It's amazing, I say, how pervasive it's gotten. They're putting ads on apples in the supermarket now. On room keys at the hotels. On the seat back in front of you. And now, on uniforms at the ballparks?

"If the owners agree to it," Ed says, "is the players union going to stand in the way? No way. Not if it's going to give them more money."

"Sort of like an out-of-control, greedy version of Little League," I say. "Remember that movie *The Bad News Bears*? Tatum O'Neal and Walter Matthau? Everybody in the Little League needed a sponsor to pay for the uniforms. So on the first game of the season, you see the backs of all the little players: Denny's. McDonald's. Baskin-Robbins. And then one of Walter Matthau's players turns around, and you see: 'Chico's Bail Bonds.'"

On our right, the Wayside Motel. Fake sheep on lawns, and a pink flamingo. Farm stands, weathered gray barns, the world's largest kaleidoscope. A tractor pulls a haycart. We move up steeper grade, in the low Catskill hills at Andes, New York.

"This is like Forrest Gump town," Ben says.

"Look, that looks like the Addams family house," says Bret.

"Hey!" says Ed. "Look at those plastic balls of cowshit!"

Cornstalks drift by, and wheat, and stands of blue spruce. Wash flaps on the line. Irene says it'll probably rain. You can tell: the cows are lying down.

We roll into Cooperstown. It's a postcard town, professionally quaint: along a movie-set Main Street lined with potted geraniums, dozens of little shops offer hats and jerseys and memorabilia and autographs. The Short Stop Restaurant. Cooperstown Bat Company. National Pastime Gallery. Doubleday Cafe. Bullpen Bagels and Coffee. A sign in a window at Mickey's claims: WE HAVE THE BASEBALL CARDS YOUR MOTHER THREW AWAY.

We waste little time. The Wojciaks check into their bed-and-breakfast, and I throw my stuff into my room at the budget Baseball Town Motel. A half hour later, we stand in front of the Hall. We pose for pictures.

"Holy bejesus," Ed says.

"Oh," says Brandy, "my god. Ohmygod."

We walk inside.

"You're supposed to genuflect, Ed," Irene says to her son. He gives a couple of quick two-handed, palms-down bows: "I am not worthy, I am not worthy."

In the first gallery, we're flanked by long rows of bronzed faces: plaques of the legendary players, and the words of their deeds. Lou Gehrig: the Iron Horse. Frank Chance: the first base link of "Tinker to Evers to Chance." Big Ed Walsh: won forty-one games in 1908; started and won both games of a doubleheader. Charles Comiskey: the Old Roman, fifty years of baseball, beginning with the St. Louis Browns in 1882.

Irene stops in front of Bill Dickey, the old Yankee catcher. She reaches out. The tips of her fingers touch his bronzed face. Tenderly. "I saw him play," she says softly. She stands there for a long moment, staring into his likeness, and moves away slowly. A moment later, she cries out, *"Luke Appling!"* as if the man were an old best friend, standing, alive, in front of her.

Brandy comes back to report that Ted Williams has been sent back for restoration. "So many people touched him," she figures. Touching, here, seems to be encouraged.

We reach the first black man in the long line of heroes. Jackie Robinson. I ask Irene, what did you think when he started playing? A long pause. "We thought it was—*different,*" she says finally. "But he was a good player." Jackie's plaque is in excellent condition.

And on down the gallery: Spahn and Feller. Snider and Greenberg. Koufax and Drysdale. Campanella and Mathews and Mantle and Ford. And Hank. Smiling, with the "A" on his cap. Too bad he didn't choose to wear the "M" for posterity.

A few steps away, glass cases exhibit the jerseys and uniforms of Mark McGwire and Sammy Sosa in the home run chase of 1998. McGwire's case dwarfs the one for Sammy. "Why couldn't he get one the same size as of McGwire?" Irene asks me. I look at her quizzically. I sense she's trying to tell me something. "Food for thought," she says.

We look at the diagram of the Hall, and map out our two-day journey. Yankee exhibits are everywhere; it is all Ed can do to keep from drooling. There's an entire room for the Babe. Next door stands the shrine for the Hammer. This we will wait for; we'll do Hank last.

We go upstairs. Within moments, Ed is high on Yankee greatness.

"Can you say, twenty-four world championships?" he asks me. We're in the Room of Champions. "New York *Yankees!*"

"Can you say, one World Series appearance?" I grumble, evoking my hometown Brewers.

"And what did they do?" Ed grabs his throat and rasps, like he's got a chicken bone in his throat.

The man is merciless. I tell him: a testament to our lasting friendship has been my willingness to endure heaps of abuse from Your Exalted Yankiness. "And what do you think of the basic essential unfairness of my small-market team getting clobbered by your big rich sons of bitches?" I ask.

"I think it sucks," Ed says. "And I really feel sorry for you." Then he starts laughing.

"For some reason I don't sense a lot of compassion."

"Don't know what to tell you. I feel sorry for you. I wish to hell you can get yourself some money and buy yourself a team. The Brewers? They'll get there one more time, probably, before you die. And that'll be it. But only—*only*—if they're incredibly lucky."

The man is relentless.

"If baseball's still around," I mutter. "If it hasn't collapsed on the basis of its own greed." I might actually start sulking here.

"I admire your stick-to-it-iveness," says Mr. Appointed Greatest Yankee Fan. "I have to give it to you. You know, the

Brewers are *never* gonna win a World Series. And you know, it's amazing that you're still a fan. You haven't come over to the Yankee side yet."

"So are you saying that if the Yankees weren't any good, you wouldn't root for them? So you are the Fair Weather Man?"

"Noo . . ."

"I've found your Achilles heel."

"No."

"Achilles Heel Man."

"No."

"Achilles. Heel. Man."

Between the razzing we actually learn something. A hundred years ago the Chicago Cubs were known as the Orphans. The Braves were called the Beaneaters; the Phillies, the Worcester Brown Stockings; the Dodgers were variously the Brooklyn Bridegrooms, the Superbas, the Robins, the Trolley Dodgers.

A lot earlier—"In the beginning," a display says—"after God created heaven and earth, there were stones to throw and sticks to swing." Two thousand years ago, we learn, people were playing with bats and balls in Egypt.

"They're stretching it here," Ed says. "We all know it started in New Jersey."

We look at a small, brown, bruised-looking ball, used in an 1854 game between the Knickerbockers and the Gothams.

"There was baseball around Elizabeth in 1850, 1860-something. They played across the river with the best teams in the New York area."

So now, it's not enough that Ed can hammer me with his

Yankees; now, he says he's from a place that *invented* the damn game.

At a display in the next room, I eke out a thimbleful of revenge.

The Milwaukee Braves. 1957. The year Hank clinched the pennant with a homer (eleventh inning, County Stadium, September 23, 11:34 P.M.), and his teammates lifted him onto their shoulders. The year he won the MVP. The year Lew Burdette was the Yankee-killer, winning three games, including the finale in New York. This is the moment set aside for Milwaukee in the Yankee-dominated Baseball Hall of Fame.

"Do you know who this is?" I ask Ed, standing in front of Burdette's picture.

"I don't know," Ed says quietly. *Quietly!* "I was too young to remember."

I am only too happy to tell him, to savor *our* time in baseball history. Maybe I was only a year old. But it feels like I remember.

O

That evening, we put away the razzing. We're in a bar, the Wojciaks and me, the night before the All-Star Game. We sit beneath a big screen watching the home run contest. McGwire and Griffey and Sosa and Burnitz (my guy from Milwaukee) blast balls over the Green Monster at Fenway. Ben and Bret play a game of foosball. Brandy talks with Ed senior and Irene over Manhattans and vodkas; they're telling her about the time at the track with Linoleum Joe, when the long-shot Matta Grosso II came in, and Irene won enough to pay for an entire semester for Ed at Holy Cross. They paid for his entire college education this way.

At the next table, I tell Ed that I've started to come back to baseball. A little bit. After the strike in 1994, I became so disgusted with the greed, I'd grown cold on the game. But Ed, I know, never left.

"Everything in America changes so much," Ed says. We watch McGwire hit a towering drive beyond the bank of lights, and into the night. He stands at the plate, watching his majesty the way Hank never did. "And baseball is the constant thing. My life is crazy. We have two restaurants. My head is spinning half the time. But by the end of the day, I go coach baseball and for those couple of hours, I forget all about that. And I'm in some other place. I'm into the game. I'm into the kids. I'm into the situations. I'm into the proper way to do the double cutoff. At the ballpark, watching a game—Phoenix, or Yankee Stadium—you can sit back and reflect. In between pitches. In between innings."

"At the same time we were talking about all the changes—the corporations and all the ads—"

"But that's not the game." Ed jumps in to cut me off. "That's the other things that are involved in formulating your team and paying the money. I don't give a shit about how much money you make. I don't keep track of that stuff. It's how you play the game. That's all that counts. I go by, Can you hit a left-handed pitcher who's got a wicked slider? Are you going to hit the ball in the clutch when your team needs you with two outs and a guy on in the bottom of the ninth? Are

186

you gonna hit the cutoff in that clutch situation, when you have to throw somebody out at the plate? When the pressure's on?"

Will you deliver, when it matters?

"I love the game of baseball. Whoever invented it, and wherever it came from. They say New Jersey. It's a wonderful thing. It's the greatest thing ever invented."

O

The Baseball Hall of Fame is a kind of secular church. Ritual is preserved in scraps of cloth, and stitched cowhide, and silver trophies encased in glass. Tradition is recorded in the seasons between frosts, and replenished in a mountain pilgrimage. Images are touched until they are worn, and made ever new again.

Upon the highest mantel rests the image of George Herman Ruth. This is so, say the experts, because the hard-swinging Babe saved the game from the disastrous "Black Sox" scandal of 1919, when eight players on the Chicago White Sox conspired with gamblers to fix the World Series; and because Babe lived life large. "I swing big," Babe used to say, "with everything I've got. I hit big or I miss big. I like to live as big as I can." And so Cooperstown is not only a Church of Baseball, it is a Church of the Babe. His big-as-life carved wooden statue greets you when you enter; his records shout out from the walls; his souvenirs stuff the shelves of the gift shop; and upstairs, in a large space crammed with worshippers, he is the idol of the Hall's largest shrine. Unlike anyone else in Cooperstown, the Babe has a room of his own.

The second day, we enter the Ruth shrine, through a ballpark turnstile. The walls are done up in white columns, coliseum-style, a replica of the façade of Yankee Stadium. Beneath, fifty-two images: Babe in the children's hospital. Babe in his Packard. Babe, in his camel hair coat, with his wife and daughter. Babe signing autographs. Babe, dropping his bat, looking deep toward right field, beginning his home run trot.

Inside the Babe memorial, and out, the place is choked with people: midsummer vacationers, like us, on their own long pilgrimage. What's amazing, as I count to 50, 100, 150, 190, is that I cannot see a single African American face. Everyone here, at this moment, is white. Every single one of us, jammed into these exhibits, has entered the Hall by walking beneath the sign with Jacques Barzun's famous quote: "Whoever wants to know the heart and mind of America had better learn baseball—the rules and realities of the game." The reality in the Hall of Fame is that we're all white, and the exhibition two rooms away, called "Pride and Passion: The African American Experience," is nearly empty. We walk over.

In the 1880s, we learn, there was discussion over whether to allow blacks to play baseball with whites. An early major league team in Toledo, Ohio, included black players. So did minor league teams in other towns, though whites often refused to pose for pictures with their dark-skinned teammates. The resistance to integrated baseball included grotesque Currier & Ives caricatures of thick-lipped, long-armed blacks, made to look like animals. The cartoons clearly implied that these men possessed neither the skill nor the intelligence to play the emerging American pastime. Looking at those early racist portraits, just a generation removed from slavery, I think: They were *afraid* to let blacks play. They were *afraid* that the strong, strapping, scary black man would succeed. At the heart of the ridicule, it seems, was not only the doctrine of white superiority, but a fear that this doctrine, put to the test, would be disproved. Hence the necessity to ban blacks from the "major" leagues.

And so they played in separate worlds. Ed and Irene and I stand before a poster for a game between the New York Lincoln Giants and the Baltimore Black Sox, on July 5 of an unnamed year. Perhaps it was 1952, Hank's one year in the Negro Leagues. He probably played against some of these same guys; little did he know he'd retire twenty-four years later, as the last major league player from the Negro Leagues. The Giants–Black Sox game was to be a benefit for the Brotherhood of Sleeping Car Porters, whose founder, A. Philip Randolph, was a prominent labor and civil rights leader. The 1963 March on Washington, most remembered for Martin Luther King's "I Have a Dream" speech, was Randolph's idea.

"Clash of the Season," the poster promised. "Let's see that we have positively the biggest event of the year. For the first time in history the Yankee Stadium is extended to the colored people of Harlem. . . . Grandstand, $1.00. Box seats, $1.50."

"They played in Yankee Stadium," Ed says. "They played in Comiskey, they played in all the major league ballparks, just when the other team was on the road."

"But they didn't get any coverage," says Irene.

"I read this book called *Only the Ball Was White*," Ed says. "And they played Negro League ball in Elizabeth, too. What's that park up the street from the field I used to play?"

"Brophy Field," says Irene.

"Right, Brophy. They'd play up there. And these guys were awesome. And they never got a chance to play with the white guys. The only time they got a chance to play against the major leaguers was like a barnstorming tour."

"I wonder how those games turned out?" I say.

"Oh, the white guys lost most of them," says Ed. "Satchel would just kick their asses." Satchel Paige, who after a spectacular twenty-year career in the Negro Leagues helped the Indians win a World Series in 1948 at age forty-two, and pitched with the Kansas City Athletics at *fifty-nine*. He even made the Braves' roster in 1968, at age sixty-two; Hank was his chaperone. Though Satch didn't play, Hank recalled a man who still threw hard. His baseball stories covered five decades, including many barnstorming games against the white players. In his prime, he once struck out twenty-one major leaguers in an exhibition. "They were afraid to play him," Ed says. "Ty Cobb would struggle against those guys so bad, he'd say, 'To hell with this.' And he walked off the field one game, supposedly. They threw him out stealing and everything and he just said, *pffft!*, I don't want to play you guys. And he left."

I'd heard a story about Cobb and the black players from the oldest living Negro Leaguer—a man named Ted "Double Duty" Radcliffe, the ninety-seven-year-old former pitcher and catcher, still sharp enough to remember his performance against Cobb in Cuba. "I threw his ass out twice," Double Duty told his audience at a Negro League luncheon I'd been to in Milwaukee. "He said, 'You ain't gonna throw me out again.' I said, 'Well, that means you ain't gonna run no more.'"

I think of the black ballplayers I grew up watching—Hank Aaron, Bob Gibson, Lou Brock, Willie Mays, Maury Wills, Ernie Banks, Billy Williams, Willie McCovey, Willie Stargell, Curt Flood, Paul Blair, Joe Morgan, Bobby Tolan, George Scott, Frank Robinson—and know that, without them, we could not have called it "Major League Baseball." So, how could we before? And how could we even decide who was the best player? After all, as Jesse Jackson had pointed out to me, Babe Ruth never had to face Satchel Paige. "Prior to 1947, you really didn't have the major leagues," Reverend Jackson had told me. "You had the white leagues and the black leagues. In 1947, you could begin to see who was the best in the *major* leagues."

That year, Jackie Robinson endured the same kind of hate Hank would face a generation later, though not in such volume. "We are going to kill you if you attempt to enter a ball game at Crosley Field," one letterwriter threatened. "We have already gotten rid of several like you. One more is fine." Irene stands before the letter, eyes narrowed, staring intently, hand over her lips. She, and I, and the rest of the Wojciaks, are the only ones in the room.

○

He's sittin' on 714. Here's the pitch by Downing. Swinging, there's a drive into left-center field. . . ." Milo Hamilton's voice drifts over from the next room. I've held back till the last. To see how Hank is recognized, and how they tell his story. My friends have held back with me. And now we enter.

And Hank has a wall. There's his locker, and a television set, with the home run playing over and over. And a picture of Tom House giving Hank the ball after 715, and his comment about seeing Hank's tears for the first time. And a picture of him getting a standing ovation weeks later, in Congress.

And that's about it. Nothing about the tension of the Chase. The hate mail, the death threats. What he endured. What the record meant. What kind of hero the man is. Nothing about how he delivered, when it mattered. In the Baseball Hall of Fame, this journey is not acknowledged.

The air has gone out of me. I have a funny feeling in my heart and in the pit of my gut.

My friends are quiet. Irene comes over. We look at the picture of Hank, smiling, with his mother squeezing him tight. I tell her she thought he was getting shot.

"It looks," she says, "like a scared smile."

I whisper to myself: This place is small. Cramped. Wedged in, next to the walk-in mausoleum for the Babe. Why doesn't Hank have his own room? What is it about 714 that meant so much more than 715? Or 755? How many would he have had to hit, to get a room of his own? I think of Jesse Jackson's question: *When number one is not enough, what do you do?*

"It's insufficient," I say to myself. To Ed, I say, "Maybe I should offer my letter."

"Yeah," he says, gently. "Just ask for the curator. The museum guy."

It's a good idea. And so, armed with my letter and the scrapbook, that's exactly what I do. Unannounced, at eight-thirty the next morning, I am ringing the bell at the business offices of the Hall of Fame. After a short wait in the reception area, a surprised, gentle, white-haired fellow comes out to see who I am and what I want.

We sit in a conference room. He looks at my letter from Hank. It's a remarkable thing, I tell him, for a guy who's in the middle of a chase to take the time to write a letter like this. I wrote Hank, I say, because of all the hate mail he got. And I noticed you don't tell that part of Hank's story. You display a letter that was sent to Jackie Robinson—but Hank got so many. And the picture, I tell him, of his mom: she thought her son was being shot. And that's not explained. So, I say, maybe, you'd want to consider taking my letter, or maybe even my scrapbook . . .

The man tells me it's very possible that in the library, where they keep all the archives, they might be interested in my letter.

I was thinking more in terms of letting the public know what he went through.

We are thinking of changing our exhibits, the man tells me, to focus more on baseball as part of American culture.

I see. Baseball and how it fits into the heart and mind of America—the rules and realities of the game. Hank's experience would certainly fit in there.

I see that coming, he says.

I want to ask you one more thing, I say before getting up to leave: Why does Babe Ruth get a whole room and Hank Aaron a wall and a locker?

Maybe, in the future, he says, Aaron will be treated to a bigger area. They have some space restrictions up there. But it's more than home runs: And he talks about how Babe lived large. And he says, "Babe put baseball on the map" after the Black Sox scandal. "It's what he did for the game."

It's what he did for the game. Fine. I have no problem measuring it that way. Here's what Henry Aaron did for the game of baseball: He came out of the Negro Leagues, and in 1953 went to the last bastion of segregated ball in a part of the Deep South that Dr. King and Rosa Parks hadn't even started in on. With his teammates Felix Mantilla and Horace Garner, he broke the color barrier. He endured a season's worth of "nigger" and "coon" and "alligator bait" and separate water fountains and separate restaurants and separate hotels, while batting .362 and winning the league MVP. He played so well, league officials believed he had begun to transform the racial attitudes of thousands of white southern fans. Then he went north, to Milwaukee, and lived in the black neighborhood as he was told to do, until he broke the color barrier there, too. In the suburbs, kids taunted his little sister so bad she had to go back to Alabama. But most people loved him there, and they went crazy when he won them a pennant with his home run in the eleventh in 1957. Nine years later, in the midst of King and Abernathy and Young, he helped a new city become part of a New South.

What Hank Aaron did for the game: From the late 1950s until the early 1970s he became the most consistently excellent player in baseball history. At a time when home runs didn't come cheap, he hit more than 40 in a season eight times, at least 30 home runs fifteen times and 20 or more for twenty consecutive years. In the nineteen-year heart of his career, from 1955 to 1973, he *averaged* 37 home runs per season, yet never hit more than 47. He had more home runs, more runs batted in, more extra base hits and more total bases than anyone who ever played this game. He's near the top in doubles, and in runs scored. He was so good that you could take away all his home runs, and he'd still have 3,000 hits. Incredibly, as a slugger, he's among the all-time leaders in stolen-base percentage. He stole 24 of 27 one year; 31 of 36 another. He was one of the first members of the 30–30 club in single-season homers and stolen bases, and he won three Gold Gloves. Unlike the waddling Ruth, Hank was a brilliantly complete player.

What didn't Hank Aaron do for the game? He didn't flaunt it, didn't shout it out from the window of a twelve-cylinder Packard, didn't spend his nights whoring around, didn't stand at home plate and watch his home runs land. Unlike the Babe, who ordered his assistant to throw away all his mail, except the checks and "letters from broads." Hank didn't ignore his young fans who offered only encouragement. And he didn't stop playing, coolly, intensely, in his understated way, like "grace in a gray flannel suit," as the sportswriter Jim Murray wrote, "like a poem with a bat in his hands." Not when they called him "nigger" in his home park, not when armed guards took his children to school, not when they threatened, again and again, to kill him, certainly not when some sportswriter suggested he stop at 713, to honor Babe Ruth. "I didn't play baseball," Hank would write twenty-five years later, "to honor Babe Ruth." And in the years after he became the home run king, and the endorsements dwindled, and people stopped talking about his as the greatest record in sports, and sportswriters wrote that DiMaggio was the greatest retired player, Henry Aaron didn't lose his cool, or his pride, or his dignity. "Your dignity," Jesse Jackson would tell him much later, "was non-negotiable." Instead, Hank chose to speak out, as he had before, advocating fair treatment in hiring black managers and front office people, in a sport with a long history of denying them justice.

"Negro players are getting to the point where they're really beginning to wonder what the game is coming to," Hank told a reporter from Minnesota in 1969. "We're at a stage where the owners will have to let us show we can do something other than hit and run and slide. They're going to have to do something for us. They'd better start opening some doors to Willie Mays, Ernie Banks, Frank Robinson, Bill White and me." More and more now, Hank was using his platform of excellence to speak out for justice. Years later, he'd say: "Baseball has got to change. There is racial prejudice. It is real and it has been for a long time. I cannot honestly say that baseball has been absolutely fair with blacks. I cannot look myself in the mirror each day and not speak the truth. And I will continue to say it for the rest of my life." These things never concerned Babe Ruth.

Babe Ruth saved the game? Imagine the game without Hank, without the generation of blacks that came up with him. *They* saved the game, from being slow, and plodding, and far, far less exciting, less graceful, less beautiful than it would have been.

Why doesn't Hank Aaron have a room of his own? Later, when I ask Dusty Baker his opinion, he doesn't mention the Black Sox scandal, or the Roaring Twenties, or how Babe Ruth lived large. He just looks at me, and says: "It's America, dude. It's America."

O

The streets of Cooperstown are as white as the Hall. "I'd say one in a thousand is black," says John Kurdziolek, owner of the Third Base Cap Company. "I don't know why. It's just a white tourist town. I shouldn't say that—I'm not racist in any way. I notice it, and I think about it, but it doesn't trouble me. This is a family town. You go to see it as a family. But obviously, it's a middle- to upper-class kind of place." Yet there are many middle- and upper-middle-class black tourists; they just don't seem to come here.

Lines of hats, from major league teams present and past, march down the wall behind him. Kurdziolek sells jerseys, batting gloves, and memorabilia, and tens of thousands of caps a year, including specialty caps with Hall of Famers' names and numbers. He finds almost no interest in stuff for Hank.

The same is true, I learn, at the other souvenir shops that line the Norman Rockwell main street. And, I'm told, at the card dealers.

"Well, Babe's presence, that's the thing," says Ray Hines, who, like dozens of other dealers, rents space in the summertime at the Cooperstown VFW Hall. He's trying to take a break; I've caught him on his way downstairs, clutching his Styrofoam box lunch. "Nobody could kiss the Babe's shoes in terms of his persona. In what he did for the game"—this again—"they're not in the same league."

Hence, Ray says, there's far less interest in Hank's old cards. And maybe there's another reason. "You know, people have a tendency to stick together," says Ray, who's white. "You look at card collectors: black collectors typically collect Aaron, and Hispanic collectors gravitate toward Hispanic names. I don't think all these people are prejudiced. I just think they stick to what they're comfortable with. Now me, I collect Cleon Jones," the Met outfielder from the 1969 team, who is black. "So, I don't know. I just know, my observation is, people stick to groups they are comfortable with."

"I don't think that way," says Tony Porter, a collector in the next room, when I ask him if race plays a role in how few Hank cards he sells. "I'm sure it's possible, but I wasn't brought up to think that way."

He doesn't understand why there's so little interest in old Hank cards. I look down at his collection. He has about ten different Hank cards, preserved in plastic sheaths. I'm looking for the 1964 card, the one that Kath bought me at The Popcorn Stand. Somewhere along the way, it seems, I've lost it. Tony doesn't have that one. But I buy two others: the 1975 card with the Brewers, where Hank finished his career, and the one from the year before. He's beaming, in his Braves cap. The card has a crown on it. It says: HANK AARON: NEW ALL-TIME HOME RUN KING.

"It's a shame," Tony says of the low demand for the Hammer. "He was the best. I mean, every time Hank came to the plate, you heard it—*crack,* and you knew it was gone."

"Excuse me," says a woman to my right. A customer, breaking the reverie. She's standing with a blond boy who looks to be about ten. "He wants to buy a Hank Aaron card, but they're too expensive. We can't afford twenty dollars."

Tony and I look at each other. He smiles, raises his eyebrows. This is amazing. One minute ago, I'd bought two Hank cards. Now I tell the boy, You take your pick. I want you to have one.

Are you sure? his grandmother asks.

I have never been more sure, I tell her. I introduce myself and learn that the boy's name is John, and that he is from Troy, New York.

John chooses Hank as a Brewer. The kid has a taste for the underdog.

"When I was about your age," I tell John, "the Braves left Milwaukee. I used to listen to them on the long-distance radio. Do you know he got a lot of mean mail?"

"Yeah," he says. "Because he was black."

I tell him about the scrapbook, and about the letter Hank sent me.

"Did he sign it?" John wants to know. Yeah, I say.

"Cool."

Hank, John says, "was an awesome player."

Where did you first hear about him? I ask.

"In the Baseball Hall of Fame."

O

199

Ed and I sit on a bench in front of the Baseball Town Motel. I await my taxi to Albany. I'm leaving a day early, to get home, and pack up again for a late summer trip to Milwaukee.

After we left the Hall yesterday, we went to lunch. I asked Ed and his mom whether it seemed Hank wasn't getting his proper recognition. And why some crucial parts of his story—the hate and the death threats—remained untold by the Hall of Fame.

"Maybe," Irene said thoughtfully, "they were embarrassed by it."

Think about the contrast, I'd said, between McGwire and Sosa's chase, and the one Hank endured a generation earlier. It would be no wonder, Ed said, if Hank had ended up bitter, and angry.

"It should have been a happy time," Irene said of Hank's chase. "But it wasn't."

Now Ed sits facing me, one leg folded on the bench, thinking back on the last couple of days. "It's like after you finish a big meal," he says, looking relaxed in his shirtsleeves and shorts. "Very satisfying. You realize how much stuff is in that building. Oh my! It's amazing—all those gloves, and the shoes, the sweat, every time they played. You remember those moments. It's like when my mom went up and touched Bill Dickey. I was like, Yeah, I know that guy. I lived through that. My mom always wanted to come up here. And I always have, too. It's always been the temple. The church."

Ed frowns and looks at me. I notice how gray his eyes are. "You go to the Hall of Fame and relive those memories from your past, or my mom's past, those stories of games she saw, players she saw, but then you also learn about stuff you didn't know. You would think that some of the people that go there would want to learn something about the black history of baseball. There's a lot to learn about. I was surprised that exhibit was so empty. It really pisses me off. Or, you know, you go to a ball game. How many black people do you see at the park? You go to Phoenix to see a game and there are no black people there.

"It bothers me," my friend says, his gaze boring into me. "Maybe their interest does not lie in baseball anymore."

The taxi comes and swallows me up. I ride down the hills, past the yellow-topped wild carrot, and rows of planted onion, potatoes and Indian corn, thinking about our pastime, its rules and its realities.

9

BIG BLUE

Milwaukee County Stadium, July 20, 1999

Hank Aaron sits on a folding chair in the grass behind home plate, looking at his notes. Ten thousand fans stand by quietly, waiting. Next to Hank sits the commissioner of baseball, and a balding old pitcher whose tie flutters in the wind.

"Baseball fans!" the emcee begins. "Welcome to Edie's–Jewel–Osco–Hank Aaron night!" As faint cheers die, there are introductions to be made, and scholarships to be handed out, for the Hank Aaron Youth Leadership Fund. Hank reaches over to shake the hands of two black youths from Milwaukee's inner city. I wonder if they know what this graying man did.

"He hit one of the most famous home runs in history," says Bud Selig, the Milwaukee native and friend of Hank's for forty years. The baseball commissioner's voice bounces through the empty seats. "In September of 1957, off of the St. Louis Cardinals, to win the National League pennant. He hit 195 home runs in this ballpark, more than in any other park. Hank, you brought a lot of glory and a lot of happiness to Milwaukee. And as you know, you're still number one here. Welcome home, Henry."

In late 1974, Selig, then the Brewers' president, worked out a deal with the Atlanta Braves to bring Henry Aaron back home to Milwaukee. For Hank, it was a bittersweet homecoming. The Braves had fired manager Eddie Mathews, but team officials didn't even ask Hank if he was interested in the job. And the team was going with younger players. The Braves offered Hank a low salary to keep playing in Atlanta, according to the newspapers; then they tried to entice him into a public relations job in the front office. "I ride in the front seat of the bus for years and then they say, 'Go to the back, you can't do anything else for us!'" the home run king said. "I don't want to be a houseboy. I want to make a contribution to a baseball club." He said he would prefer to go back to Milwaukee. "This was a city that showed me respect."

When Selig heard that, he pounced. He made a deal with Bill Bartholomay, president of the Braves, the man who had taken baseball away from our town nine years earlier. "Gosh, I will never forget it," Selig would recall years later. "I remember the thrill, thinking, 'Oh, my goodness: Hank Aaron is going to be playing for the Milwaukee Brewers!' That really put us on the map." Like Babe Ruth and Willie Mays before him, Hank was coming home at the end of his career.

Everyone looks up to the scoreboard behind center field. Even the Brewer players, warming up along the right field foul line, stop playing catch and look back, to a time when many of them were in preschool. From July 20, 1976, a video plays, black-and-white and grainy on the message board. Number 44 is at the plate, in a Brewer uniform. He flicks his powerful wrists, and the ball jumps off good wood, in a quick, tight loop, curling inside the left field foul pole. Home run number 755. As Henry Aaron lopes around the bases for the last time, and the Brewer mascot slides into his giant keg of beer in the bleachers, a cheer comes up from the small crowd, twenty-three years later. Down the first base line, I see Dave Nilsson, the Brewers' burly Australian slugger, with his glove tucked under his arm, clapping, and clapping.

Crouching there with my notebook, twenty feet from Hank, I notice I have tears in my eyes. Back then, it seemed an anonymous home run on a forgettable night. Hank hit a fastball from a relief pitcher named Dick Drago of the California Angels, who now rises from his folding chair, a rounded man in coat and tie, acknowledging his connection to history. Barely 10,000 fans had watched Hank hit number 755 in County Stadium that night; with nearly half the season left, no one figured the time for his last had come. Except, perhaps, Hank himself. "Each time I hit a home run," Hank had told me in Atlanta, "I thought it was the last one, because I didn't hit many that year."

This is a night for anniversaries. Thirty years ago, men first walked on the Moon. I was thirteen, on a canoe trip, on an island in upper Michigan, looking out through tent flaps at the sky. Before the rains came and the tents flooded, we saw the silver crescent, dancing in and out of clouds. Our counselor asked us to imagine; we did. Tom, my brother, turned twenty years old that day. Tonight, at County Stadium, he is fifty.

We sit in the upper deck: Tom, his wife Priscilla, their six-year-old boy Casey; my mom, her friend Fred Berman, and his two sons, Joe and Jon; me and Yam.

"I'm so grateful for all the fans I had a chance to play before," Hank had said moments earlier. "I have always said that it started here. If it hadn't been for you fans, I just don't know where yours truly would be. Thank you very very much from the bottom of my heart."

In the fourth inning, by our prearrangement, a Brewer employee brings Tom a birthday package: a pen in the shape of a bat; a Happy Birthday ball; a Brewer totebag. Casey is excited. He uses the pen bat to draw tattoos on our hands. My brother smiles: a proud-dad smile for his son, fading into a good-sport smile for his own anniversary. He's the first man in the family to turn fifty.

During that long-ago summer in the nation's capital when Tom was born, my parents dreamed that Dad would one day launch a career in politics or the Foreign Service. One of his fellow law clerks at the Supreme Court was Elliot Richardson, the future attorney general who would stand up to Richard Nixon in the "Saturday night massacre"; another was Warren Christopher, who would later become secretary of state. Years later I found Dad and Christopher's correspondence, warm and cordial, in a sheaf of letters in Mom's attic.

Mom and Fred are sharing a hot dog. He is a kind man, a painter, printmaker, and art professor emeritus at UWM, where my mom taught for years. The Berman kids grew up in our neighborhood. Fred's son Joe, four years older than I am, was a Milwaukee Braves fan with the best of them. He tells me he never saw someone hit a ball as hard as Henry Aaron. Once, he said, Hank hit one so hard at the shortstop, he was afraid the man wouldn't get his hands in front of his face before the ball creamed him. Another time, Joe recalls, Hank swung at a ball over his head, and tomahawked it just above the shortstop's leap. "And then the ball began to rise. Like a rising fastball. And all of a sudden—*poom!*—it was in the left field stands. I don't think it made the seats by more than a few feet. Just a rocket." Later, in Atlanta, at a park nicknamed "the launching pad," Hank would begin to loft the ball more. He had Ruth in his sights; more than ever, he was swinging for the fences.

In the summer of 1972—with the Hammer at about 650 and the hate mail pouring in thick—Mom and Dad took John and Yam and me on a vacation in Colorado. John and I had both recently been diagnosed with curvature of the

spine, so for twenty-three hours a day we had to wear back
braces that went from the pelvis to the chin—bulky metal
things that ate through our shirts. Of the five of us traveling
the Rockies that summer, only Yam and Mom looked normal.
Once, we stopped for the night near the Royal Gorge. After
we checked into our cabins, we went for dinner: Dad in his
wheelchair, with his paralyzed right hand, John and me in
our back braces. Flesh and bone and metal, walking and
rolling into the dining room. Afterward, Mom reported, a
well-meaning man in a soft southern accent took her aside.
Were you all in some terrible accident? he asked.

The ball is floating, up in the lights. Figures in white con-
verge on the infield grass. A man opens his glove and swallows the small white sphere. Out in right, a player stands
motionless, looking in, arms at his sides. I look beside him, at
the long line of chalk that ends at the warning track; and beyond, past the bleachers, to the twisted, slumping hunk of
steel that has fallen on the new stadium.

Seven days before, Big Blue, one of the biggest construc-
tion cranes in the world, was maneuvering a 400-ton section
of steel into place for the new roof at Miller Park, the stadium whose luxury-box income, it was promised, would save
a small-market franchise. It was windy, too windy to be safe.
Big Blue buckled, hurtling earthward, and smashed into another crane, crushing a "manbasket" containing three construction workers. They were killed instantly; as they died,
the rest of the crane landed in a twisted heap inside the new
stadium. Damages were later calculated at $100 million.

Big Blue now hangs limp upon the lip of the new stadium. It's the end of the fifth inning. Tom's name appears on the board with the other birthday people, and our crowd of nine musters a cheer. I ask Tom if he has any special County Stadium memories. He does: Waiting for autographs after a game, only to be driven away by an angry Warren Spahn banging on the fence as he walked toward the clubhouse. Hearing from his fourth-grade teacher in 1959 how she was booed when she left Harvey Haddix's perfect game in the tenth inning, because she had to teach the next day. (Haddix was perfect for twelve, and lost in thirteen.) Buying a beer for Bowie Kuhn in the bleachers during the 1970s. Sitting with Terry Perry's sister Sue as she flirted in her pink sweater with Yankees left fielder Roy White. Watching drunken fistfights in a whole section of the upper deck when the White Sox and their fans came to town in the '80s. Witnessing Sammy Sosa hit home runs 64 and 65, in the chase with McGwire in 1998, and the Brewers coming back to win the game when a Cub outfielder dropped an easy fly ball.

But these memories he would tell me about later. Tonight, he is not too excited to be turning fifty. "I'm not too sentimental," Tom says, looking out at the field where he watched Lew Burdette mow down the Yanks nearly forty-two years ago.

Hank Aaron has gone up into the press box, to visit on the air with his old friend and teammate, Bob Uecker, the Brewers' announcer. Hank tells Milwaukee how sorry he is about the accident; how tragic the loss of the men, and the fall of Big Blue; how we have to keep up hope. In center field, a flag flies at half-mast.

O

"Hey, *butterball!"* Tom yells through cupped hands, at a pitcher whose name, Parque, evokes our memories of an old margarine ad.

"Yeah, pass the Parque!" I yell. "It's Kraft at its best!"

It's a sunny afternoon, and Tom and I have come to the ballpark again. We sit together in the Diamond Boxes behind home plate. His boss at the *Milwaukee Journal Sentinel,* the new, merged paper where Tom is an editor, has given him the tickets to see the Brewers take on the Chicago White Sox. When Parque hits Jose Valentin, the Brewer shortstop, with a pitch, we unleash, amidst waves of our laughter, at the unfortunate pitcher from Chicago:

"Hey, Parque! You're melting!"

"Hey, *butterball!* Whassa matter, ball *slipping* away from you?"

People turn their heads, frowning the frowns of civilized fans.

"My editor's going to hear about this." Tom laughs, looking around the elite section of season ticket holders, where attendants come to take your order for microbrews and high-end corned beef. *You said sausage, sir? Will that be bratwurst, Polish, or Italian? And would you like the Secret Stadium Sauce with that, sir?*

We take our sausage heritage seriously here in Milwaukee: an early campaign to promote the city carried the banner "Monarch of the Sausage Kingdom." Hence, after the fourth inning, we get the sausage race. Men (or women, I can't tell) wrapped up like 3-D cartoons—impersonating the Italian, the Polish, the Hot Dog and the Brat—come scurrying in from the left field warning track: sausages on the run, elbowing for position in the race toward home plate.

Italian breaks the tape.

A teenage boy in an apron strides down the Diamond Box steps: *Hey, get your bottled water here!* Now *there's* a line I haven't heard. So long, frozen malt cups encased in bricks of steaming dry ice, and salted-in-the-shell peanuts tossed halfway down a long row in a packed grandstand, and wiry guys hauling two cases of bottled beer, popping the long-necks, pouring in a flash till the foam licks the edge of the paper cup. Hello, bottled water.

I look to the left field bleachers, toward the trusty sign above the top row: TRUE BLUE BREW CREW. This silent statement of loyalty has been there since the 1970s. Except now it's gone. In its place: PIC 'N' SAVE.

Beyond the outfield scoreboard, we can see what's left of Big Blue, an inverted V atop the damaged new park. We speculate: Though the Brewers haven't said so yet, there is no way Miller Park will be ready for the 2000 season. Tom has been editing the Big Blue stories for the paper, and it's apparent that the damage was considerable and that the cleanup alone may take months. County Stadium, which was to be demolished at season's end, will stand for another year. Already, the Brewers have abandoned this year's club slogan, "Bringing Down the House," in recognition of its sudden perversity.

In their quest to stay in Milwaukee, and keep the city major league, the Brewers have worked multiple angles. They got the big bucks from a corporate sponsor—of course it had to be a brewer—and then went after a handout from the tax-payers. The team lobbied hard for a sales tax surcharge that would help pay for Miller Park. A donnybrook ensued in the state legislature; when one opponent switched sides, and gave the Brewers a one-vote victory, his constituents recalled him. Bud Selig, the team owner, now had the tenth-of-a-cent sales tax from consumers in southeastern Wisconsin to finance part of the construction. Selig had also insisted that the park be in the same venue as the old stadium, rather than downtown, where some civic leaders preferred. And he fought to keep the considerable parking revenues for the team, even though many of the lots are on county property. These were, Selig insisted throughout, essential sacrifices for the community: modern-day rules and realities necessary for keeping a small-market town in the major leagues. Skyboxes, and taxpayer dollars, and corporate identity, would keep baseball in Milwaukee. But many in the divided city continued to ask, *Who is this place for?*

"It's about a way to get white people's money," my brother tells me. We've hiked to the edge of the grandstands in the right field corner, to get a better look at the disaster. "Baseball, to me, just seems empty now. It's just about money." Years ago, Tom wrote a piece for *Milwaukee* magazine, describing the love affair between the city and the Brewers of the early eighties—blue-collar types like Pete Vuckovich and Ben Oglivie and, especially, Gorman Thomas, who'd crash his body into the center field fence in pursuit of fly balls; whose "gorgeous space-shot home runs," Tom wrote, typified the man who was "the heart of the team" on a "team of the heart." Like Hank, Gorman had worn number 44 early in his career, but he gave it up when the Hammer came home. Now, the team is no longer a reflection of the community. It hasn't been for a long time.

When I had gone to a game with Tom's old friend Terry Perry, she'd looked around the ballpark, through the Diamond Boxes and the grandstands and the bleachers, and the upper deck where her little brother was almost born, and said: "You used to see a lot more regular folks, working-class folks, people of color out here. I don't know what happened." The crane, Tom suggests now, and the damage it caused, are emblematic of deeper rifts. "Look at what's in front of you," he says. Around the blue crane, an intricate mesh of sea green steel lies twisted and contorted, like a busted erector set. It's a perversion of what was meant to be.

O

"When something like this happens, we say, 'God don't like ugly.'" The blunt remark belongs to Annette (Polly) Williams, a state representative from Milwaukee's inner city. We're sitting over lunch at the Savoy, a black bar and restaurant near Martin Luther King Drive. She says she's had a few "God-don't-like-ugly" calls in the week since Big Blue came crashing down. Her constituents didn't want to pay a cent for the new stadium, Williams tells me. Not at a time when the state now known as a "pioneer" in welfare reform was beginning to implement its tough new program, and federal funds for food stamps and family assistance were being slashed. Next to that, she says, no one sympathized with the idea of paying new taxes for a stadium they had no desire to go to. Even if they wanted to go, she says, they could never afford the games. "That stadium is not for people of color," she says. "We need skyboxes for the rich so they can watch the game in plush pleasure? I resent it. That Brewers' stadium is nothing but entertainment for the rich."

Fair is fair, Williams had said in the legislature; if you want the stadium tax, how about a tax to invest in low-income neighborhoods? Or incentives to keep what's left of the factory and brewery jobs from flying out of town? Her words were unheeded.

Polly Williams's parents, James and Louise Wade, came up from Mississippi in the 1940s. Her mother knit gloves at Krasno Brothers and later sewed upholstery at American Motors. Her father pulled hides at the Albert Trostel tannery—dangerous, smelly, grueling work that involved dipping maggot-ridden cowskins in vats of lye and pulling out the hundred-pound, hairless hides with hooks. Some of the Trostels were neighbors of ours on the east side. Tom, my brother, worked as a longshoreman at the Port of Milwaukee and recalls the overpowering smell of the raw, brine-cured hides. So does Polly Williams. "It really stunk," she tells me. But it was work. "A.O. Smith, Allis Chalmers, the breweries. This was a blue-collar town. You didn't have to have an education. Just a strong back, and you could support your family. We didn't have a lot of the problems that we have now. We had stable families."

In the early 1980s, the big factories started to close. Tens of thousands of workers got pink slips from the giant manufacturers once at the heart of our town: Allis Chalmers, makers of tractors and turbines; Harnischfeger, the builders of cranes and hoists; Bucyrus-Erie, where they churned out steam shovels and dredges. At Allen Bradley, home of the largest four-face clock in the world (bigger than Big Ben in London, England), automation came in, and three thousand jobs went to Mexico. In less than four years, writes John Gurda in *The Making of Milwaukee,* the area lost 56,000 manufacturing jobs—"more jobs, in absolute numbers, than Milwaukee lost during the Depression." Tom once had an old poster on his wall, with the slogan of the city's soul: MIL-WAUKEE FEEDS AND SUPPLIES THE WORLD. Now those were just words. In black Milwaukee, where the closing of the tanneries had already hit hard, the silence of the factories was devastating. Black unemployment more than doubled; black families' income, once about two-thirds of whites', plummeted to below 40 percent. Two out of every five black families in Milwaukee now lives in poverty—four times the rate of white families. "When they left," Polly Williams says of the factories' exodus, "it was a real blow here."

In the days before the lines shut down, the Wade family would tune in the Braves on WTMJ, the station named after its parent company, the *Milwaukee Journal,* where a rising executive named Irwin Maier was soon to take the reins. Polly Williams recalls how she and her parents and her brother Jesse would stop whatever they were doing when Hank stepped in to hit. "We were more involved when we had people like Hank Aaron and Billy Bruton," she says. "They were here." For Hank's first three years in town, before he crossed the color line from the inner city, he lived in black

Milwaukee. His first year, the monthly rent was seventy-five dollars—paid in two installments, his landlord Jay Gilmer said, because "athletes did not make the big bucks as they do now." Billy Bruton lived nearby. And in 1956, Felix Mantilla moved into the neighborhood. "They were part of the community," Williams says.

In those days, before the good jobs disappeared, and before integration made middle-class black flight possible, there was a vibrancy to the community, Polly Williams says. Third Street, she remembers, was filled with places "run by black people for black people": small businesses and social service agencies. It was before the street was called Martin Luther King Drive.

"It was nothing to see law offices next to barber shops, next to dentist offices, next to funeral parlors," my old Campus School friend, Rodney Franks, had told me. "Third Street was the locus of black commerce in Milwaukee previous to the integration movement. That was there out of necessity because black folks could not go to Water Street"—where my dad's law office was—"or Kilbourn or whatever. You *could* go there but you may not be treated well. And with the advent of integration, lawyers moved their offices off of Third Street, other professionals moved their businesses away from the community. As a result of that, a lot of the black community's essential images of influence for young black people were gone. They were not on Third Street anymore." On Martin Luther King today, you can ride past Booby's and Tiny's Lounge and a soup kitchen and a blood bank and Duke's Unity Club and empty lots and a Dr. King health center and a Taco Bell. Lately there are a few signs of change, but especially compared to thirty years ago, the professional addresses are missing.

Just beyond the borders of the black community, downtown, near Usinger's sausage factory, King Drive is called something else: "Old World Third Street." White people work down there. "They do not want Martin Luther King's name in the white neighborhood," a black community leader told me.

Rodney's parents took the family out of black Milwaukee, into suburban Brown Deer, in the late sixties. The family had fought the access battles—Rodney's father was a community organizer, and for years had marched with Father Groppi and black community leaders for fair housing and employment. Now, the family walked the walk, out of the inner city, and like Hank, became black pioneers in a new racial vision for America. "Later on," Rodney told me, "I remember saying, 'Did my parents move out here to give me a better environment, a better education?' I'm sure the educational part was achieved. But the environment—moving from central city out to Brown Deer—was that really a good environment for a fourteen-, fifteen-year-old kid who up to that point was in a truly urban situation? Did we really benefit from moving out into the suburbs? Because a lot of black people with means were getting the hell out. They were moving out west, you know? Was that healthy? Was that a healthy move for the big picture? And the jury's still kind of out on that."

The jury's out for Rodney; not for Polly Williams. "I never had a dream like that," she says. "They had this whole dream of living in a utopian society. I knew it was a joke. Living next to a white person—that has no value to me. I live where I live by choice. It's all black. I love it." Integrated education, she says—like the kind Rodney and I experienced—is no better. "These people get an integration experience by having a few black kids come to their schools. But not one of those white liberals ever sent their kids into our part of the city. It's always about black folks leaving their place to come to a white base where they have no strength or power." Because of integration, Williams says, black athletes no longer live in the community. And community leaders, she says, have to struggled to get black players from the Packers or the Bucks to even talk to inner-city kids, because they're too busy "signing autographs for a bunch of white people." She thinks this agenda is set by the white agents. "There's this fear that you can't allow black folks any opening. To maintain this power, you can't lose an inch. So you just can't have Aaron topping Babe Ruth. The white has to be in control."

Polly Williams often prefers sharp words to soft ones. Once during our conversation, she says derisively, "You know how white people are." But if her words provoke or irritate white listeners, she doesn't seem to mind. And when you consider baseball and see how few blacks are in management, on the field and off, it is hard to argue her point about whites needing to be in control. Fifty-two years after Jackie Robinson broke in, twenty-five years after a black man first wore the home run crown, there are so few black managers or general managers that the commissioner himself, partly at Hank's urging, has made this a central plank of his tenure. For the 2000 season, the Brewers' new president, Wendy

Selig-Prieb, heeded her father's words: Davey Lopes, an African American, will be the team's new manager.

But the management positions are only baseball's obvious failings; there are more subtle examples. Consider the importance of the third base coach. He flashes the signs to bunt, to swing away, or to steal a base; he tells a runner rounding third to stop or to try to score. He is a key decision maker, whose call can mean the difference between winning and losing. A first base coach mostly just stands there, pats the runner on the rump after he's crossed the bag safely, and tells him to watch the coach at third for a sign. During the 1999 season, of the sixty base coaches on the thirty major league teams, twenty-one were minorities; of those, however, only six were third base coaches, and two of those were on teams with black managers. "Third base coach, he has to be the smart one, to give all kinds of signs," Felix Mantilla said, laughing, when I asked him about this. "So they have to put the white guy in." It was an inside joke, he said; common knowledge in the separate, black world of baseball. When he played against the Dodgers, he would tease Junior Gilliam, L.A.'s black first base coach. "Hey, Junior," Mantilla would say, *"First base!"* Mantilla laughed as he remembered, but it was a better-than-crying kind of laugh. The unfunny part was that Gilliam was considered a brilliant baseball man; when he died, he was still coaching first base.

One morning over breakfast not long before, I had asked Hank's close friend, Joe Kennedy, about the base-coaching issue. Yes, Kennedy said, years earlier Hank had put the question to him: "How many third base coaches are black? As opposed to first base coaches?" At the time, Kennedy didn't know the ratio; he only sensed, correctly, that the numbers were highly skewed. "I think a lot of this is unconscious," Kennedy told me matter-of-factly. Unconscious, he meant, to whites.

○

"**We** are angry, and intend to stay angry until America worries about freedom here instead of just worrying about freedom abroad," Vel Phillips, the mother of my schoolmate Dale, called out in the Milwaukee Common Council chamber one evening. It was the summer of 1967, a touchstone season for me: Hank was closing in on 500 home runs in Atlanta; baseball came back home, if just for a game, to a packed County Stadium; Dr. King came north, fighting for fair housing and employment in Chicago; Bobby Kennedy considered a run for president; my father's M.S. became clear, and present, and potent; cities burned across America. That summer, Milwaukee too erupted in racial violence, the National Guard arrived with its armored personnel carriers (APCs), and 1,700 people were arrested—few, if any, in my neighborhood. The night Vel Phillips spoke in the Common Council, another alderman stood up to denounce Father Groppi, leader of the NAACP Youth Council Commandoes, as a "preacher of hatred." With two hundred civil rights advocates in the room, the atmosphere crackled. Every night, on the streets, Father Groppi, Mrs. Phillips (the "Queen of the Commandoes") and the others had kept up the pressure, demanding social change.

"When we was out there marching," Jesse Wade says

thirty-two years later, "I would risk my life for him." The Commando bodyguards would start Groppi's car for him, in case it blew up; they would ring the marchers with their presence, taking a brick before the others. Wade, the older brother of Polly Williams, is a stout man for whom breathing no longer comes easy. He sits in his first-floor inner-city flat, in an armchair, beneath a portrait of Malcolm X. Of Father Groppi, he says, "He didn't really believe that white people would do things that they were doing. He kept saying, 'We're not like that.' And then we'd be marching, and some guy would throw a bag of shit at you.

"He was white," Jesse Wade assures me of the son of the Italian grocer, "but his nature changed." Dick Gregory, the comedian and civil rights activist, had said much the same, in one of his frequent visits to the city: "Father Groppi proves that black and white is no longer a color in America, but an attitude." The priest's 1965 trip to Selma, and the calls there to bring the movement home to communities across America, had stirred Groppi to action in Milwaukee.

In May 1967, three months before the riots, Jesse Wade had been on the sidelines. "It wasn't my thing," he remembered of the marches. "Music and boxing was my thing. I was blowing the saxophone." They called him "Hook"—they still do—from the way he used his fists at the Y, and on the street. Like a lot of guys, his heroes were Muhammad Ali and Hank. "If you said something about them in a negative way, you could get your ass kicked," he remembers. "Because they was so loved by the people."

If the movement in Milwaukee was not Hook's thing, it became his thing in an instant one day that month, as he sat idling in his car. Marchers blocked the avenue, standing face to face with a line of blue uniforms. "The police decided to charge the marchers, with those big long sticks," Hook remembers. "And there was this big old cop—he looked like he was six foot six—he runs across the street, and he looks at this little girl—ten, eleven years old—and then he just took his club and whacked her right in the face. He hit her so hard she jumped in the air. And she was just laying there, trembling, you know. And all the blood was shooting out of her head. And he stepped back and kicked her. And a flash went through me. I put my car in park, stashed my keys and ran across the street. I saw nothing but blue."

Hook was a little guy, but his reputation, he says, was of a fearless man. "And I just dove on their backs. I just grabbed them from behind and took about four down with me."

Hook was arrested that day. The next day, he joined the Commandoes. He was twenty-seven years old. "We were just the click of a movement in Milwaukee. It was all over the country. But I thought we were going to change the balance in Milwaukee, because we were hot on some issues, and we were making people think."

I tell him how vividly I remember the Commandoes on that night across from the Arena, when George Wallace came to town. About how the Wallace supporter I confronted called me "pumpkinhead" and told me to get lost, and how I'd crossed the street, to watch the Commandoes, marching in step. I was twelve. "There was something about the way the Commandoes carried themselves," I tell him. He reminds me: polished black shoes, creased blue jeans, blue jean jackets with the Commando patch, black T-shirts, black berets. The uniforms worn by the Commandoettes were much the same. With Wallace in town, and his supporters rallying, Hook tells me, their berets were cocked to one side: a signal of battle mode.

In late July 1967, on Third Street, someone threw a rock through a window. Within minutes, the situation escalated to bricks and fires. Race riots had hit dozens of cities that summer; the worst were in Newark and Detroit. As Detroit smoldered, Wisconsin's white leadership wanted swift action. They wanted control, and quickly. Hours after the first rock flew, 4,800 National Guardsmen were on their way to the city. A policeman, Bryan Moschea, was dead, along with two elderly women. The mayor imposed his martial law declaration: taverns closed, filling stations shut down, mail delivery was suspended. Grocery stores opened for two hours each afternoon; other than that, no one was allowed to move. In the inner city, a mother was arrested for venturing out to buy milk for her baby. Police patrolled with M-16s, "the kind used by the troops in Vietnam," according to the *Journal*; some officers even rode through the inner city in Brink's armored trucks.

"The Inner Core was tightly sealed with a ring of steel," the *Journal* reported as the conflict began. Nevertheless, whites harbored terrified fantasies of black rioters coming through the front door. Many loaded their hunting rifles. This was the time we sat in our backyard—my mom recalls hearing distant explosions—wondering what would become of us and our city. Black fears were based on the actual presence of riot police and Guardsmen and fires down the street; Rodney Franks was among the thousands who watched the armored personnel carriers with their .50-caliber machine guns rolling through their neighborhoods. "This is occupied territory," decried one black leader. Another called the inner city an "armed camp." Of the 1,700 people police arrested in those few days, 98 percent were black. Clifford McKissick, suspected of hurling molotov cocktails only moments before, was shot, unarmed, by Milwaukee police; he bled to death in his mother's arms, on his living-room floor. "There need not be a funeral today," Father Groppi called out to mourners a few days later. The shooting, he said, was "a wild, irresponsible act. Don't let his death be in vain, or next week we'll go to the funeral of another black man." McKissick was the same age as my brother Tom and was in his first year at Whitewater State University. His cousin, Daniel Gregory, told me that in earlier years, he and Clifford would spend summer days at the Boys Club behind Clifford's house; a highlight of their young lives was the day, perhaps in 1962, when Hank Aaron came to speak. "Just knowing somebody important cared," Daniel told me. "That meant a lot. It gave you things to look up to. It gave you hope that there was something better out there for you. That they weren't all against you."

In an exhaustive study of the cause of the riots across the country that summer, the Kerner Commission in 1968 declared that the roots lay in racial oppression and economic deprivation. Blacks in Milwaukee agreed: they blamed the riots on discrimination, poor housing and police brutality—the very things Phillips, Groppi, the Commandoes and hundreds of other blacks and whites were marching to protest that summer. The next year, 1968, the city finally passed the open housing law.

In the ensuing years, the Commandoes evolved to focus more on grassroots social service work; for a generation, Jesse Wade was their leader. He ran the Commandoes' youth leadership programs. "We tried to do something for our community," Hook says. In a corner, a television plays softly. Hook recalls the after-school field trips to the zoo, and barbecues at the lake. He remembers the breakfast programs, where neighborhood kids served the elderly. And the sewing classes, taught by his mom, where teenage girls learned to make clothes. And the days when young Commandoes built wheelchair ramps and installed them at the inner-city homes of the disabled. "We were *in* our community," he says. One of the biggest Commando programs was summer camp. And one of that program's biggest supporters, Hook says to my surprise, was my grandfather, Irwin Maier. "He was crazy about the Commandoes," Hook says. They used to talk in Grandpa's office. One time Hook went to get help for the 270 kids he was taking up north to Indian Mound. "Anything that we wanted for the camps, he got it," Hook says. "He'd call up one of the grocery stores and says, 'The Commandoes are going to camp, what are you going to do?' Not '*Can* you help,' but 'They need some food up there, what are you going to give them?' He talked like he was the king! And then he'd hang up and say, 'Don't worry. Kohl's [a local grocer] is going to take care of you.' He was a tough man. But he was a good man."

Once, Hook took three busloads of kids to Atlanta for Hank Aaron Appreciation Day. There was no game scheduled that day; just a time set aside to acknowledge Hank. When the buses from Milwaukee rolled in, Hook couldn't believe it: there were only about five hundred people at Fulton County Stadium, almost all of them black. "And I said, 'Something ain't right about this shit.' I said, 'Where the fuck is the whole town?' I guess they figured Hank Aaron ain't no Atlanta boy. He's from Milwaukee." Afterward, Hook said, he and a few of the Commandoes made it over to Hank's house. Billye Aaron met them at the door. "She said, 'They really hate my husband, because he beat Babe Ruth out.'"

Hook's sad eyes regard the white man from the east side. "It's all gone now," he says of the Commandoes' dreams. "I feel we lost all of them. Yeah. For all that hard work we put in back then, it's even worse now."

Polly Williams says there is no longer a tradition of "strong black men, protectant of the community"—nothing like in the days when her brother Jesse ran the Commandoes. Hook had even sent a few Commandoes down to Atlanta to shadow Hank, after hearing about the death threats. "We said, 'You stay around, and be as close as you can to Hank Aaron without him knowing,'" Hook recalls. He told them, "Play it low key, man. Keep yourself always in a respectable way."

The Commandoes could relate to what Hank was going through. "We struggled," Hook says, "as a group." For a guy like Hank, he says, you were willing to lay it on the line. Now, "there is nobody," no hero like that. Not even Michael Jordan. "I mean, he got a lot of fans, but they don't outright love him. He could move over there and they would say, 'The hell with it.' Jackie Robinson couldn't move over there. Hank Aaron couldn't move over there. They would go over and get them and bring them back: 'You belong to us, man.' Now, it's all about the buck."

But this meaning of Hank is for people of a certain age, Hook says. Among the young, even Henry Aaron is losing his legacy.

"I talk to some of those young guys," Hook says. "They always call me Old Man, the Vet, Papa, and all that. I want to put something in their head a little bit, some of the gang members. They look at me and say, 'Let me tell you something, Old Man. Your day was a good day. You got a mother and a dad, don't you?'

"'Yeah, I got a mother.'

"'Well, I got a mother that ain't worth a shit. I don't know where the fuck my father is. If I seen him I wouldn't know him anyway. I don't love him 'cause I don't know him. Then my mother has to go out and turn tricks. That's what she said she has to do to feed us.' He is looking cold. And I kind of back off a little bit because he is getting angry.

"I said, 'You can't fault your mother for what she had to do to feed you, man. If she didn't do it, you wouldn't be here.'

"He said, 'You know what? I really don't give a damn if I am here or not. We see that we can't make it. So we gonna take it. We take from you. We take from anybody. 'Cause we don't give a damn. 'Cause we be dead anyway.'

"I said, 'You got no feeling, man?'

"He said, 'Man, when you get to this point, there is no feeling. I hate this. But don't worry: I'm not the only one. There is a hundred thousand of us, just like that.'"

Hook looks over at me. Above his head is a photograph of his parents, from the 1940s. It is a beautiful image: a young, attractive, well-dressed couple—he in his gray suit and necktie, she in her blue and white dress, white beaded necklace and earrings—newly arrived from Mississippi, ripe with their dreams of a chance in the North.

"They had me almost ready to cry," Jesse Wade says of the young men on the street. "And I was leader of the Commandoes."

O

In late 1999, long after I visited Jesse Wade, I learned something that should not have surprised me. In the summer of 1967, in the midst of the curfew, as our family sat in the backyard, swatting at mosquitos and wondering what would become of us, my grandfather was meeting with the mayor, the governor and the police chief; this summit meeting helped ensure an ironfisted response in the inner city. Not only did the mayor call in the Guard, as many other big-city mayors did that summer, but his extraordinary declaration of martial law, according to Milwaukee historian John Gurda, contributed to a "siege mentality . . . extraordinary levels of fear were still evident months later." The city, Gurda wrote in *The Making of Milwaukee,* "was traumatized to its bones."

My grandfather was a complex man. He was involved in dialogue on race relations—with Tom Cheeks; with Wesley Scott, the head of the Milwaukee Urban League; and, as he wrote in his memoir—ghostwritten by my brother Tom—with the Commandoes. Before beginning a meeting in his office at the *Journal,* he insisted that the Commandoes remove their berets. "They readily agreed," he noted approvingly, "and we got to work." (Hook laughed when I told him Granpa's version. "He told us to take off our berets," Hook said. "But we refused! Nobody was going to mess with our uniforms. I was a general, so I was wearing a black beret. The other guys had on yellow berets. I just stood up and took off my jean jacket—this was sharp, pressed, you could wear it to any party or meeting—and put it around the chair. And then the other four Commandoes did the same. And *then* we started the meeting.")

By Grandpa's account, by Cheeks's, and by Hook's, these meetings led to some progress. Later, after the riots, Irv Maier's newspaper, and the mayor himself, would call for better housing and jobs in the inner city. But at the moment when the riots started, whatever Grandpa Irv might have learned about the roots of discrimination and poverty and racial tension in the Inner Core did not appear to inform his response. Along with the other white power brokers, Irwin Maier—lover of order in his fair city, in his office, and on the patio under his apple tree, where the metal furniture had to be arranged just so—dismissed the non-violent alternatives proposed by Vel Phillips and others in the black community.

Black community leaders said the curfew had created mass hysteria in the ghetto. They expressed outrage that they had not been involved in the official response to the crisis. "The city administration and the white system called the shots," read a statement by prominent black leaders, as the "ring of steel" was still in place. "[They] set the guidelines for communications in the traditional paternalistic manner which was acceptable to them." Indeed, Grandpa Irv recalled white leaders meeting at his house to discuss "proper action"; martial law was their solution. "Crime is crime, and must be put down by whatever force is needed," said a front-page *Journal* editorial on the first day of the riots. The headline read: ORDER MUST PREVAIL.

None of this should surprise me terribly: a conservative man, publisher of the state's biggest newspaper in a conservative midwestern town, advocates law and order in 1967. What stunned me, when I learned about it, was the disconnect. Here I was, the first night of the curfew, sitting in the backyard, thinking about Father Groppi and my Campus School pals that lived in the inner city, and wondering what might happen to our tranquil neighborhood; half a mile away, the governor, the police chief, and the mayor and my grandfather were meeting at Grandpa's home—a red brick house surrounded by cop cars and black sedans on an otherwise deserted street. The men gathered upstairs, in the library, to discuss what Grandpa would later call "proper action." "Burn, baby, burn," they'd been hearing all summer. No doubt they felt anger and fear; the swift, harsh, "proper action" would be cited later as the measures that saved the city. This conviction—that the white leaders' actions saved Milwaukee from further bloodshed—would be held almost exclusively by whites.

"I would say they perceived some kind of threat that allowed them to put their differences aside," Rodney said, when I told him about this extraordinary meeting of white leaders, some of whom rarely found much to agree on. Rodney was being diplomatic. The perceived threat, of course, was above all to the white power structure; the iron fist was about control, to reestablish order, and keep things tranquil for us whites. This way, if we so chose, we wouldn't have to think about it anymore. After all, Clifford McKissick did not bleed to death in a living room in our neighborhood. The APCs didn't roll past our front doors. Policemen were not hitting anyone we knew with billy clubs. As Gaile Aaron would say, we could afford to be detached. As much of the city can be today: while white Milwaukee celebrates an economic recovery, black Milwaukee might as well be in another country. Rates of black unemployment, housing loan discrimination, small-business ownership and child poverty are among the worst in the United States. And, despite what Jesse Wade and Vel Phillips and James Groppi marched for thirty-two years ago, the city remains one of the most racially segregated in the country.

It was small consolation for the inner city's declining fortunes, but in 1988, a deeply divided city council finally agreed to rename the 16th Street Viaduct after Father Groppi. Groppi had died three years earlier, after leaving the priesthood. He'd been driving a city bus and organizing bus drivers. In proclaiming the James E. Groppi Unity Bridge, the Common Council noted Groppi's "lasting contribution to the social consciousness of Milwaukee and to the progress toward social justice." The late father was survived by a wife and daughter.

O

"Baseball," Bud Selig is telling me, "has always been sort of a mirror of society." We're sitting in the new Milwaukee office of the commissioner of baseball, located here, on the twentieth floor of a downtown bank building, because my hometown is Selig's, too. I've just asked him about the days when the national pastime seemed more tied up in issues of racial justice, at the center of a crucial black aspiration. The commissioner says, "When you look at the Jackie Robinson experience, to the everlasting credit of Branch Rickey—that was a precursor of the civil rights movement. There's no question baseball has played a very significant role in that. And a very positive one."

As a child, Bud Selig went to Wrigley Field to see Jackie Robinson play his first game in Chicago. Selig and a cousin and a friend named Herb Kohl, who grew up to be a U.S. senator, witnessed a piece of history that day. "And I looked around and we were the only white people in the upper deck," Selig remembers. "It was really thrilling. You don't see that anymore. And I am concerned about that." He's not sure what has happened.

I offer the commissioner of baseball my theory of why black fans have left the game: That for many people, blacks included, baseball no longer represents a collective sense of civic good. That there was a time when baseball meant something more, before Safeco and Qualcomm and Pacific Bell and Miller beer parks, and before the starting lineup was brought to you by Infiniti; that it was tied into real hopes and aspirations, especially among blacks; that it connected more deeply with people's lives. Tom had told me he thought baseball had been "a theater in which such values as bravery, skill, craftsmanship, self-sacrifice and strength could exhibit themselves, as examples for the audience. Something that's been disconnected by all the money." John Gurda, the Milwaukee historian and friend of Tom's, had told me: "I think there may have been a time when baseball mirrored the community: hardworking team, blue-collar team. We actually had time off from school to watch the Braves in the World Series. The nuns would lead the prayers. It was precious. It's about money, now. My own feeling is that baseball has become fairly irrelevant to society. They've lost their moorings. They've lost any ties to the working class. They've lost the connection."

I tell the commissioner, it seems like something's missing now. I remember Andrew Young's comment about sports existing in a political context for blacks, as part of a survival strategy. In his day, Young told me, in Hank's day, "I had some social context in which to grow up, and some social context in which to feel social responsibility for the community. And that doesn't exist anymore." Maybe blacks don't come to see baseball, I tell Bud Selig, because baseball no longer represents a collective aspiration. Maybe there's just no sense that it stands for a common good any more.

"I don't know, Sandy," the commissioner says, jangling the change in his pocket. "We've spent a lot of time talking about it. Hank and I have talked about it. Talked a lot about it with Frank Robinson, Joe Morgan, Len Coleman, the president of the National League. I don't have an answer to it. I am concerned that inner-city kids don't play baseball. We have the RBI [Reviving Baseball in Inner Cities] programs and a lot of stuff going on—125,000–130,000 kids are in inner-city play now. We are getting there. We have a long way to go."

Selig rejects the idea that baseball has become too expensive. I argue that four-dollar hot dogs and three-dollar bottles of water are not going to attract anyone on a budget. But, Selig counters, "baseball tickets are the cheapest by far of any sport." He has a point; prime seats for the Milwaukee Bucks games, for example, where you'll see many more black fans, cost sixty-five dollars each. "The Brewers have discount nights," he goes on, "take a family of four for twenty-five dollars. Ticket, hot dog, Coke and something else for every person. You couldn't even go to a fast-food operation for less than that."

Still, I remember the old Knot Hole Gang: poor kids could get into a game for a quarter. As Andrew Young had told me when I'd visited him in Atlanta, when he was growing up, "Baseball was a poor people's game." Now, it's a luxury-box game. Baseball, it seems, still is a mirror of society.

Bud Selig gets up from his desk; we walk over to the west-facing window. He peers through the plate glass toward County Stadium, and Miller Park just beyond. On a clear day, you can almost see Big Blue, slumping over the new park, freezing its progress. Today, haze shrouds the disaster.

"It was one of the most heartbreaking, emotional traumas of my life," the commissioner of baseball says, still squinting out, hands clasped behind him. The three stadium workers are not long buried. "I was just back from Boston and the All-Star Game, which was a huge high. Hank Aaron, Willie Mays, Carl Yastrzemski, Bobby Gibson, Robin Yount. It was special. And about five-twenty, my secretary Lori came running in and turned the TV on. And my daughter Wendy called me from the ballpark." Wendy Selig-Prieb took over the Brewer operations when Bud became commissioner full time in 1998, but the stadium had been her father's child. "And Wendy said, 'Dad, this is bad. You have to come out here.' I spent the night there."

We go back to the desk. I talk Milwaukee: My friend T's younger sister, Angela, was a good friend of Wendy's in college. "Wonderful girl," says the commissioner. "Wonderful family." I tell him that T and I used to go out to the White Sox games, when he brought baseball back before the Brewers came. In fact, we'd just been to "Turn Back the Clock Night" at County Stadium, where the White Sox came to town and played in their uniforms from 1969.

"I am sure you heard this from thousands of people," I tell Bud Selig, "but we were so fired up that you brought it back. That first game after the Braves left—the Twins and the White Sox—"

"My first foray into baseball," the commissioner interjects. "July 24, 1967: Fifty-one thousand, one hundred forty-four. We roped off the field and put in extra fans. And that was really the beginning of the second phase of Milwaukee baseball. I was just a kid—thirty-three years old. In fact, your grandfather was one of the first people I went to talk to. And he was really for it. He was a wonderful man." He tells me my grandfather was instrumental in getting County Stadium built in time for the first game of the Milwaukee Braves, in April 1953.

The next year, out at the park, Selig saw a rookie named Henry Aaron hit the ball as hard as he'd ever seen it hit. Smoking line drives. Three years later, on a late September evening, Selig, then a college student, skipped an accounting class to sit in the upper deck at County Stadium; Hank's eleventh-inning homer that night clinched the pennant. Soon afterward, the two young men became friends; in the off-season they'd get sideline passes to the Packers games and listen to Vince Lombardi scream at his players. Perhaps no one appreciates the talents of a man like Hank Aaron more than the commissioner. "I saw his first game here with the Braves, and his last game here with the Brewers," Selig says. "And, man, he was fun to watch play. He was magnificent. I never saw Hank throw to the wrong base. I never saw Hank make a base-running mistake. He was phenomenal. He was magnificent. He was quiet. He was dignified. I never saw anything like it."

I tell the commissioner about my trip to Cooperstown. The room for the Babe, the wall for Hank.

"In defense of Cooperstown," Bud Selig says, "I think Hank today is getting the recognition he deserves. Babe Ruth—Sandy—Babe Ruth in my judgment is the most famous athlete of the twentieth century. Period. Nobody even close. I think baseball historians would agree that Babe Ruth carried the game on his big broad shoulders and skinny legs. He set records in the dead ball era that were just incredible. I think there's no question that Babe Ruth is the greatest player of all time. And maybe the greatest athlete of the twentieth century. So, I don't think that Hank is getting shortchanged at all in that regard. I think Hank has now been recognized." Selig has played a big role in that. This year, the twenty-fifth anniversary of 715, he unveiled an award for each league's best hitter, modeled after the Cy Young Award for pitchers, to be called the Hank Aaron

Award. Under Selig's direction, baseball celebrated the anniversary with ceremonies in nearly every ballpark. Hank was also prominent and visible at the All-Star Game, and at the World Series, where he was named to the All-Century Team.

And look, Selig says, at another measure of progress: how differently the nation responded to the chase between Mark McGwire and Sammy Sosa, fifty years after Jackie, a generation after Hank and 715. "I think it was a manifestation of how far we've come," he says. Perhaps. I wonder, though, what the reaction would have been like if Sosa had been number one, instead of being portrayed as the sidekick to the white guy. Would he have gotten hate mail? "The thing with Hank," Bud Selig is saying, reminded of another generation, "was so wrong and so unfortunate. So awful. And he had done so brilliantly. And he was so remarkable in so many ways. And to have to go through the pain; I know when I got him up here, he was obviously still in pain."

When Hank came home to Milwaukee in 1975, he did not have the 30–35 homer years we all dreamed of. But we didn't really care. He came up here to be with us again. "He gave us everything he had," Selig tells me. "He gave us two good years." And we loved that. Maybe the numbers dropped off because Hank had turned forty-one before he ever put on a Brewer uniform. And maybe it was because of the pain the Hammer was in; the pain Selig began to notice. He hadn't really understood what Hank had been through. Not until his daughter Wendy got to know Hank's secretary, Carla Koplin, and got a taste of the hate mail. "I was stunned," Selig says. "I had read about it, and heard about it. But until Carla really started telling me, and Hank told me, I never understood. I could not imagine. *Could not imagine.* It was *embarrassing.*"

Bud Selig thinks his old friend's wounds are finally closing. "I think the last two or three years have been very helpful," the commissioner says. "I know that Hank was quite angry at one point. But I am happy that all that bitterness—" He stops in mid-sentence. "And it was bad," says the commissioner of baseball, remembering what his friend endured. "It stuns me to this day."

10

VALUES

New York City, January 1999

The bunting, in red, white, and blue, made the room look like the upper deck at Yankee Stadium. "Take Me Out to the Ball Game" drifted through the overhead speakers, followed by Abbott and Costello's "Who's on First?" Under the lights on a semicircle of tables, in the care of a small auction house from the Upper East Side, lay forty-one items of American value: Sammy Sosa's 66th home run ball, from 1998; a ball signed by Cy Young; another by Babe Ruth; by Ty Cobb; by Roger Maris. And the centerpiece, what everyone came to see, and a few would try to own: Mark McGwire's 70th home run ball. The ball had been imprinted with a DNA code for authentication, and its owner, a fan from St. Louis, had transported it to The Theatre at Madison Square Garden in an armored car.

"Lot number one," the auctioneer said as the auction began. The ball rested on a pedestal beside her, in a square lucite case. She began her dignified calls.

The bidding for the McGwire ball began at $400,000 and quickly rocketed upward. *The bid is at one million dollars. Who would like to bid for one million-one? One million-one is the bid, would anyone like to bid at one million-two?*

A million-two. A million-three. A million-four, and five, and six. A pause.

Is there any interest at one point seven *million dollars? One point* seven *is the bid, would anyone like to bid at one million-eight?*

Several dropped out of the bidding; others wouldn't dare scratch their noses.

The auctioneer was smiling. No ball had ever reached half the current bid. *Two million dollars is bid!*

Whoops and hollers from the crowd. Now it was down to two: a maker of neckties, standing nearby, and an anonymous man, whose voice came through the speakers overhead.

Two million-two. Two million-three. Two million-four.

"Two and a half million is the bid. Is there any interest—"

"Two million six," said the necktie mogul. Another pause.

"Two million seven," said the anonymous voice.

"*Selling at two million seven* . . ." Necktie paused. *Last chance* . . . Necktie gave up; the gavel came down.

Sold, to the anonymous caller.

Gasps, then cheers.

"It was a spectacular event," said the auction house representative.

"I'm telling you, this is a great country," said the necktie mogul.

"This is America," said the fan from St. Louis. "Anything's possible."

The new owner's identity was soon revealed. He was Todd McFarlane, a maker of action figures, whose acceleration to wealth was powered by the originality of his Spider Man drawings; whose official biography boasts of his rise to "comic superstardom"; who, when toy manufacturers wouldn't give him full control over his Ultra Action figures, started his own company, "because those guys said I couldn't make my own toys."

"It was feverish," the auction house rep, Amye Austin, recalled later, of the bidding for Mark McGwire's ball. "There was an obvious desire to possess it."

Staring out from one of his Web sites (www.70hrball. com), McFarlane clutches his famous ball, wearing the smile of possession. This object of American desire, signed by the Paul Bunyan who hit it, was put up for bid by Guernsey's, an inventive auction house attuned to particular American cravings. On this day at the Garden, Guernsey curators were still fresh from sales of the personal belongings of President John

F. Kennedy: a JFK rocker, for $325,000; a tie clip ($6,500); a lunch bowl ($2,750); two pairs of long underwear ($3,000). Soon, Guernsey reps would select items to auction from the archives of Graceland: an Elvis pink leather matchbook cover ($4,250); an Elvis paperweight ($11,000); an Elvis black jumpsuit with a mint green neckline ($65,000). Later, with millennial zest, they would offer the "Gift of the 20th Century": the sale of the necklace Princess Diana wore on "the last official engagement before her tragic death." The lucky buyer was promised a stunning piece: "A brilliant cut diamond and marquise diamond scroll motif centre with a South Sea cultured pearl five stone and marquise diamond fringe drop . . . mounted in platinum, claw set." Initial bids were expected at $500,000.

On that January day in the Garden, there was another item up for bid: the ball hit by Henry Aaron for his 755th home run. That ball represents the greatest feat in baseball history. That ball marks 41 home runs beyond the old Record That Couldn't Be Broken, the old Greatest Record in All of Sport.

The ball itself has a story to tell. It was not marked with invisible ink, like Hank's 715th, or McGwire's 70th, or his 62nd, 63rd, or 64th, or Sosa's 66th. When it hooked inside the left field foul pole at County Stadium in July 1976, it rattled around for a while before being chased down by Richard Arndt, a member of the Brewers grounds crew. Officials of Bud Selig's team told the young man to turn it over. He said he didn't mind; he just wanted to present the ball to Hank himself. Team officials said no. When Arndt refused to give them the ball, he was fired and the Brewers deducted five dollars from his paycheck to cover the cost of the ball. Later, he moved to Albuquerque, put the ball in a safe-deposit box, and eventually got Hank to sign it. Arndt, now a furniture salesman, did it on the sly: it was at an autograph show in Phoenix, and he didn't tell Hank the significance of the ball he was signing. Now that he was putting it up for auction at the Garden, Arndt wanted Hank's blessing. He got it by agreeing to donate a portion of the proceeds to Hank and Billye Aaron's charity, the Chasing the Dream Foundation.

Compared to the frenzy over McGwire's ball, the bidding for Hank's was quiet, and the desire to possess it not so obvious. The ball never reached its minimum asking price of $850,000, and the item was withdrawn from bidding. (Number 755 sold later, at a lower price; Arndt donated a quarter of the sale, about $156,000, to Hank's foundation.) To Austin, the young Guernsey's representative, I put aside the question of whether any sphere of stitched cowhide should be worth $850,000, and asked her instead to compare Hank's record to McGwire's.

"It was a bit more impressive," Austin ventured, of 755. McGwire himself agreed; he called Hank's record "the greatest ever." Then why the disparity in bids? I asked Amye Austin. "I can't really speculate," she said, before excusing herself to attend to the pressing deadlines of the Graceland auction.

○

Eight months later, I stand in the second-floor office of Danrick Sports Enterprises. It's a fancy name for a business ensconced in a spare bedroom of a *Leave It to Beaver* house on a quiet side street in the Jersey burbs. Charlie Danrick spends his days making copies of old baseball games. It's a simple operation: a couple of cassette machines, an old reel-to-reel player, piles of index cards, and boxes of audiotapes lining the walls from floor to ceiling. On the tapes: deep, honeyed voices Danrick has captured and stashed away, to be copied and mailed out for a price.

"Name a game!" says the round-faced, square-glasses man, laying out a challenge. Danrick is sixty years old; he looks fifty; his expression suggests he just raced home from school to play catch.

"Hank Aaron's first game as a Milwaukee Brewer," I say. "First home game, in Milwaukee. April 1975."

"I can show you *exactly* where that is," Charlie Danrick says. "Watch."

He pivots, grabs three boxes, plunks them to the floor with a rattle, straightens up, reaches in, plucks a cassette, hands it to me: "4/11/75. Cleve. at Milw. Hank Aaron returns to Milw."

Boy, what a thrill today, huh? Bob Uecker's younger voice calls out from the County Stadium press box. *Unbelievable. Greatest crowd ever here.* On a cool April afternoon, Henry Aaron, in his twenty-second year in the big leagues, took a bow before 50,000 fans. They sang "Welcome Home, Henry," to the tune of "Hello, Dolly!"

"I have twenty-two hundred tapes in here," says Charlie Danrick. "My wife walks into this room and she says, 'What the hell, what is going on here?' And I say, 'Can you believe it? Just give me a date and I can pick out any game from any box.' She says, 'You don't even know where your socks are!'"

Don't be fooled; Danrick's business is licensed by Major League Baseball. He has his own Web site—www.baseball-tapes.com. And he sells "many thousands" of tapes per year, though he is careful not to say just how many thousands.

"As a kid, I remember having a little Philco radio," he's saying. "And I got interested in what was called DX—meaning if you tuned the dial carefully between your big high-powered stations, and the conditions are just right, you will be able to hear the other stations." Sounds familiar.

Growing up in Passaic, a couple of exits south, young Charlie Danrick was already listening to the New York games across the river: Russ Hodges for the Giants; Mel Allen at the Yankees' microphone; Red Barber with the Bums in Brooklyn. Now he started tuning in to Gene Kelly, and the 1950 Whiz Kids out of a station in Philadelphia. And he followed the rise of the great Pirate teams of Mazeroski and Clemente and Elroy Face from KDKA in Pittsburgh, Bob Prince at the microphone.

"The Gunner," Danrick says. "And his sidekick, the Possum. He had a buzz cut. But I was a big Brooklyn fan. And I used to tape games just for my own interest. And I had hundreds of old Brooklyn games on reels, put away. And I went away to college and my folks threw out the whole thing, thinking it was garbage."

Later, Danrick got his hands on a few precious games—the Cubs and the Dodgers in June of 1957, the Yankees and Red Sox three years later. He made master tapes. He bought a duplicating machine. And he took out an ad in a monthly called *Sports Collectors Digest.*

"I wanted to see what would happen. And lo and behold, thousands of dollars came in. In a week, I saw there was unbelievable interest in this stuff."

The thing took off. He was making a living. Then he got a registered letter from the Yankees. "And I thought, Holy Smokes, George Steinbrenner is after me!" Charlie remembers. "I was bootlegging Yankee games. But George Steinbrenner liked the idea! They invited me to Yankee Stadium to sit down with the Yankees' magazine brass. They wanted me to sell my tapes through the magazine. I could not believe it!" Lawyers for Major League Baseball were less enthusiastic: they sent letters ordering Danrick to cease and desist. But once the entrepreneur Peter Ueberroth took over as commissioner in the mid 1980s, both sides recognized a mutual interest: for a percentage share paid to the Game, Danrick could continue.

As he cranked out the tapes, he soaked in the different styles: Mel Allen ("probably one of the most recognizable voices in the country—he had that southern twang"); Red Barber ("the same way; he was the Dean"); Vin Scully ("unbelievable, there isn't anyone who can come close, no way could anybody draw a word picture like that"); Bob Prince ("a cheerleader as an announcer"); Jack Buck, out of KMOX in St. Louis. ("The guy had a velvet, velvet voice, and he made one of the great calls of all time—Kirk Gibson's home run in the last of the ninth inning in Game One of the '88 Series: 'I don't believe what I just saw. *I don't believe what I just saw.*'")

But for drama, or for tape orders, nothing will approach

the call of Bobby Thomson's shot heard 'round the world to beat the Dodgers. *The Giants win the pennant! The Giants win the pennant! The Giants win the pennant!"* Russ Hodges shouted on October 3, 1951. Danrick has a tape of that same moment from Liberty Broadcasting's Gordon McClendon. More than any other tape, the shot heard 'round the world helped build Charlie Danrick's business.

"I sold thousands," he says. "I can't estimate." McGwire's 62nd home run is another big seller. And the 1949 World Series between the Yanks and Brooklyn, with Allen and Barber calling the action.

What about Hank? I ask. What about number 715?

"It doesn't sell," he says. "It just lays there. People don't buy it." Not even Braves fans?

"I was contacted by Bob Hope, the director of merchandising for the Atlanta Braves," Charlie tells me. "And Mr. Hope wanted to sell that game of April 8, 1974, in the Braves catalogue. But he needed someone to do the taping. So he contacted me."

Danrick told him he had Vin Scully's description—*A black man is getting a standing ovation in the Deep South for breaking a record of an all-time baseball idol. And it is a great moment for all of us. . . .*

Hope was not interested in that version. The Atlanta marketer wanted Milo Hamilton's more conventional call: *There's a new home run king of all time, and it's Henry Aaron! . . .*

Charlie told him he didn't have that version. Hope said he could get it to him. He did. Charlie then sent Hope fifty copies and the Braves put it in their catalogue.

"And it bombed!" Charlie tells me. "It actually bombed. I never got a repeat order. Look at me. I advertise in *Baseball Digest*. Century Publishing, wonderful people. *Baseball Digest* reaches 350,000 a month. But even in *Baseball Digest*, it doesn't sell.

"It must rank as one of the greatest single events ever to happen in baseball. What Hank did is incredible! It just shattered an icon—it proved that records could be broken. When I got that game, I thought I had the premier selling game of all time. Something that would rival the Bobby Thomson game of 1951. Or even surpass it."

At the Guernsey's auction in New York, the furniture salesman, Richard Arndt, had said the same thing about 755—he thought Hank's ball might get as much as McGwire's. Not so there; not so for Charlie Danrick and the tapes of 715.

"Old World Series games dwarf that sale," Danrick tells me. "*League Championship Series* games dwarf the sale of Hank Aaron. He's at the bottom!"

Even now, I ask, in the twenty-fifth anniversary year? You must have had a *little* bump.

"No. Not one in every hundred tapes. I would say, one in every four hundred or five hundred tapes. It's ridiculous! Until this day, I can't believe it. I know; I see the facts before me. But it is difficult for me to understand."

Actually, when he thinks about it, it's not.

"I think it's racism," Charlie Danrick says. "It is racism. Why would an achievement like that—breaking Babe Ruth's record—not be recognized, not be sought by baseball fans all over the world? And the only thing that I would think of was that the record was broken by a black man. That's all. That is all."

In another time, a hero's worth would not be principally measured by his ability to generate sales. But in an increasingly commercial society, as value is defined more and more in terms of money and nothing else, marketability is a powerful indication of how a hero is considered in the culture. Fifty-one years after his death, Babe Ruth remains a potent marketing force, generating more than three million dollars a year in licensing fees for wristwatches, plastic figurines, ads for Lipton tea, American Airlines, Wheaties. "His name is fabulous," said Darci Ross, president of CMG Worldwide, which licenses the dead hero's image. "He's just a wonderful person, and everybody knows who he is." When I spoke to her earlier, she mentioned his popularity with kids—something Ruth cultivated with highly publicized hospital visits to sick children. By contrast, Hank's commitment to children has spread across decades and has sprouted a multimillion-dollar foundation to assist inner-city youths. But just as Babe is seen as the bigger hero, he's also seen as the kids' guy. And his past of womanizing, whoring around, even ordering the tossing away of fan mail that wasn't money or "letters from broads"—none of this, of course, is part of the image CMG is crafting of their long-dead client.

"You look at Babe Ruth," Ross told me, "and I've heard some of these things—not that it's cute, and I hate to say it, but he can get by with it, because he overshadowed that with his great side, the caring compassionate person with a great personality." Hank, of course, would never have been afforded the privilege of whoring around and having people think of it as cute. But it is not only Ruth's lingering power in the market that says something about how Hank is considered in the culture. If Hank Aaron's ball is pulled from the bidding, while Mark McGwire's soars to absurd heights; if Charlie Danrick can't make a sale of the greatest record in all of sports; if the home run king didn't pull down the big endorsements, it says something about the value of Hank in mainstream America.

Is this purely racial? Probably not; Michael Jordan, the biggest Gatorade–Wheaties–Ray-O-Vac–MCI–Chevrolet–Hanes Underwear–Space Jam man of all time, who, by the way, also played basketball, has proved that race need not limit a man from becoming a human product endorsement. "Michael Jordan transcended the issue of race," Richard Lapchick, the director of Northeastern University's Center for the Study of Sport in Society, had told me. The irony, he said, is that "he was able to do that because he never delved into issues of race." If Jordan had been like Hank, Lapchick said, and spoken out about racism, "he would never have been allowed to become a commercial success." So Hank's sustaining lack of popularity has to be considered in layers. Yes, he played in small markets; yes, his style was unassuming. He didn't have the flash. But the man had everything else you could ever want in a hero: strength, courage, perseverance; kindness, humility, consideration; speed, power, grace; a great smile, a loving family, humble beginnings; and a remarkable ability to triumph over adversity, over hate, over injustice. What a great American story. In considering how the gods of fame passed over Hank Aaron for so long, one can't ignore the color of his skin, or the fact that he was willing to talk about what he, and the other blacks of his sport, endured for so long.

"I know he suffered," Danrick says. "But you know: It will never change. In this country you're never going to have acceptance of minority races. You may have acceptance but you will never have appreciation. You're going to find bigotry. It's allowed according to the Constitution. It's just a part of America. There is no law that says that I have to like minorities. And this is what's going on here. What are you gonna do? What *can* you do? We can't change history."

We talk about Jackie Robinson and the hate he suffered when Branch Rickey brought him up in 1947. This, Charlie Danrick says, is what finally brought Jackie down. "It just ate him up and killed him." Danrick has a tape from a WMCA talk show on the day Jackie Robinson died, prematurely at age fifty-three, in 1972. "He had to fight these terrible battles," Roger Kahn, the author of *The Boys of Summer,* recalled on the program. "The letting loose of a black cat on the field, and saying, 'Here's your brother.' The holding up of shoes and saying, 'Porter, shine these.' The manager for Richie Ashburn saying, 'When you go into second base, I want you to slice the nigger.' This is the climate into which he came. And I think that prematurely aged him. It took years off his life."

"At least," Danrick tells me, "it didn't kill Hank Aaron. Thank God."

He looks at me, curious. "Seeing as you know Hank Aaron"—I smile, allowing the truth to be stretched—"is Hank Aaron bitter?"

Is Hank Aaron bitter? I recall Ed Wojciak's comment in Cooperstown: *Wouldn't you be bitter?* And from Ed's mom,

Irene: *It should have been a happy time. But it wasn't.* And from the commissioner, a remark aborted in mid-sentence: *I know that Hank was quite angry at one point. But I am happy that all that bitterness—*

Is Hank Aaron bitter? "I can't tell," I say to Charlie Danrick. "I think he's a lot less bitter than he was."

In 1992, eighteen years after Hank broke the record, a writer named Mike Capuzzo spent time with Hank for a piece for *Sports Illustrated.* Hank went up in his attic and pulled out a box of letters. *This,* he told Capuzzo, *changed me.* The article described a man who still kept a lookout for strangers approaching. Who still checked his rearview mirror for a car on his tail. Who still worried that his drinks could be poisoned. Who still felt unsafe, unless he was sitting at home, behind his ten-foot fence and electronic sensors. *SI* called the story "Prisoner of Memory."

Seven years later, I tell Danrick, I found Hank less like that. Though his daughter told me he still wouldn't ride in a convertible, Hank had seemed more at peace. With Capuzzo, he had shed tears, and said: "So many bad things happened. Things I'm still trying to get over." Seven years on, he told me, "It was tough, no question about it." But he added, "When I first got out of baseball, I was an angry man, probably. But now, I don't have time to worry about that."

For years, it seems, friends worried that Hank would not let go. In Milwaukee, I met an old teammate of Hank's from the Negro Leagues, Sherwood Brewer of the old Indianapolis Clowns. They played together in 1952. Brewer remembered Hank as an awkward second baseman, "but could he hit. Everything on a line." Of the hate mail, Brewer said, "He told me he doesn't know why he keeps that stuff. He'll still sit down and read it once in a while." Not only did the hate mail still have power over Hank; so did the ghost of the Babe. "Babe Ruth will always be number one," he complained to a reporter years after his retirement. He later said, "Throughout my career, I've known as long as you're black when you come into this world, you'll always be considered a second-class citizen." Reverend Jackson had told me that Hank was contending with long-lasting "racial mythology. Myths of superiority—that's what people were defending." And not just of the Babe. "Isn't it funny," Hank said in 1979. "Before I broke his record, it was the greatest of them all. Then I break his record and suddenly the greatest record in baseball is Joe DiMaggio's hitting streak."

By the time I talked to him, Hank didn't seemed worried about any of that. He told me, "I think about some of the things that my mother often tells me—things I have no control over, don't worry about."

Perhaps the relevant issue, I tell Danrick, is not whether Hank is bitter, but rather what lessons he took from this experience. Did it cause him to reshape his view of the world? I tell him what Hank had said in our interview: that a part of him had been carved out, and would never be regained. That part he identified as "not trusting people, I guess." So much accumulation; even among the well-wishers, so many people were unaware of his struggle or had the privilege of forgetting. Millions of white Americans *had* wished Hank well. Bob Costas told me he thought Hank had put "too much proportion" on the hate over the years, and not enough on the goodwill of white Americans. But Costas also acknowledged,

"You can hardly blame him, because he had to live through all the threats and racism. Emotionally, the greater impact was delivered by the hate." And Hank's sister Alfredia told Mike Capuzzo, "The bad memories are more profound. If someone dumps urine on your head during a game, it can spoil everything, spoil the two home runs you hit that day." And if you get 10 tons of hate mail, it can spoil the 20 tons of good wishes.

"I actually have no control over what happened, and how people think, and why they think the way they do," Hank told me. "Sometimes you think about it, and then it just passes you by. And I say, 'Hey, that's all right with me.'" Perhaps what Hank learned to do, ultimately, was to shrug his shoulders: *This is how people are; you can't change it.* And, *Be careful who you trust.* And, perhaps, another understanding: "My father has told me this," Hank's daughter said to me. "He said, 'Gaile, I want you to know that there is a black world and a white world.'"

No white American context exists for understanding what Hank experienced. It makes no sense to say, "If a white athlete had suffered this," and then compare the two, because in America, it would be impossible for a white athlete to suffer this. There is no parallel. In sport, the closest example might be the abuse Roger Maris received in breaking the Babe's single-season home run mark in 1961. But Maris's troubles were beans next to Hank's. As a black editor of mine, Sue Goodwin, once pointed out: "No one was saying, 'My gun is watching your white ass,' to Roger Maris."

There is also no white American parallel in the *expectation* of how Hank was to respond to the abuse. Anger was out of the question. "You can't react normally because of the white world out there," the Harvard psychiatrist Alvin Poussaint tells me one day when I visit him in his office in Boston. Dr. Poussaint, who is African American, has long been concerned with the portrayal of blacks in the media; he worked with Bill Cosby in developing the characters of the Huxtable family for *The Cosby Show*. "They didn't expect Jackie Robinson to show any anger when people yelled racial slurs at him," Dr. Poussaint says. "They didn't expect Hank Aaron to go raving and angry because he was getting hate mail. They wanted him to understand—you know, there are people like that." I ask the psychiatrist what kind of effect this could have on a man, keeping his rage inside like that.

"In some unconscious ways, you can just repress it," Dr. Poussaint says. "But other times you have to actively *suppress* it. You feel that if you in any way let it out, it's going to damage your public image—that the white community in particular wouldn't understand. Anger from black men is one of the things white America fears, consciously and unconsciously. When Hank Aaron was playing, you had the Black Panther Party, and it terrified America. And I think, because of the slavery and all the oppression, the lynchings, there's a feeling that the black man is a very threatening creature. Even with slavery, black men in particular learned that if you were accommodating, and looked the other way and didn't get angry, that you were rewarded."

Sammy Sosa understood this psychology perfectly, Dr. Poussaint says, during the next mega–home run chase, twenty-four years after Hank's. "He played the American psyche so well," Poussaint says. "He understood that if he was in any way threatening or boasting about how he was going to 'get' this guy, he would have been rejected by the American public, and they would have been down on him, hoping he would lose. I think he realized that by being into this brotherhood, and the 'best man,' and 'McGwire's great,' and so on, that he would play much better with the American people. And then he did the thing on *Saturday Night Live*"—Sosa parodied an old skit in which a stereotyped black Latin ballplayer says, *Baseball been berry berry good to mee*. "He just took it and turned it around. Like it was a joke. So he came across as someone who was kind, and he stood tall, and I think he gained support for that. Even though the American public was still with McGwire."

A year earlier, the inverse image of this had occurred when the basketball player Latrell Sprewell put his coach in a chokehold after a confrontation in practice. The incident generated months of coverage, despite the absence of pictures for television. Every piece of the narrative was duly noted: fines, suspension, the player's public acts of contrition, and whether they were sincere and made the man worthy of reinstatement. By contrast, when a white football player, Kevin Greene of the Carolina Panthers, attacked one of his coaches on live television, the story received little play. The Sprewell incident may have been more serious, but not by much: After a powerful shove of his coach, Greene kept coming, grabbing the coach by his collar; his physical abuse was limited only by the strength of the large men holding him back. Neither act was defensible. Yet, while Sprewell's attack was greeted with shock and discipline, Greene's was viewed as a "family disagreement."

"It was love taps," said one teammate. "We're all in this together," said another. Greene was suspended for one game,
an action couched in tones of regret by his head coach, Dom
Capers: "It's an emotional game. Emotions run high." Even
the coach who was attacked, Kevin Steele, said, "Football is
an emotional, aggressive game. Those guys are out there
fighting, okay? Kevin is a good person." And the following
day, Greene felt comfortable enough to joke about it: "I'm
sure someone did—at one time or another through high
school or pee wee football—probably want to jerk a knot in
some coach's tail. So I did it for all those guys so they can
help pay my fine. Send your dollars here to Ericsson Stadium." That comment provoked no public outcry; the NFL
took no action against Greene. He resumed play following
the team's one-game suspension and the incident was
quickly forgotten.

Why the sharp contrast in public awareness of the two in-
cidents? Is Latrell Sprewell somehow scarier to mainstream
America than Kevin Greene? If so, why? Alvin Poussaint says
this about black men and the deep fears harbored by white
America: "Should his anguish be let loose, he will become
even more dangerous, and he will be [among] the warriors
who will stir up the masses to attack white people." Kevin
Greene, as a white man, enjoyed benefits Latrell Sprewell
did not. This is what the presidential candidate and former
basketball player Bill Bradley calls "white skin privilege."

"When I was a rookie in the NBA," Bradley said in a 1999
speech about race relations in America, "I got a lot of offers
to do advertisements, even though I wasn't the best player on
the team. My black teammates, some of whom were better,

got none. I felt the offers were coming to me not only because of my biography, but because I was white." Bradley
calls white skin privilege "the flip side of discrimination." In
his speech, at Cooper Union in New York City, the former
New York Knicks star said, "While discrimination is negative
and overt, white skin privilege is negative but passive. It's a
great blind spot more than a painful boil, but in a subtle way,
the result is often similar. Most whites are unaware of it.
What I call privilege seems normal to them. It seems normal
because it is not seen in contrast with the experience of
someone who doesn't possess it."

Henry Aaron did not possess it during his home run chase
in 1973; twenty-six years later, Ray Rhodes did not possess it
when he took over as the head coach of the Green Bay Packers. When I went home for my twenty-fifth high school re-
union, an old classmate I hadn't seen in years made a joke
about the new coach. He took the old Packer fan vow of a
return to football glory—*The Pack Will Be Back*—and in-
serted a racial twist: "The Pack is black," he laughed grimly.
Rhodes and his two top assistants, Sherman Lewis and Em-
mitt Thomas, are African American. For generations, Wisconsin fans have thought of the Packers as family. "And for
many of them," wrote Eugene Kane, a *Journal Sentinel*
columnist who is black, "it was like coming down for breakfast each Sunday morning and finding Rhodes at the head of
the table."

The pressure on Rhodes when he took over for Mike
Holmgren, the white coach who had taken the team to two
Super Bowls, was immense. Blacks in Wisconsin, and else-

where, were rooting for him the way they used to pull for Hank; they badly wanted him to prove something by his success. Whites in Green Bay, meanwhile, were not accustomed to blacks in positions of authority, especially of their most beloved institution. Blacks make up less than 1 percent of the city's population; when I interviewed a black labor leader in the area ten years ago, he said he was constantly being stopped by well-meaning citizens asking him, "Which Packer are you?" And, as with any coach coming in, fans in Wisconsin expected Rhodes to bring the Packers immediately back to the Super Bowl; anything less would be failure. In a way, the man couldn't win. To make matters more pressurized, each day, on his way to work, he drove down streets named after his legendary white predecessors, Mike Holmgren and Vince Lombardi.

Early in his first season, when the team lost three games in a row, Packer fans lit up the radio talk-show phone lines: Rhodes had to go. A discussion followed in the press: Was Rhodes being given the chance a white coach would? The new Packers coach was barely halfway through the season. Was racism driving much of the criticism? "I have a difficult time accepting that it is," wrote *Journal Sentinel* columnist Cliff Christl, a self-described "aging white curmudgeon, born and raised in Green Bay when it was as white as its toilet paper." Christl didn't deny that racism exists among Wisconsin sports fans; he just doubted it was central to the calls to fire Rhodes. But Christl might have reconsidered had he spent half an hour browsing through his own paper's on-line Packer forum. A sampling:

I am just very depressed that RW [Ron Wolf, the Packers' general manager] has let RR ruin one of the most storied franchises in the NFL.

I guess everyone knew it was Holmgren who was the brains behind the offense.

I would like to know what the players really think of this clown. Don't hire people based on color, this is a great example of that.

One topic that never seems to go away is the fact that the NFL lags well behind the other major sports in the hiring of black head coaches. Well, what's the big urgency here? I mean, black head coaches in the NFL have for the most part done horribly and none of them have ever won anything.

Rhodes for water boy!

RR is a stinken monkey.

If you look back to Rhodes' glory days when he managed the astonishing number of TEN wins with the Eagles (and this stands out as the best coaching job EVER. He should be elected into the hall of fame immediately. In fact, they should rename the entire city of Dayton "Rhodesia.") who were his quarterbacks? Rodney Peete and Randall Cunningham. BLACK quarterbacks. . . .

they juked, they jived . . . they got JIGGY with coach Rhodes.

Instead of validating Rhodes' obviously Africanly–Americanly superior gameplan, Favre, the southern redneck, has taken it wholly upon himself to sabotage this ebony-born vision of glory. I think he [Favre] should not only be waived, but be charged with hate crimes! . . . RACISM! RACISM! RACISM!

Not a single fan objected to terms like "JIGGY" or "stinken monkey" or "ebony-born vision of glory." I counted just one fan in the entire forum who argued that Rhodes, with a record of four wins and five losses midway through his first season, should be given more of a chance. One sentiment prevailed:

Let's kick Ray out of Green Bay!

The calls for giving Ray Rhodes the quick hook struck one *Journal Sentinel* football columnist as "hilariously premature." But by the end of the season, when the Packers finished 8–8, out of the playoffs for the first time since 1992, general manager Ron Wolf agreed. After only a year on the job, Rhodes was fired. Was Wolf simply making a sound football decision? Everyone agreed it was a disappointing season. Reports indicated that Rhodes had effectively lost control of the team. Yet it is hard to imagine a white coach getting fired after going 8–8 in his first year. The only other Packer coach fired after a single season was Scooter McClean, who finished 1–10–1 in 1958. The Wolf move shocked many Packers; some black players expressed anger and disappointment. A black columnist for the *Journal Sentinel* called the firing "bizarre." For whatever reason, Ray Rhodes was not given much of a chance. How much that had to do with the public discomfort with a black man in charge of "one of the most storied franchises in the NFL," it is hard to say. But in analyzing Hank's chase, Dr. Poussaint talks about the problem some white fans have in transferring from white icons to black ones. In this analysis, for some fans, Ray Rhodes—no matter how good he would have become, no matter how many Super Bowls he might have won—could never have reached the status of a Lombardi, or even a Holmgren, just as Hank Aaron could never have been Babe Ruth or Joe DiMaggio.

"They were attached to Babe Ruth being the king," Dr. Poussaint says of fans in the era of Hank's chase. "So in terms of identification you have this bond, because they were white and he was white. And then the icon supposedly would become Hank Aaron, but they couldn't identify with him because he was a black man. Part of not wanting to identify with him was they didn't know how to. So in a sense you were taking away the opportunity to identify with the next icon. If there had been another white man breaking the record, they could have moved on to the next era. But it was difficult, still is difficult, for many whites to make the jump. Psychologically very uncomfortable."

O

The day after my visit with Charlie Danrick, I sit in the head-
quarters of the largest advertising firm on earth, waiting for
the Young Creatives. McCann-Erickson, with 1,000 employees in this midtown Manhattan building alone, has billed
more than $16 billion to Exxon, General Motors, Coca-Cola,
Microsoft, DuPont, Nestlé and thousands of other clients in
127 countries in the past year. The firm also handles the account for MasterCard. And MasterCard, through the Young
Creatives, has discovered Hank Aaron, twenty-five years after 715. He's part of their "Priceless Campaign," which
features life's moments you can't put a price on—"and for
everything else, there's MasterCard."

"It's a campaign of responsibility," Susan Irwin, the advertising giant's senior vice president and director of corporate
communications, tells me, without a speck of irony. The athletes chosen, she says, "should not be the brats of the world.
This is a value-based campaign, so athletes must reflect the
value system that MasterCard stands for." A generation removed from the heat of a race-based chase, Henry Aaron—
smiling, gray, and retired; showing no visible anger; a threat
no longer—has finally been chosen by Madison Avenue. He
is to personify the value system of a credit card company.

Just now the first of the Young Creatives walks in. He is
Eric Goldstein, twenty-eight, clad in hiking boots, jeans, a
black V-neck and a two-day stubble. Part of his creativity, I
surmise, derives from the fact that he gets to come to work at
a multi-billion-dollar ad agency dressed however he likes.
Eric's work for the campaign centers on crafting the images
for baseball's All-Century Team, which MasterCard is spon-
soring. The ad entices fans to use their card to win a chance

to go to the World Series with Hank Aaron and Willie Mays. Hank, Eric says, is at last being recognized as the greatest living ballplayer.

"And when you think of players of the century, you know, Hank is just at the top of everybody's list, I would think," Eric says. I enjoy hearing this from a guy who was three years old when Hank cracked 715. The McGwire-Sosa race, Eric believes, "made people look at Hank—like, 'Wow,' recognizing what an incredible feat it was. And that's why you're seeing him being covered more. But I think what we're saying—society's saying—we have this national treasure that we haven't recognized in such a long time. Let's embrace him. The increased love of baseball has really helped reestablish him."

He pops a tape into a VCR. We see hand-held images made to look like a dad's home video: "Camcorder, four hundred dollars" (a blond boy and girl waving from the family's front lawn); "three-hour tape, seven dollars" (the kids in the back of the station wagon, and a sign pointing to the stadium); "extra battery, twenty-five dollars" (the boy bounding down the steps, into the box seats); "home movies with Hank Aaron and Willie Mays—Priceless" (the Hammer, smiling and waving at the camera, his arm around the little blond boy).

"This is the wonderful Priceless Moment," Eric says.

I ask Eric if he's heard anything about what Hank went through to break the record. Yeah, he said, he'd seen something on ESPN about the death threats. "That's just another thing to admire about him," the young man says. "What I remember seeing on television was him reliving the moment he crossed home plate, where his mother just grabbed him and hugged him and wouldn't let go."

The next Young Creative walks in—Tim Bayne, twenty-seven, in leather sandals and shorts. Tim spent forty-five minutes talking with Hank on tape for another MasterCard spot, the one that relived 715. "Going down there I heard people that were saying bad things—that he was very bitter. 'You're not going to get anything out of him. He's angry because he didn't get the recognition that he should have gotten.' He wasn't bitter at all. He was really nice."

In researching his interview with Hank, Tim learned something of what Hank endured. The interview was also to be part of the Priceless Campaign, but only the happy reflections. For his spot, Tim showed the homer, with Hank's comments in a voice-over. As he rounds the bases, we hear: "I can remember the home run. . . . I hit the ball, and sixty thousand people start blowing! And they just blew it right out of the ballpark. It was a tremendous thrill. And especially my mother's face. She was in the stands smiling, and coming down to home plate. I felt like I made her very, very happy."

As Hank crosses the plate, we see his mother, charging through the crowd like a fullback, Hank's bodyguard with a hand on her back.

"You see him running, the mom running, and we just thought that was a fantastic video," says Tim.

"Can you rewind back to that point and freeze it?" I ask. The spot begins playing again. "Freeze it right there," I tell Tim. It's virtually the same picture I have in my scrapbook: Hank in a broad smile, and his mother with her back to the camera, arms flung around him. "So what's that image projecting there—right there? What is that saying?" I ask.

"It's like, you did something great and you're glad that

your mom was able to share it," Tim says. "It was just great to do something that made his mom and dad very proud of him."

Eric agrees. "If you take away the cameras and take away the crowd, it's still a child making his parents proud." This is why, the two young men tell me, it was chosen for the Priceless Moment.

"I want to tell you something that I learned about this picture," I say to Eric and Tim and Susan. I tell them about my scrapbook and the letter from Hank, and how I'd met Gaile Aaron, and what she'd told me about the bittersweet embrace. "And you hear, *pop, pop, pop,* and the cannons are going off—and you see his mom coming tearing through there," I say. "His mother thought he was being shot."

"Oh God," Susan Irwin gasps under her breath. The young men are quiet for a moment. "Eric and I didn't know that inside story," Tim says.

Not that they can be blamed; Hank himself had only told Tim he'd made his mother "very, very happy." Was it because Hank didn't want to relive it? Or because he was talking to one world, not another? Or because he knew this was not the kind of memory that would make for a Priceless Moment?

O

February 1999 had marked the beginning of an official reassessment of the value of Henry Aaron. It began in Atlanta, on the occasion of his sixty-fifth birthday. Yam and I were in town for the event. It was early afternoon, and we were outside Turner Field. I was hoping to find James McClain; after seeing him outside Hank's office a month earlier, I had told him that I would be back for the Gala.

A man was selling Braves T-shirts and Atlanta Falcons pennants across from the stadium. He said James usually shows up around this time; just hang tight and you'll probably run into him. I told the man why we were in town; he was not impressed. "It's been overdue!" he said. "Why you have to wait 'til his birthday party? He's just getting his recognition tonight for all the stuff he did back then, so what's up? It's just something they're doing for him. That *should* have been done. Lot of things should have been done, ain't done, what's up?"

I asked him what he remembered of the Chase, and the hate mail. "Well, we've been going through that all our lives," he said. "So what's up?"

Just then the man spotted James across the street, walking toward us in a red windbreaker. "James!" he yelled. "James, come here, boy!"

It was really good to see him. We had spoken once by phone, but he wasn't sure which day I was coming in. I told him Yam and I had to get to a press conference—Bud Selig was going to unveil the Hank Aaron Award—and then the Gala following. We made plans to meet later, at 11:00 P.M., in the parking lot of the Kentucky Fried Chicken, across from Turner Field.

"I'll take you down Ashby Street," James said with a big smile. "The barber shops are open late on Fridays!"

The Gala for Hank Aaron was black tie. I sat at a table in the back. The Temptations showed up, and the singer Jeffrey Osborne, and Mr. Cub, Ernie Banks, and Sammy Sosa and a

couple dozen other players, and Bud Selig and Evander
Holyfield and Jane Fonda and Ted Turner, who had brought
Hank back to the Braves' front office in 1977 and later pro-
moted him to vice president. Bob Costas emceed the event.
John Lewis was there, and Maynard Jackson, and Maxine
Waters, and the governor and ex-governor of Georgia. Jimmy
Carter sent a message by videotape. Andrew Young told the
story of the parade in 1966, and the good old boys outside
the American Hotel, and what that said about Hank and his
social impact.

President Clinton arrived, to polite applause, fresh from
his impeachment trial in Washington. When Jeffrey Osborne
rose to sing his pop hit, with the lines "I wanna wooo-wooo-
wooo," Hank and Jesse Jackson gladly took their turns at the
microphone for harmony. Osborne invited Bill Clinton to do
the same. The president declined; "I wanna wooo-wooo-
wooo" would not have been the best message to send to a
Senate that still had his fate in its hands.

"Presidents don't come to ballplayers' birthday parties,"
Reverend Jackson told Hank as the testimonials began. The
two men went back more than thirty years; in *I Had a Hammer,* Hank credited the "country preacher" with teaching him
that "the struggle is not to drink at a water fountain; it's economic." Now, Jackson told the Hammer, "It's about what you
did beyond the lines. Your adversity seems to have made you
better and not bitter. You turned pain into power." He recalled how Hank was never afraid to speak out when he saw
discrimination, unlike modern athletes obsessed with the
lure of marketing. "Many a giant between the lines," Jackson
said. "But moral midgets just beyond the lines. With all their

fame, they're indifferent to the crisis of the common people. I should never forget when the Bulls were playing the Lakers, and fifty-five people had been killed after the Rodney King explosion, and the media went to the athletes on both teams and said, 'Make a statement, what do you feel about fifty-five people dead?' They said, 'Don't bother me, I have no opinion, I am into my free throws.' You never chose your free throws—your home runs—over dignity. And so you are a citizen, a voter, a civil rights activist, you never put marketing over manhood, that's why you're not selling a lot of candy and shoes. And like David and Samson, the great biblical athletes, you're in that tradition of athletes who transform culture. Beyond class, beyond color, is something called character. You're in that rarefied air."

The Gala, Gaile Aaron would tell me later, "made up for a whole lot of stuff." Two thousand people filled the ballroom that night, and Hank and Billye Aaron had harnessed the occasion to do good. Tickets for the Gala were five hundred dollars (the press got in for free), with the proceeds—a million dollars—going to the Chasing the Dream Foundation, set up to help inner-city kids in Atlanta and Milwaukee.

It was past ten-thirty, and the president still hadn't spoken. I knew James would be waiting in the KFC parking lot, and I left the Gala early. James was pacing the lot. "I thought you weren't going to make it," he told me.

We swung back downtown to pick up Yam, and cruise the darkened streets. Yam drove; James sat in the front. "You're over here in Hank Aaron's area," James said. "Ashby and Martin Luther King Drive. And this right here is called Vine City, better known as the Bluff."

The streets were quiet; all the barber shops and rib joints were closed. "Did you ever play baseball when you was young?" James asked.

"I played in the park, every summer day I would play," I said.

"I played high school ball," he told me. "I was pretty good."

We rode in quiet for a time; for a few moments, I dozed.

"Right over there." James pointed. "Thousands of soldiers died in that ravine, what they call I-20."

We made a big circle around the city. Then back to Turner Field. Yam and I were leaving the next day. We got out to say our good-byes, and James pulled something out of his coat: two pieces of stone, scraping softly between his hands.

"These right here, when they tore down the old Braves stadium, this was marble off the old Hank Aaron statue," James told me. "I have a big chunk of it. It took me an hour to break these pieces off. This is what I do: I give this to you," he says, handing one to Yam. Then he turns to me. "And this is your piece. And what I want you to do is try to embronze something on it. Something related to us. And that's all I have to give you right now. But you've got a piece of history right there."

And then James McClain turned and walked off into the early morning darkness.

11

INHERITANCE

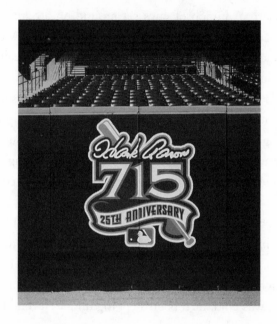

Atlanta, Georgia, September 1999

During the summer of 1999 I returned to Atlanta several times, seeking pieces of Hank's legacy. Each time, I tried to find James McClain. I wanted to see him again, to watch a

271

game with him at Turner Field, to talk more about Hank. First I tried the neighborhood—Georgia Avenue, past the stadium and across Hank Aaron Drive. I asked the guys hanging out at the KFC: "Popeye?" they said, calling him by the nickname born of his glazed right eye. Yeah, they knew him; no, they hadn't seen him in a few months.

Someone told me to check a liquor store downtown. This surprised me; James hadn't struck me as much of a drinker. I went there. A bunch of guys sat around on a curb, sipping sweet hard wine. No, they'd never heard of James McClain; nobody called Popeye sounded familiar either. I called the post office, and asked Wyman McElroy, the man who delivers the mail in James's old neighborhood, if he'd seen him lately. Months earlier, McElroy had been nice enough to get a message to James. "I used to see James McClain just about every day," McElroy told me. "But it's been a long time. I think he may have left town. Or maybe . . ." His voice trailed off.

James had been sick; one night he'd called me at home in Massachusetts, coughing from what he said was bronchitis, asking if I could wire him some money for penicillin before his cough turned to pneumonia. It was winter, and northern Georgia was cold; he'd been sleeping under eleven blankets, he said, in a shed somewhere near the stadium. Before we hung up, he said he was looking forward to taking in a game with me in the summertime. I sent him fifty bucks by Western Union.

Now, back in Atlanta, a friend here suggests James may have checked into a drug rehab. But he didn't have a drug problem, I tell her. Doesn't matter, she says. He might have said he did, so he could get a bed and meals for a couple of months. But if he's gone there, she says, it would be hard to know; they keep everything confidential. You could always try the homeless shelters, she tells me; there's a whole bunch of them. Or, you might consider that if he was sick, and sleeping outside, you know, maybe . . .

The next afternoon I stand at the corner of Peachtree and Pine, a few blocks from the gleaming center of downtown Atlanta envisioned by Mayor Ivan Allen and the Boss, Robert Woodruff, in the days when Hank and the Braves first came to Atlanta. There, in the upper floors of the skyscrapers that carved a new horizon, I had visited Andrew Young, and Maynard Jackson, and Congressman John Lewis. That heart of the New South is over my shoulder; in front of me is the Peachtree-Pine shelter, where five hundred homeless men sleep each night. It's a drab brick warehouse; inside, it looks like a converted parking garage. I'm thinking that somewhere in here, I might find James.

"James McClain," says a guy sitting at a computer terminal near the entrance. His head is shaved, the hair starting to come back again, stubble on pate. "Don't have the name. But that doesn't necessarily mean anything. Some guys don't like to use their real names. You can have a look upstairs. That's where the guys sleep."

A cluster of men gathers around a television, yelling and cursing and calling out encouragement: the Atlanta Falcons aren't doing so well. I wonder where these guys were on April 8, 1974—what lives they were living, what dreams they had in mind.

I stop to talk to a clean-shaven man, with a gentle smile

and boots of cracked leather. John Martin associates Hank's dream and struggle with the years of his own higher life: the life of a "suit and wingtip man," who read the newspapers every day and listened to National Public Radio driving to work; a man proud to put his daughter through college. It was "before my downfall," Martin says. "I got caught up in a fraud case." The feds, he says, "broke me like a twig." He did two years in federal prison, "came out and never really been able to crank it back up. Lost my family and everything that was dear to me." For eight years he's lived the cycle of the street: shit work, drugs, alcohol, souplines. I learn that a soup kitchen called The Cup starts feeding at 6:30 A.M. on Sundays; Blood and Fire feeds at noon. "It has changed and it has not changed," Martin says, assessing a dream and its progress. "I know in my lifetime change has been phenomenal. I guess a slaveowner coming back today, seeing Atlanta, he would probably want to go back to his grave. But there is that whole process now—the rift between those in the upper area and those in the lower area has grown even wider."

Nearby, a man my age named Carl tells me that back in April 1974, "The only dream I had was living to see twenty-five. I didn't think I was going to live that long, because of all of the things I'd been going through. A lot of people went through a lot of things like Hank Aaron did, that's just not advertised." When he was eight years old, Carl and nine other black children desegregated a public school in rural Georgia. "When we got off the bus, they were throwing things and singing these songs: 'One little, two little, three little niggers,'" Carl remembers. "I got beat up every day. And I had a teacher that took me to the back of the class and tell me that she don't teach niggers and told me to sit right down and draw pictures all day. And that's what I had to do. I even had a teacher tell me that in order to get treated like the rest of the class, I needed to get some Clorox and wash the black off me. And I went home every day and got my mama's Clorox and try to wash the black off me. I really grew up feeling like I was gonna be a target. And I feel I like I *am* a damn target. Because of my skin color. So Hank Aaron," Carl tells me, "hasn't been through nothing like what I have been through."

Next to Carl, sitting on the cement floor, is a middle-aged man named Terry. "I am very happy for Hank Aaron," he says. "He's got two chicken places over here on the West End. He employs black people. I am glad he played baseball. I am glad his wife Billye is a beautiful person. God bless Hank Aaron, and I hope when he dies—two thousand years from now—he's got a beautiful cloud waiting on him. *God bless Hank Aaron.* But Hank Aaron's reality has *nothing* to do with the average black man's reality in America. I got a dollar twenty-two in my pocket."

I climb the stairs to the second floor, still in search of James. I emerge, and stop short. In front of me is a vast in-door space, big as a college gymnasium, lined with hundreds of mattresses. There are as many as three hundred men here, sleeping, sitting, reading, leaning against their packs and rolled-up bundles of clothes, staring up at the ceiling. Almost no one is talking. The air is thick with the sweet-sour smell of men who've labored hard all day in the southern heat, for the minimum wage—vans ferry many of them to construc-tion jobs—but have no means to stand under a cool stream of water at day's end. The mattresses go on and on, blending into an indoor horizon. In the dim light, in the dank room, it looks like they go on forever. It feels like I've walked into some kind of Dickensian London in late-twentieth-century America.

"You can talk to the guys here if you want," says the young black man who helps run the shelter. "I mean, if they want to talk to you." But I can't do it; I can't walk up to each man's mattress and say, "Do you know James McClain?" I can't shout out, *"James! James McClain!"* and cut the quiet din of men who'd like to maintain whatever privacy they can imagine in their twelve square feet. So I just stand there, for a long time, taking in the view. James is out there, somewhere, within these walls or beyond, but I'll not find him here.

In fact I never would find James McClain. I would not get a chance to talk to him again, about his family, about his time in Vietnam, about where he felt his life was headed back in 1974, on the April night when Hank made history. But in looking for James, I'd meet a man who'd been there on the day when Hank caught up with the Babe. "I was in Cincinnati," the man tells me. "I was there when he tied the record. April 1974."

It's just before five on a Monday morning. The man is leaning against the brick wall outside the Peachtree-Pine shelter. I've come back because I'd heard about the fleets of white vans that swoop down from the suburbs to haul the legions of black men to their labors for the minimum wage. I came to see this. "Ah, you're here to see the slave ships," laughs the man from Cincinnati. "Been here and gone already."

The man's name is Thomas Duett. He wears a dark shirt,

dark plaid pants and a baseball cap that says "Gem City Steel." On the sidewalk beside him is a worn leather bag with a worn leather strap. We stand under the street lights; downtown glows, almost within reach. Draped halfway to the sky, there's a big red "H." The Hilton. That's where I'm staying.

"It was exciting," Thomas remembers, of 714. He was eleven years old; now he's thirty-six. The same age as Yam. "But you know, one minute, you want to be happy for him, but your joy is like sprinkled with a little terrorism. Is this man gonna die because he broke a record? A *baseball* record?"

Thomas tells me that he usually tries not to stay at a place like Peachtree-Pine. It's the bottom of the bottom, but it got late and he ended up here last night. He signed in as Frank L. Wright. "They don't know who Frank Lloyd Wright is." He laughs. "I mean, you got guys coming in here, they will sign Leonard Bernstein, you know what I'm saying? The people in charge, they are not culturally enlightened to a lot of different things. A guy can come in here with a Ph.D. and be sitting right here. You wouldn't even know it. You got guys with Master's degrees, welders, medical technicians, you got dental technicians. Every section of society is represented here. Sixty percent of these guys were the haves before. See, I used to think everyone out here belonged here. Until I was put in that position. And it has been a real struggle trying to get back."

It's no longer just a race thing, Thomas says. "It is a class thing. If you ever go to a place like India—it's a caste system. We have that but we don't admit it." Consider, Thomas says, what would happen to him if he went down to Turner Field to sleep. "Police will come and get you up outta there." During the 1996 Olympics, police made thousands of arrests of homeless people; one charge was "acting in a manner not usual for a law abiding citizen." "But if the Braves are in the playoffs," Thomas says, "you can run down there and camp for tickets." Like I did, with T, for the Packers games in the 1970s. "What's the difference in a hundred and fifty white people laying down here at the stadium to buy tickets, and me being down here this morning because I had to be?"

Sometimes Thomas works the labor pools. He has pounded nails, washed dishes, run a garbage landfill, boxed wine bottles on an assembly line, worked as a sous chef at a high-end strip joint. "Labor pools are part of the system," he tells me. "You gotta think, if you're running a major company, no matter what your name brand is, figure you got fifteen hundred employees—you can come in here and use the labor pools. It's cheaper. Build a facility, pay less money, use one-third of your workforce as temps and save on your benefits." In a town with a poverty rate of close to 20 percent, there are plenty of guys willing to do the work. "When the disposable diaper came out, you figured, 'It's not worth the hassle, I can use this and throw it away and buy another one when I need it,'" Thomas tells me. "That's how we do people now. We have disposable people. They are expendable: 'I can use this man. He's a temporary. I don't have to wash him. I don't have to re-fill him, I don't have to use him over. I can use him up and throw him away, because it is cheaper to go out and get another one.'"

Thirty-five dollars a day take-home will only let you eat and wash your clothes, Thomas says; even fleabag hotels run nearly two hundred dollars a week. As a result it has been almost impossible for him to get off the street. He says he fights depression all the time. But whatever anger he holds doesn't play on his face, doesn't rest in his eyes.

"Your grandfather worked at one job all his life," Thomas tells me.

"Yeah, fifty-six years," I say. "How did you know?"

"My grandfather did the same thing. They worked one job forever."

First light is creeping up; the downtown horizon softens. A jogger with a Walkman glides past.

"You know," Thomas is saying, "I don't run around preaching and all that, but I try to listen. Like, if I had an opportunity for anything I wanted, I would ask for what Solomon asked for: wisdom, understanding, and knowledge. You know, that is all he asked for. You can know something, and you can understand why, but if you don't have the wisdom to pursue it—like Hank Aaron. Seriously. He didn't make a fuss like they do now, all the trash talking. He didn't do that. He quietly set about doing what he was doing. And he accomplished his goal. Facing death threats and everything. Actually, he let me know that when a man really wants something, if you stick at it long enough, you can do it. If you keep with it, you can overcome any obstacle out there." It seems there are thousands more obstacles facing these men than there are genuine opportunities, but the prospect of accomplishment helps Thomas consider his days. Above all other trades, he's a chef, and at that, something of a gourmet. He wants to start his own restaurant.

I wish him luck, and look around. We've been on the sidewalk talking for two hours. Pale blue ventures up in the east. A Federal Express truck rumbles past. Atlanta's week is starting. I have one more question. "You told me that Hank Aaron shouldn't have the burden of a civil rights leader put on him," I tell Thomas, who had said earlier that he didn't think it was Hank's responsibility "to come and get these guys off the streets."

"And yet," I tell Thomas, "what he was doing at the time became part of something larger. I remember being twelve years old in 1968, and being aware of a struggle that a lot of people felt, a common struggle to add more water to the lake, and lift up all the boats. I mean, if that was a dream then, what is the dream now?"

"Whose dream?" Thomas wants to know. "His, or mine? Or the community's?"

"The community's," I reply.

At first Thomas speaks generally. He talks about affirmative action, and how it has little to do with the poor; about welfare and broken families; about black police hassling poor blacks much the way white cops used to hassle all blacks. "They are embarrassed by a lot of our situation," Thomas says. "Which I am, too."

Then he takes another crack at my question, through the prism of Hank. "To see a man win is an inspiration," he says. "Any time you see one of your own, so to speak, to come from sharecropping background, you know? Not so many generations removed from slavery. To see somebody rise like that, there is an inspiration. Seriously. If he can do this, then I can go out here and go back to school and reeducate myself to be

able to deal with today's society. But as far as the overall impact, you ask the average ten-year-old or seven-year-old black
child, or white child, what did Hank Aaron mean to society.
You get—'Who?' They don't know."

Thomas gazes down at the sidewalk, then up into my
eyes. "I think, on the one hand, if Hank Aaron had it to do all
over again, he would like to knock down the barriers in baseball," he says. "But on the other hand, I doubt seriously that
he would choose to break that record. Because he would
look at it like, it put undue burden on him. It caused a lot of
problems. You see, when I came to Atlanta, I got into the
shoe care business. Shining shoes in an upscale shoe shop,
making decent money—Executive Shoe Care Center, on the
corner of Spring and Mitchell, called Excellent Shoe Care
now—and he was one of my customers. And I met him per-
sonally and talked to him, and told him all about the game in
Cincinnati. We used to pick up and deliver shoes from CNN
and all that, and he would come in and pick up his shoes.
And he really looked like he was tired of all this. I mean, I am
looking at him in awe, like this is one of the greatest men
ever. We talked just as freely as you and I. But I am telling
you—he is a very subdued man."

The rush hour has begun; in an hour, I'm supposed to see
Dick Cecil, the Braves executive, at his house near Piedmont
Park. I say goodbye to Thomas and drive to the Hilton, to
shower and change. On my way back out, I stop to pick up
my rental car from the parking valet. A white woman has
been waiting for her car for nearly five minutes. Arms crossed,
tapping her feet, she is furious. "This is *supposed* to be a spe-

cial service," she fumes. "You'd think if it was busy, they'd get more *people*." Her week is off to a bad start. On another day, I might feel just as she does.

Twenty minutes later I am moving through the sensuous greens of the Deep South and turning into Dick Cecil's driveway, under a brick portico and up to his work studio. He greets me with a warm smile. With his broad, freckled face and quiet, gentle way, he looks like the Nebraska man he is. For that matter I can picture him standing by a farm silo in Wisconsin.

"I figured you came for these," Cecil says, sliding open a black file drawer labeled "Baseball" and plucking two sheafs of letters. I have read excerpts of the hate mail and the threats. But I haven't seen them for myself. I want to reconnect, one last time, with what Henry Aaron experienced in the terrible time leading up to the greatest record in sport.

"It wasn't just southern hate," Cecil says. "It was Yankee hate. It was universal hate. Vicious stuff."

He leans back—dock shoes, blue slacks, a gray athletic jersey, buttoned down halfway—and watches me leafing through the mail.

> *Niggers are the same as apes and have the morals of an alley cat and are Parasites and the Scum of the Earth. The time has come to send the niggers back to Africa and the Jews to Israel for the good of this country and then send the nigger lovers to hell. Hitler did the Jews. He was a good man. Hitler got rid—*

"Jesus Christ," I whisper. Cecil is looking intently at me. He wears a pained smile—it looks a bit like Felix Mantilla's better-to-laugh-than-to-cry smile. I start looking through more letters, thick and heavy between my fingers, but really, there's no need to read more.

"When the first threats started coming, I went to the FBI," says Cecil. He was a vice president of the Braves at the time. He arranged to bring in Atlanta policeman Calvin Wardlaw to be Hank's personal bodyguard. He arranged for Carla Koplin to wade through the mountains of mail. He tried to screen a lot of mail from Hank's eyes. As the record approached, he called up George Plimpton to write a book chronicling the night of 715. He got Pearl Bailey to fly in for the national anthem that night. And, day after day, he talked to Hank. "No athlete," says Cecil, "has ever gone through what Henry went through. I mean, some guys get a death threat and they are out for three days. Henry had threats for almost a year, continually, and he kept playing. I don't think he missed a day because of the death threats.

"And I will tell you who helped him through it," Cecil says. "It was Billye. Billye had a lot to do with him getting through it." And, when the time came, Hank made it clear that there was someone else there for him, too.

"One of the proudest days in my life is when they did the premiere of the film"—*Chasing the Dream,* the one Denzel Washington produced a few years ago—"they sent me an invitation and I didn't reply. I went to it at the last minute. Henry got up and he started talking, and he said that there were two people that really helped him through that period. 'And one of them isn't here today.' And Ted Turner said, 'No, he is here. He's in the back.' And Henry gave me credit. Me and Billye. He said, 'Those are the two people.' Totally unexpected. It was just an unbelievable moment for me, to be recognized for what I didn't know that I did during that period."

Behind his steel-frame glasses, the rims of his eyes look red. "Henry and I are very, very good friends," Dick Cecil says.

As we speak, the votes are piling up for the All-Century Team, sponsored by MasterCard. Soon, an old bugaboo would come visiting Hank again: Though he got a lot of votes, he didn't make the starting lineup. Ted Williams is starting in left field; Willie Mays in center; Babe Ruth in right. Hank is on the bench.

"Ruth came at a time of spanning World War I and World War II," Cecil says, seeking to explain Hank's Ruthian problem. "Baseball was king at the time and Ruth was king of all baseball. He was a folk hero. The Japanese during World War II would use his name in trying to provoke the Americans. He was a figment of the grandfather's mind. And you know, maybe Henry—in fifty years—maybe when he's dead, he'll get the recognition that he deserves."

O

On my last day in Atlanta, I head south, toward the exclusive neighborhood of Cascade Heights. For months, I've been trying to reach Billye Aaron. She has been busy, in and out of town, and, perhaps, wary of a guy who claims to be writing a kind of tribute to her husband. A lot of white people have sought to make money off of Henry Aaron over the years—

Richard Arndt, the man who caught 755 and surreptitiously got Hank to sign the ball years later, is only the latest. Why should I be any different?

For those reasons, it seems, Hank has declined to talk further with me. I assume that he has grown skeptical of my motives as the project progressed. And why shouldn't he be skeptical? "Not trusting people" was his own assessment of the legacy of racism. And I suppose I can't blame him if he sees me as just another white guy hoping to make money off his name.

Billye Aaron, though, has agreed to sit with me for a short while. And now I am turning past a sign warning of guard dogs, and up the circular drive to my old hero's red brick, white-pillared house. Mrs. Aaron greets me, cordial but cool, at the family's front door. We sit in wingback chairs in the entranceway. Fresh flowers sprout from a large vase on a table.

I ask her first about the chasm in memory: How the African Americans I've spoken to, almost without exception, remember vividly what her husband endured; how the whites, with some exceptions, do not—and express shock or even denial when told about it.

Mrs. Aaron's own roots in the civil rights struggle go back to the early 1960s, long before she met Hank. Her late husband, the Reverend Sam Williams, was a prominent figure in the movement. He was a founder of the Southern Christian Leadership Conference, and taught philosophy at Morehouse College. One of his students was Martin Luther King, Jr. Mrs. Aaron wades slowly into my question. "When you compare the differences in the memories of the experience itself, it doesn't surprise me that whites have a very different memory of or understanding of what was happening then," she says. "That selective memory exists today."

I tell Mrs. Aaron what I've learned about what her husband and Felix Mantilla and Horace Garner experienced in the Sally League in 1953; how Felix told me that, after forty-six years, no one had ever asked him about his story.

"And this surprises you?" she asks.

"Not anymore," comes my reply.

And I would not be surprised a few months later, when a white pitcher playing for Hank's team, and young enough to be his grandson, lit into minorities, gays, and immigrants in an interview with *Sports Illustrated*. John Rocker's venomous comments against foreigners, Japanese women, "some queer with AIDS," and a black teammate he called "a fat monkey" must have not really surprised Hank very much—not after living the life he's lived. When WSB Television asked him about it, he sounded tired. "Someone who feels this way," the Hammer said, "is a very sick person." Some observers would see an opportunity for education. "Here in the South, we have witnessed change in even George Wallace," Andrew Young would write in the *Atlanta Journal-Constitution*. "Why not John Rocker?" Saying that Rocker's "deep-seated prejudices" came to the surface in frustrating moments after the Braves lost the World Series to the Yankees, Young would suggest that the young man cracked under pressure in the face of a "ferocious" New York press and repeated taunts from Yankee fans. "Rocker might learn something about dignity and restraint," Young would write, "by reading about the experiences of Jackie Robinson and Hank Aaron, who endured the indignities of segregation and ugly race-baiting. . . . The crowds and the atmosphere were worse for them than Rocker could ever imagine. Yet Robinson and Aaron never lost their cool." Later, Young would give Rocker a copy of his civil rights memoir, *An Easy Burden.* "Welcome to the struggle," Young would inscribe. Then the old aide to Dr. King would take the young pitcher out to see the home run king. They'd meet at Hank's new auto dealership, Hank Aaron BMW. When they emerged, Hank would say, "I'm glad I had the chance to talk with him. What he said was very offensive. But I do forgive him."

So no, I tell Mrs. Aaron, thinking back on Felix Mantilla's experience, I guess I should not be surprised that no one ever asked him what he went through.

"What surprises me," Mrs. Aaron laughs, "is that you'd be surprised. That white people would have any particular interest in this. In the hardship. As a matter of fact, I guess in some ways many of them seem to feel that if you've been fortunate enough to have the skills to play the game, I mean, what more can you ask for? You're there, you played in the game, you are quote-unquote reaping the benefits. They don't stop to think about the fact that just being a black person in an extremely racist country where everything is predicated on color—there are all the differences in the world."

Mrs. Aaron is reflecting a separate reality, a common knowledge among so many American blacks. She quotes W. E. B. DuBois, the noted black intellectual who taught at Atlanta University in the early 1900s: *The problem of the twentieth century is the problem of the color line.* "You cannot escape it," she tells me. "Any way you look at it, it all boils

ME AND HANK

down to: Are you Mark McGwire or are you Hank Aaron? If you are Mark McGwire, you get all of the adulation, all of the accolades, all of the everything that white America can put on an achievement like that. If you are black and you do it—put the shoe on the other foot. Sammy Sosa would not have gotten that kind of attention. His baseball will not be as valuable to white America as a Mark McGwire baseball." (At the Guernsey's auction, Sosa's 66th homer ball sold for $150,000, 5 percent of McGwire's 70th.) "And Hank Aaron's 755th home run ball was nowhere near as valuable to white America as Mark McGwire's 70th home run ball."

I know, I tell Mrs. Aaron.

She looks at me curiously, through large frames. Her hands are folded in her lap. Her demeanor is serene, unflappable. Her hair is gray. I hear laughter coming from the next room. It sounds like Hank's.

I tell her about my reaction to Cooperstown: the room for Babe and the wall for her husband. Billye Aaron says, "That's America."

"That's exactly what Dusty Baker said," I say.

I tell her I'm aware of her own roots in the movement. And yet I wonder how much of her own analysis was shaped specifically by her husband's experience. "How much of your witness to that shapes what you are saying right now?" I ask.

"I have lived in this country all my life," Billye Aaron tells me. "I have lived in the South all my life. I've lived it, I've breathed it. I have survived it. And nothing really is new or surprising to me. Because I know white people better than they know me. And I know pretty much what one can expect. And I'd rather be pleasantly surprised."

We're running short on time. An architect has arrived to consult with Mrs. Aaron on a remodeling project. I have time for one other question. And so I ask her what I asked her husband—and Andrew Young, and Maynard Jackson, and John Lewis, and Dusty Baker, and James McClain, and a man on the street named Thomas: Was Henry Aaron's struggle part of a larger movement?

"It happened," Billye Aaron says of the Chase, "during the time when many African Americans were coming face to face with the whole reality of racism and oppression, and how we had not been able to partake in the American Dream. And we were all assuming a certain role for taking on the responsibility for freedom. For gaining our freedom. And without anybody putting a label on it, without anybody saying, 'Oh, I'm going to do this'—you just got caught up in it. And it became a self-edification, if you will, to express one's humanity. And to say that this had been going on too long, and too many people had died.

"Sometimes," Mrs. Henry Aaron says, of her husband and of so many others, "you just had to do what you had to do."

O

Henry Aaron could have spent his retirement on the golf course, or sitting behind an autograph table, or doing the rubber chicken circuit. Surely he is no stranger to a nine iron, or to the baseball card shows that are the stock in trade for many a retired ballplayer. But for years, Hank's deepest commitment—more than his business ventures with Church's fried chicken, or Arby's roast beef, or BMW, or the CNN Airport Network, or even his vice presidency of the Braves—has been to young people.

Hank has always been into the kids. Not in a mugshot-with-the-sick-child-in-the-hospital-and-then-off-to-the-next-photo-op kind of way. He's done his share of those visits, but mostly, it seems, Hank's connection to youth has been made quietly. A few years ago, former Atlanta mayor Maynard Jackson saw Hank walk into a basement room in a building at Morehouse College and take a seat in the back. It was an anonymous fundraiser and there were no cameras. Hank was just showing his quiet support. Decades earlier, during his chase, he'd made it a point to respond to the young people who'd written to support him; I have the evidence, with yellow tape marks on the corners. There wasn't much written about that, either. And there were no reporters present on the day in 1961, outside of County Stadium in Milwaukee, when Hank stopped to sign an autograph for a ten-year-old boy. The child, Terry Stephens, had been waiting patiently outside the clubhouse. All his friends had left; all the fans had left; all the other players had left. When Hank emerged, it was just him and the boy. Hank signed Terry's glove and asked him how he was getting home. "On my bike," Terry said. It had been a day game, during the week; rush hour was approaching. "You don't want to be riding up 35th Street in that traffic," Hank told Terry. He put the boy's bike in his car, stopped and bought him a hamburger, and drove him home.

"Everything about Hank," my friend Vic Thomas would recall thirty-seven years later, "was always storybook." To this day, Vic added, "he is very concerned about the kids, and the youth, and the future. And I think that's very cool."

INHERITANCE

O

The day I turned eighteen—January 15, 1974—my father honored me with eighteen baseball tickets of my choice to the upcoming Brewer season. This was to be the year Hank would break the record in Atlanta, the year before he came back home. The birthday certificate was written like a legal brief, on parchment-like paper, and on it Dad had pointed out that I could choose "Eighteen (18) (xviii) tickets to one (1) (i) game, or one (1) (i) ticket to eighteen (18) (xviii) games, or nine (9) (ix) tickets to two (2) (ii) games," and so on, and then it was embossed with a notary stamp, and, with the flourish he could muster from his frozen hand, his fountain pen applied: *Thomas L. Tolan, Jr.* When he gave me the certificate, he could not suppress his glee at this use of his legal skills.

Three and a half weeks later, on February 10, we checked my father into Columbia Hospital, the place where I was born. He was forty-nine years old. He'd been complaining of a stomachache; I remember hoping he didn't have an ulcer. My mother, as it turns out, was more concerned.

Six days later, Larry Tolan died. A doctor told us it was cancer, and that he'd had it for a long time. That pack a day of Camel straights would be the culprit. Because of the M.S., the man said in his doctorly way, Dad could no longer "appreciate pain." It was the lone mercy of the disease: he didn't feel the pain, didn't even know he was sick, until the end.

In those five sleep-short days before he died, everyone was home. Mom and the six kids. At the hospital, we'd take turns watching over my father, who was mostly comatose but not completely unaware. As Mary sat with him, he suddenly opened his eyes. Fingering his hospital gown, he said he'd been sure to put on his finest for her visit. Another time, as John got up to leave, saying he had to go do his homework, Dad's eyes opened again. "Well, John," he said, "it's been a scintillating conversation." At some point during the last hours, Tom and Mary and John stood at Dad's bed, singing *Chattanooga Choo-Choo* and *I Got a Gal in Kalamazoo* and *They Can't Take That Away From Me.*

As for me, I slept on a cot beside my father, a little while before he died. In the middle of the night I woke up to a terrible moaning, coming from somewhere deep within him. *Dad?* Nothing. *Dad? Dad, can you hear me?* No response. Just the pain, riding on ghostly moans. Was he thinking anything? Did he hold in his mind a picture of my mother, maybe, at a lake in Maine in the summer of 1948? Or the Tolan eyes of his son Tommy, staring back at him a year later? Or perhaps he was considering some mundane detail, like the family station wagon, still stuck over with Howie at the Downer Garage. Or was it just the pain? I wonder if he even knew he was dying.

When spring came, I chose my eighteen (18) (xviii) tickets: Nine games of two tickets each. I watched another eighteen-year-old, Robin Yount, play shortstop that year. Mary, my sister, had a crush on the kid who was bound for the Hall of Fame. That year, I went often with T, and with a close family friend, Michael Brickley. Once, when a pop foul came our way, I chased, and misjudged it. It landed behind me: on my seat, next to Michael. He looked down at it, curious, as a boy came and snatched it. I raced back and struggled with the kid for a moment, then realized I was now a man. I let go.

In the numbness after death, I readied my scrapbook for the coming 1974 season. A strong man in Atlanta, at the risk of his family and his own life, was seeking justice; seeking to overcome what history was throwing at him. And I was going to record it.

Fifty-one days after my father died, I wrote the numerals "715" in large block letters. I filled in the letters with a red ballpoint pen. When I open my scrapbook to that page, I see how I did it: furiously, in tight up-and-down strokes, filling the blocks, making them vibrate.

O

It's a summer night, warm and clear; as perfect for baseball as perfect could be. Banks of lights gain strength against a gathering dusk. On the inside, there's a hum, an intensity: The division leaders from Houston are in town. On a Monday night, the stands are filling up. The pennant stretch drive is upon Atlanta.

From the press box at Turner Field, I gaze out at deep green in the shape of a diamond, and the earthen paths where grown men play. "When we were little kids," Phil Niekro had told me, "we were trying to play a man's game. As soon as we got to the big leagues, we were men playing a little boys' game." The diamond is empty, now, but I can narrow my eyes and see the Hammer, again, breaking on the pitch, sliding hard and safe into second. Or lacing one into the power alley in left, against the wall on a line, digging into third with a triple. Or charging from right, coming up throwing, a rocket to third to nail a gambling runner. Or rounding the bases as cheers thunder down, the pennant is won, and teammates prepare to hoist him upon their shoulders. In that last moment, it is 1957, and my father is thirty-two years old, embracing my mother, hollering for joy: witness to a younger man's speed, and power, and brilliance.

Sportswriters look over their notes, the public address man at the microphone clears his throat. I walk back to the grandstand, down the ramp, and out of the stadium, against the flow of fans coming in. At the corner, by the KFC, I look back at the stadium, glowing like a great spaceship.

"Excuse me," comes a voice from the sidewalk. A man and his wife are sitting at the edge of the parking lot. "We're trying to get to the game, and we're a little short of the cash."

I don't know if five dollars will help, but that's what I offer. I join them on the curb. His name is Kevin McThan; she is Dollena, a cardiovascular technician, out of work—been that way, it seems, for a long time. She's in a faded yellow tank top, gym shorts and beat-up Coca-Cola flip-flops; he wears running shoes, but no socks. He's a sheet metal man, experienced in heating and refrigeration. He, too, is unemployed. But he has an idea.

"I'm not going to be a millionaire, I'm going to be a billionaire," he says. His dream is deeply rooted in the American Dream: to develop a new idea, claim a patent, sell it, and rise above the masses. His invention, Kevin says, would "change the automotive industry." All he needs is an investor.

"I just need that one person just to listen to me," he says. He sips his can of beer from a paper bag. Got it for sixty-three cents at the gas station. Previously, Kevin says, he came up with a theft-prevention device for shopping carts—once you leave the lot, it starts beeping and a brake comes on. And he developed a gadget for dispersing a shot of cleaner into the toilet bowl every time you flush. Each time, he says, someone beat him to the patent. But now, he's sure he can make it. He asks for my help.

I tell him I'm just a journalist, not a corporate guy. "I don't move in those circles," I say.

A white limousine pulls up across the street, drops off its passengers, then glides away. "We've been going through a lot of *changes*," says Dollena. The government, she says, tore down the place where they were living, in order to build a jail. They've been struggling to find a stable place ever since.

Dollena says she loves to write poetry. And now she is scribbling, pausing, looking up, scribbling, on a loose sheet of my notebook paper. Kevin tells me, We just want to go sit in the ballpark for an evening. "It's something to relieve our tension. To take off the stress. To think. To relax." These are the same reasons my friend Ed Wojciak likes to go to the games.

Now a black limousine pulls up at the same far curb. "They've got booze in there somewhere," Kevin says. "And with my invention, they sit there in their limo, and they hit a button and booze will come into their car. I have something that can go in any car. Forget about booze, anything you want."

I tell Dollena my story of Hank. "Hank *Aaron*," she says, eyes brimming. "That moved you *real good*. I'm going to write a poem about that."

As dusk deepens, the glow from the stadium lights grows sharper. The national anthem drifts over the walls. The black limousine rolls away. Fans stream in, backpacks slung on shoulders, foam tomahawks in hand.

The McThans live poor; I'm not sure they really intend to spend their scant resources on the game, its four-dollar hot dogs, its five-dollar beers. But they insist: they're going in. We part, and they walk toward the ticket booth. I stand back, in the open plaza, beside the bronze statue of Hank, watching to see if they will enter the stadium. In line for tickets, they glance back and wave; I wave back at them. I look away, out of respect; when I look back again, they're gone.

O

The game is beautiful to watch. With my press pass, I move around the park, wherever I please, amidst 40,000 fellow Americans. It is humid and windless and the beer is cold. The grass is well mowed, in stripes dark and light. By the left-field foul pole stands a bottle of Coke, forty feet high.

In the late innings, the pressure builds. The game is tied and the Braves have two men on base. A Houston coach walks to the mound; thousands chop the air and make a war chant. A man comes down from the grandstand to snap a picture from the field-level seats. A rookie steps in to pinch-hit. It is all electric. The rookie swings, and drives the pitch on a line. It lands inside the chalk, on the soft grass in front of the left fielder. The Braves take the lead; the place is like thunder, mad with delight. It is a deep delight, abiding, of a kind not confined within these walls.

"The Mets play Atlanta starting Tuesday!" my sister Kath would write me from Brooklyn a few weeks later. Thirty-five years after bringing me to The Popcorn Stand, to the Braves, and to Hank, she has rediscovered baseball. She still has her Duke Snider glove from the 1950s; in the spring, in Central Park, she taught her daughter Alice how to throw and catch. "I'm starting up conversations with strangers now!" she would write as the playoffs approached, reminding me of the possibilities embedded in the game.

"All restraint is out the window and imagined divisions like race or age or gender or class—forget it—we're fans. Yesterday I had to leave the game in the fifth inning to do some errands and check in with Alice at the music school. Up out of the subway I see two guys (black, twenties, cool) in a car sitting waiting for the light to change. The game is on. I yell to them, What's the score? They look at me, don't understand, I have to yell it twice more and they tell me 3–2, the Mets.

"We thumbs-up, I go on, walk up and down Second Avenue, finding a liquor store with the game on, the guy graciously allows me to watch until it goes into extra innings and I have to get Alice and take her up to the bus that's going to East Hampton where her friend Mara and Mara's family are for the weekend. I get her on the bus, take the subway down to Dean & DeLuca to get some fancy bread and salad greens, go into the subway, loaded down with Alice's violin and backpack and the grocery bags. There's a guy reading the sports page. He's not reading about the Yankees but about the Mets. I go up to him, say, Excuse me. He looks up abruptly, quickly trying to assess whether I'm dangerous, insane, should he step back from the track. I say, do you know who won the Mets game today? No, he says. I back off. He relaxes, explains he just got out of work. Two guys are standing nearby. They tell me the Mets won, 3 to 4. But they don't know how. When I get home, I learn it was Todd Pratt, subbing for Piazza because Piazza has a swollen thumb. Piazza kept telling Pratt during the game, 'It's okay. You can hit off these guys.' And he did."

Pratt, the substitute for the star, hit the game-winning homer; that day, New York went crazy.

"It's a great game, Sand."

Someone is riding a hard rhythm on the organ at Turner Field. Delirium continues. The rookie, who delivered when it mattered, is in the dugout, getting high-fives all around. I take a long, cool drink and sweep my eyes across the bleachers, right to left. Bud Light. UPS. Porsche. Bell South. Kodak. Napa. Home Depot. Panasonic. Delta Airlines. And there, out in left field, nestled amidst all the shouting, is a simple number, silent and dignified:

715.

I gaze at the number, until it blurs. Again I see the lope around first base, the forearm shiver at second, the handshake and slap on the butt at third, and the young teammate, Ralph Garr, standing at home, taking hold of the older man's leg, for his last step. Guiding it home. And his mother, racing toward him at all costs.

But it is not memories of the man—of his dignity, his

courage, his brilliance that seemed to come without effort—
that I carry with me most. It is more deeply imbued. It is a
grace, from a silent teaching that Henry Aaron offered. He
offered it by standing up under a terrible burden. He offered
it by writing to a kid to tell him he was not going to let him
down, and that he was grateful for the kid's support, and that
everything was going to be all right. He offered it by fighting
for possibility in the midst of the threats of terror, in the
midst of deep denial about his proper place in American history. And by risking his life for the ideals we say we hold. In
the words of Reverend Jackson, Henry Aaron "had to fight
America to fight for America. I mean, that is our story."

And Hank Aaron offered his silent teaching in ways I am
only now beginning to recognize. As I left the ballpark on
that warm, sticky night and drove north, I was thinking about
this teaching—how it had a lot more to do with justice than
it did with baseball. It occurred to me, alone in the car, that
that old raggedy scrapbook—its pictures falling out, its pages
slowly flaking away—was my first work in journalism. A doc-
umentation of one man's dream, and of all the pain and possibility within. Hank helped set me on my path.

"Think about all the people Hank motivated," Dusty Baker
had told me that day in the visiting manager's office. "You're
an example. I'm an example. There are tons of us running
around that Hank had a direct influence on," the manager of
the San Francisco Giants said. "Whether he knew it or not."

SOURCES AND ACKNOWLEDGMENTS

The seed for this book was a story I produced for National Public Radio. It was a story I'd long wanted to tell, and I considered myself lucky to collaborate with someone with the keen ear and sensibilities of Sharon Ball, the inspired senior editor of NPR's Cultural Desk. NPR editor Sue Goodwin helped hone the story into its final form, and my friends at *Weekend Edition*—including senior producer Ken Hom, senior editor Gwendolyn Thompkins, and host Scott Simon—put it on the air. After the piece aired, on April 3, 1999, just before the twenty-fifth anniversary of Hank Aaron's record-breaking home run, I was unsure whether anything more would come of it. I certainly didn't count on Paul Golob going out for a Manhattan stroll that morning with his Walkman tuned to NPR. Paul, a more diehard baseball fan than even I am, thought this story would make a good book. As a senior editor at The Free Press, he was in a position to do something about that. Paul contacted me, and in a short time we had a working plan. In subsequent months, Paul proved to be an enthusiastic, good-humored, insightful, and hands-on editor, whose attention to detail and to the larger picture were vital and deeply appreciated. Thanks also to The Free Press for its enthusiastic support from the first moment of this project, from design to marketing to sales to additional editorial support. In particular, I thank assistant editor Alys Yablon, publisher Paula Duffy, editorial director Liz Maguire, copy editor Ann Adelman and copyediting supervisor Carol de Onís.

Research help came from several quarters. Elena Gustines was available for questions central and obscure (she can tell you when the first pitch was thrown in Game Seven of the 1957 World Series, or who hit second for the Braves in May 1966). Elena's speed and competence helped me face a tight deadline; thank you, Ira Berkow, for recommending Elena. Andy Fitch's research in Milwaukee included digging through original source materials—from old copies of the

Milwaukee Journal to firsthand accounts of the 1967 riots in the city. The staff at the News Information Center of the *Milwaukee Journal Sentinel* provided access to years of Hank Aaron and Milwaukee files. I'm especially grateful to Rosemary Jensen, Paula Haubrich, Linda Randolph, David Herron-Steeger and Sarah Johnson. My old friend and colleague, reporter Patricia Guthrie of the *Atlanta Journal-Constitution,* dug into the archives in Atlanta. In Gloucester, Ashley Ahearn did research and transcriptions with competence and good cheer. Anna Solomon-Greenbaum helped clear a path with vital assistance on various projects. Vincie Bertolino, office manager, transcriber, and troubleshooter *extraordinaire,* made it possible for me to leave town to write for three months without worrying about fires burning back home. A bow of thanks to Sam Bertolino, for his keyboard and his paintbrush. Transcription help also came from Sandy Nunes. Alan Weisman, my Homelands partner, provided soulful encouragement throughout, as did my dear friends Nubar Alexanian, Rebecca Koch, Abby Alexanian, Dan Connell, Debbie Hird, Joe Garland, Helen Garland, Shep Abbott, Betsy Gammons, and Steve Gammons, star pitcher, Babe Ruth League, 1963. Grateful thanks to my agent, Jonathan Matson.

Jim Schultz of the Atlanta Braves and Jon Greenberg of the Milwaukee Brewers provided access to players and facilities. Thanks also to Peter Clark and Eric Strohl of the National Baseball Hall of Fame in Cooperstown. And, to my friends at the Blue Mountain Center, where the idea for this project took root.

For additional background on Henry Aaron's life and career, I tapped into *I Had a Hammer,* by Hank Aaron with Lonnie Wheeler (HarperCollins, 1991); *The Hank Aaron Story,* by Milton J. Shapiro (Julian Messner, 1961); *Home Run: My Life in Pictures,* by Hank Aaron, with Dick Schaap (Total Sports, 1999); *One for the Record: The Inside Story of Hank Aaron's Chase for the Home-Run Record,* by George Plimpton (Bantam, 1974); *The Milwaukee Braves: A Baseball Eulogy,* by Bob Beuge (Douglas American Sports Publications, 1988); *Aaron,* by Henry Aaron with Furman Bisher (Thomas Y. Crowell, 1974); and numerous articles from the *Milwaukee Journal,* the *Milwaukee Sentinel, Milwaukee Magazine, The New York Times* and *Sports Illustrated.* Additional background on racial tensions and attitudes, the civil rights movement, and the South of the 1960s came from John Lewis's memoir, *Walking with the Wind* (Simon & Schuster, 1998); Peter N. Carroll's *It Seemed Like Nothing Happened: The Tragedy and Promise of America in the 1970s* (Holt, Rinehart and Winston, 1982); David K. Shipler's *A Country of Strangers: Blacks and Whites in America* (Alfred A. Knopf, 1997); Jonathan Coleman's *Long Way to Go: Black and White America* (Atlantic Monthly Press, 1997); James Cameron's *A Time of Terror: A Survivor's Story* (Black Classic Press, 1982); and Gary M. Pomerantz's *Where Peachtree Meets Sweet Auburn: A Saga of Race and Family* (Scribner, 1996). Robert W. Creamer's *Babe: The Legend Comes to Life* (Fireside, 1974) helped put Babe Ruth's mythology in historical context, as did *Baseball: An Illustrated History,* by Geoffrey C. Ward and Ken Burns (Alfred A. Knopf, 1994). David Maraniss's *When Pride Still Mattered: A Life of Vince Lom-*

bardi (Simon & Schuster, 1999) was a useful source for the context of sports and heroism in the 1960s, as was David Remnick's *King of the World: Muhammad Ali and the Rise of an American Hero* (Random House, 1998). The personal archives of Jim Ladky and of John Topetzes proved beneficial. John Gurda's excellent history, *The Making of Milwaukee* (Milwaukee County Historical Society, 1999), was an important source of detail and historical context for the place once promoted as "Monarch of the Sausage Kingdom." Also helpful was "A Report on Past Discrimination Against African-Americans in Milwaukee, 1835–1995," by Ruth Zubrensky; *City with a Chance,* by Frank Aukofer (Bruce Publishing Company, 1968); "Through One City's Eyes: Race Relations in America's Heartland," a television documentary produced by Janet Fitch and Alison Rostankowski (The Duncan Group, 1999); *The Economic State of Milwaukee,* Marc V. Levine, principal author (Center for Economic Development, University of Wisconsin–Milwaukee, 1998); *Summer Mockery,* by Helen Weber (Aestas Press, 1986); and *A Career in Newspapers and Broadcasting* (The Journal Company, 1981), by Irwin Maier, who told his story to his grandson, Tom Tolan.

Thanks to those who shared their experiences of Hank, baseball, Milwaukee, Atlanta, Cooperstown, and the social and racial atmosphere of the 1960s and 1970s. These include teammates, civil rights leaders, observers, fans in the stands and family members: Billye Aaron, Gaile Aaron, Albert Allen, Amye Austin, Jason Bailey, Dusty Baker, Lloyd Barbee, Ben Barkin, Helen Barnhill, Tim Bayne, Fred Berman, Joe Berman, Jon Berman, Don Bryant, Candice Calloway, James Cameron, Richard G. Carter, Paul Casanova, Dick Cecil, Thomas Cheeks, Dennis Clack, Steve Conrad, Bob Costas, A. C. Cotton, Arthur Cotton, Eva Cullen, Charles Danrick, Thomas Duett, Joseph Fagan, Susan Farrer, Rodney Franks, Ralph Garr, Earl Gillespie, Terry Gillick, Jay Gilmer, Eric Goldstein, Jon Greenberg, Daniel Gregory, Tony Grueninger, Reuben Harpole, Tom Hayes, Ray Hines, Tom House, John Huey, Howard Hyder, Susan Irwin, Jesse Jackson, Maynard Jackson, Joe Kennedy, Howard King, John Kissinger, John Kurdziolek, Marc Levine, John Lewis, Felix Mantilla, John Martin, James McClain, Dollena McThan, Kevin McThan, John Miley, Lukata Mjumbe, Phil Niekro, John Outlaw, Terry Perry, Vel Phillips, Tony Porter, Laurel Prieb, Alvin Poussaint, Eddie Ricker, Darci Ross, Jim Schultz, Bud Selig, Terry Stephens, Victor Thomas, John Topetzes, Bob Uecker, Gerald Vance, Bill Van Leuven, Jesse Wade, Marissa Weaver, Polly Williams, the Wojciak family (Ed, Brandy, Ben, Bret, Ed senior, and Irene), Tameka Wynn, Andrew Young, Frank Zeidler, and Carl, and Staś, and Terry.

And of course, thanks to Henry Louis Aaron, who sat down with an old fan twenty-five years after Babe's record came down; who shared painful memories of what he endured; who recommended others who might shed further light upon his journey and his legacy.

Friends, family, and colleagues who read the manuscript, as a whole or in part, helped deepen the story, adding context and detail. They include Sharon Ball; Gary Pomerantz, for the Atlanta chapters; John Gurda, for the Milwaukee portions; Dori Maynard and Joe Garland, for the entire manuscript; for important early feedback, Tom Miller. My family was a source of memory, inspiration, and thoughtful comment: Yam, who traveled with me to important stops along the way, and who gathered the photographs for this book (including a couple of his own); John, my old "Strat-O" partner, for important feedback on the nearly final manuscript; Mary, for memories shared, and for feedback on early chapters; Kathleen, who read the manuscript twice, and provided vigorous, insightful suggestions and ideas throughout the process; Tom, who combined an older brother's memory of the glory years with the keen eye of a discerning editor (and who urged me to "look at what's in front of you"); my uncle, Victor Maier, for his vivid account of a Milwaukee summit meeting in August 1967; and my mother, Sally, who brought an English teacher's sharp eye to the manuscript, and whose commitment to fairness and justice has long been a source of quiet inspiration.

It's safe to say that this is the first baseball book to have been written from Amman. Though the Jordanian capital rests atop the original Philadelphia, I didn't find any Phillies fans here. But this is where my wife's family resides—my family, too, I am honored to say—and so what I did find was an atmosphere of tremendous support, conducive to focused work. Deep thanks to Tala, Lana, Jack, Widad, Reem, and especially Margo Andoni, for the love, encouragement, delicious Arabic food, and great good times that I'll always associate with the writing of *Me and Hank*.

Finally, to Lamis, whose support as a partner was deep

and abiding; whose observations as a journalist were keen and unflinching; whose compassion as a human being always brought me back to the fundamental story. Your encouragement, passion, and humanity helped me take *Me and Hank* to a deeper place, Lamis. I am ever grateful.

PHOTO CREDITS

ABOUT THE AUTHOR

Sandy Tolan was born in Milwaukee, Wisconsin, in 1956. A freelance journalist and independent radio producer since 1981, Tolan has produced dozens of documentaries and features for National Public Radio and Public Radio International. He is co-founder of Homelands Productions, an independent public-interest journalism organization, and has reported from seventeen countries, focusing on environmental, social, and political issues in the American Southwest, along the U.S.-Mexico border, in Latin America, the Caribbean, the Balkans, India, and the Middle East.

Tolan has also written articles for more than thirty newspapers and magazines, including *The New York Times Magazine, The Nation,* and the *Los Angeles Times Magazine.* His work has been recognized with more than twenty national and international awards and fellowships, including an Overseas Press Club Award, a duPont-Columbia Silver Baton, a United Nations citation, a Nieman Fellowship at Harvard University, and two Robert F. Kennedy awards for reporting on the disadvantaged. He and his wife, Lamis Andoni, live in Gloucester, Massachusetts.